# BOUNDS OF JUSTICE

In this collection of essays Onora O'Neill explores and argues for an account of justice that is fundamentally cosmopolitan rather than civic, yet takes serious account of institutions and boundaries, and of human diversity and vulnerability. Starting from conceptions that are central to any account of justice – those of reason, action, judgement, coercion, obligations and rights – she discusses whether and how culturally or politically specific concepts and views, which limit the claims and scope of justice, can be avoided. She then examines the demands and scope of just institutions, arguing that there are good reasons for taking the claims of distant strangers seriously, but that doing so points not to a world without boundaries but to one of porous boundaries and dispersed power. *Bounds of Justice* will be of interest to a wide range of readers in philosophy, politics and international relations.

ONORA O'NEILL is Principal of Newnham College, Cambridge. She has written widely on ethics and political philosophy, and her most recent books include *Constructions of Reason: Explorations of Kant's Practical Philosophy* (Cambridge University Press, 1989) and *Towards Justice and Virtue: A Constructive Account of Practical Reasoning* (Cambridge University Press, 1996).

# BOUNDS OF JUSTICE

ONORA O'NEILL

*Newnham College, Cambridge*

PUBLISHED BY THE PRESS SYNDICATE OF THE UNIVERSITY OF CAMBRIDGE
The Pitt Building, Trumpington Street, Cambridge, United Kingdom

CAMBRIDGE UNIVERSITY PRESS
The Edinburgh Building, Cambridge CB2 2RU, UK   www.cup.cam.ac.uk
40 West 20th Street, New York, NY 10011-4211, USA   www.cup.org
10 Stamford Road, Oakleigh, Melbourne 3166, Australia
Ruiz de Alarcón 13, 28014 Madrid, Spain

First published 2000

Printed in the United Kingdom at the University Press, Cambridge

*Typeface* Monotype Baskerville 11/12$^1$/$_2$ pt.   *System* QuarkXPress™ [SE]

*A catalogue record for this book is available from the British Library*

*Library of Congress Cataloguing in Publication data*

O'Neill, Onora, 1941–
Bounds of justice / Onora O'Neill
p.  cm.
Includes bibliographical references and index.
ISBN 0 521 44232 X (hardback) – ISBN 0 521 44744 5 (paperback)
1. Justice.  I. Title.
BJ1533.J9 O64  2000
172'.2–dc21  99-056414  CIP

ISBN 0 521 44232 X hardback
ISBN 0 521 44744 5 paperback

# Contents

# *Preface*

I hardly know where to begin in stating my debts and my gratitude to those who have helped with this work. Throughout the 1990s I was helped by numerous audiences, colleagues, pupils and friends. A long list of names would trivialize what I owe in an enterprise that is necessarily in many ways collective. All I can do is to state my warm thanks. The dedication calls to mind one particular, long-standing and much-missed philosophical conversation and friendship from which I constantly learnt.

# Introduction

During the last thirty years of the twentieth century, writing on justice flourished and multiplied throughout and beyond the developed world. This intellectual movement was spearheaded by John Rawls's rightly famous *A Theory of Justice*,[1] and augmented by hundreds of other writers who have debated the issues with close and acute tenacity. Their vast body of work has been admirably engaged in at least two ways. It has been deeply connected both to academic work in law and in the social sciences and to the more practical activity of many political movements. Debates about human rights and the justice of wars, about the ending of apartheid and of communism, about Third World development and welfare states, have been continuously linked to more abstract writing on the requirements of justice. The more abstract writing has been deeply argued, diverse, scrupulous and useful. There is much to admire.

And yet, I believe, there is also much more to be understood and investigated. Beyond current debates on justice there are unresolved, sometimes unasked, questions both about the philosophical and conceptual boundaries of writing on justice, and about the political and other boundaries of just institutions. The essays in this book do not present a new theory of justice: they raise questions about the boundaries assumed in work on justice and suggest alternative ways of approaching these questions.[2]

Most protagonists in recent debates about justice have accepted John Rawls's agenda of devising a theory of justice that reaches (varying forms of) broadly 'Kantian' normative conclusions while remaining

---

[1] John Rawls, *A Theory of Justice* (Cambridge, Mass.: Harvard University Press, 1971).

[2] With one major omission: these essays say almost nothing about the boundary between justice and other ethical concerns. I have had my say on this range of topics and the opportunity to say something more systematic about requirements of justice in *Towards Justice and Virtue: A Constructive Account of Practical Reasoning* (Cambridge: Cambridge University Press, 1996).

within 'the canons of a reasonable empiricism'.[3] With few exceptions, they have accepted empiricist views of reason, action, freedom and motivation, not to mention knowledge. Of course, any theory of justice that wishes to be taken seriously must respect empirical findings; but that is not the same as accepting 'the canons of a reasonable empiricism'. 'Kantian' theorists of justice accept that ethical and political reasoning must take account of consequences of action without concluding that they must be consequentialists; they could also respect empirical findings without concluding that they must take empiricist views of reason, freedom and action.

The essays in this book explore some of the paths not generally taken in debates about justice. I have taken seriously John Rawls's thought that a theory of justice can and should aim for broadly 'Kantian' conclusions, but have suggested that it might do so better by building on less exclusively empiricist conceptions of reason, freedom, action and judgement. At many points I have found it useful also to draw on the very different views of reason, freedom, action and judgement on which Kant relied to reach the first 'Kantian' account of justice (his views on knowledge, on the other hand, lie resolutely 'within the canons of a reasonable empiricism'). However, this is emphatically not a work on Kant, or specifically on his theory of justice. Excellent work on Kant's political philosophy has been appearing during the last twenty years, and I have found much of it helpful in coming to understand his position. However, here aspects of Kant's work are used to identify and explore alternative accounts of the philosophical and political boundaries of justice.

My reason for taking Kant seriously is not only that it is reasonable to suppose that there is a good connection between his conceptions of reason, freedom, action and judgement and 'Kantian' conclusions about justice. Nor is it only that Kant, unlike many contemporary writers, insists that a fully adequate account of justice must be cosmopolitan, and so has taken a less absolute view of the justice of state boundaries than have many more recent 'Kantian' writers. It is also, surprising as it may seem, that many of Kant's views accord rather well with certain daily pre-philosophical views, particularly of action, principles and judgement.

The empiricist conceptions of action that lie in the background of contemporary work on justice often conceive of human agents as moved by

---

[3] John Rawls, 'The Basic Structure as Subject', *American Philosophical Quarterly*, 14 (1977), 159–65; 165.

preferences, beliefs and a solely instrumental conception of rationality. Those who introduce additional conceptions of reasonableness or practical reason – for example, Rawls in many of his later writings, those who are interested in deliberative conceptions of democracy – generally anchor these conceptions of reason in the shared views or the debates of fellow-citizens, so adding a normative to an instrumental conception of practical reason. In making this move they may reject aspects of empiricist theories of action, but at the cost of putting any universal claims about justice in question. Paradoxically, while processes of regionalization and globalization have surged, the deep structure of political reasoning has been increasingly conceived of in civic rather than in universal terms.

Perhaps this does not matter. Universalism in ethics and politics has acquired a bad name among a wide range of philosophers, for reasons that are discussed in many of these essays. My own view, however, is that if we are to have an account of justice that is relevant for a world in which state boundaries are increasingly porous to movements of goods, capital, ideas and people, and in which state sovereignty is increasingly circumscribed, we shall need to work on setting out a reasonable form of universalism for ethics and politics. This will not be easy because conceptions of justice which were devised with the thought that states are the primary context of justice may need a lot of stretching and remodelling if they are to do global duty. Questions about the *scope* of ethical and political reasoning and about the *boundaries* of just institutions cannot be treated as mere afterthoughts in an account of justice that is convincing and useful in the contemporary world.

Although the critics of universalism in ethics have been quite varied, their criticisms have not. Communitarians and virtue ethicists, postmodernists and certain feminists, Wittgensteinians and Nietzscheans, as well as subtle particularists, have attacked universalist ethics on remarkably similar grounds, beginning in the main around 1980. Broadly speaking, these critics have argued that ethical thinking that begins with principles of universal scope will be uselessly abstract as well as insensitive to differences between cases. Some have also pointed out that any focus on principles must be a focus on rules, and hence also on obligations, rights and (supposedly) on blame: Bernard Williams's charges against what he calls 'the morality system' articulate these suspicions particularly well.[4] In viewing principles, rules and blame as the centre of the moral life, the 'morality system' excludes ethical concerns other than

---

[4] See Bernard Williams, *Ethics and the Limits of Philosophy* (London: Fontana, 1985), ch. 10.

those focussed on obligations and rights. In Williams's view this constellation of claims is well entrenched, philosophically incoherent and ethically corrupting. The incoherence arises both because putative
obligations conflict and because their claims on us are requirements yet
indeterminate. The corruption arises because principles take no account
of difference and diversity, or of the special relationships between
persons which are fundamental to the moral life. Moral thinking,
Williams concludes, must begin closer to home: 'I must deliberate *from*
what I am.'[5]

These and similar criticisms levelled against ethical universalism have
received considerable attention in more recent work on justice. Once
again Rawls's work is paradigmatic.[6] Although he has not repudiated
universalist aspirations, and has not accepted the communitarian view
that embedded social norms form adequate starting points for ethical
and political reasoning, Rawls has argued in his later work that the
agreements of fellow-citizens have a fundamental status in an adequate
conception of the reasonable, and thereby in political justification.
Many others also take it that the discourse or debate of citizens is fundamental to justice. The thought may seem convincing if we take for
granted that an account of justice may presuppose that we are fellow-
citizens of some state, or (as Rawls puts it) of a 'bounded society', insiders who can share a common debate about justice. But the approach is
strangely silent about the predicaments of outsiders, and about the
justice of a world that is segmented into states, a world in which for each
of us most others are emphatically not fellow-citizens. It seems to me
that, on the contrary, an adequate account of justice has to take seriously
the often harsh realities of exclusion, whether from citizenship of all
states or from citizenship in the more powerful and more prosperous
states. Why should the boundaries of states be viewed as presuppositions
of justice rather than as institutions whose justice is to be assessed?

Some of the essays in this book have appeared elsewhere, more or less
in their present forms; others have been very extensively revised; yet
others are published for the first time. I have tried to select and to revise
in ways that reduce overlaps and repetitions, without short-changing the
coherence of arguments. Since all the essays grow out of an integrated

[5] Ibid., 200.
[6] See in particular John Rawls, 'Justice as Fairness: Political not Metaphysical', *Philosophy and
Public Affairs*, 14 (1985), 223–51 and *Political Liberalism* (New York: Columbia University Press,
1993).

view of the role of ethical and political reasoning, I cannot hope to have been wholly successful in avoiding repetitions.

The sequence of topics is quite straightforward. The essays in the first part of the book, 'Philosophical Bounds of Justice', are about a number of the philosophical boundaries of justice. The focus moves from practical reason, to freedom and action, to principles and judgement before turning to certain aspects of justice.

The initial essay, 'Four Models of Practical Reasoning', surveys the structure and authority of various conceptions of practical reasoning often used in writing ethics and politics and considers what each presupposes, what claims each has to be thought either a partial or a complete conception of reason, and how it can shape and ground normative conclusions, including a conception of justice.

Practical reasoning and normativity will neither of them have a role unless there are agents. The second essay, 'Agency and Autonomy', considers some of the problems created for thought about right and justice by reliance on preference-based models of action and some of the advantages of relying on alternative, principle-based conceptions of action.

In 'Principles, Practical Judgement and Institutions' I take up the fear that there may be a lack of connection between principles of justice and their actualization in particular institutions, policies and acts. In it I try to look at the structures of deliberation used in practical reasoning that begins with principles, that works *towards* action and policy making. In particular, I discuss the difference between the conception of practical judgement which principle-based judgement uses and the surprisingly influential conceptions of ethical judgement as quasi-perceptual and retrospective, aimed at assessing or appraising action.

'Kant's Justice and Kantian Justice' tries to set the themes of the preceding three essays in context, by contrasting some features of Kant's work with aspects of contemporary Kantian work. In it I try to disentangle differences between abstraction and idealization, and argue that their conflation lies behind many of the criticisms made both of Kant and of contemporary Kantian work.

The last two essays in Part I focus on some of the implications for an account of justice of the revisionary views of action and practical reasoning discussed in preceding essays. Any account of justice will need to have some way of distinguishing coercive from non-coercive action, yet it is surprisingly hard to devise one within the accounts of action favoured by those who seek to stay 'within the canons of a reasonable empiricism', in which threats and bribes alike appear too straightforwardly as mere incentives that change preference orderings. 'Which are the Offers *You* Can't Refuse?' suggests another way of looking at coercion; readers will, I hope, be relieved to find that I discuss the Mafia and terrorism rather than the philosophical literature on coercion. 'Women's Rights: Whose Obligations?' rehearses reasons why, having taken agency seriously, we shall find grounds for treating principles of obligation as more basic than rights in thinking about justice. The case is made by considering debates about women's rights, but the arguments can be extended to other aspects of justice.

In the second part of the book, 'Political Bounds of Justice', I turn to the political and institutional boundaries of justice. Institutions generally have boundaries: they have a place and a time, a beginning and an end, and often an edge and a middle. Institutional thinking therefore always raises questions about scope: who is included and who excluded, and what are the physical and temporal boundaries of justice? In the modern period it has been common to think of justice as instituted and confined within state boundaries; improvements and set-backs to justice are commonly identified with the historical events in the histories of states. On a happy view of the matter, states taken severally secure justice for all. However, these assumptions have been increasingly queried as processes of globalization have begun to change economic and political life. State boundaries, I argue in this book, can no longer be seen as legitimate bounds of justice: they are themselves institutions whose justice can, and often should, be queried.

'Transnational Economic Justice' sets out ways in which the statist assumptions of certain theories of justice fail to engage with the increasingly global realities of economic life. 'Justice, Gender and International Boundaries' considers ways in which the vulnerabilities created by boundaries and their inevitable exclusions can compromise justice: an adequate account of justice has to address ways in which state boundaries and gender divisions can marginalize and exclude, so creating vulnerabilities and thereby ready contexts for injustice. 'Identities, Boundaries and States' looks at some arguments that have long been used to justify state boundaries, and suggests that arguments which try to connect (senses of) identity to bounded territories are less robust than is sometimes thought: states and their boundaries can be justified only in so far as they create no injustice for those whom they exclude; where they create injustices, there is some case for compensation. 'Distant Strangers, Moral Standing and Porous Boundaries' addresses the justice of political boundaries from the perspective of individual agents rather than of states: it proposes a way of determining to which others, and in particular to which distant others, we have reason to accord full moral standing.

The most basic thought that lies behind all these discussions is that fruitful work in ethics or politics must be *practical*. It must address the needs of agents who have yet to act, who are working out what to do, not the needs of spectators who are looking for ways of assessing or appraising what has already been done. This practical task is not furthered by seeing agents as the prisoners of their preferences, or even of the norms and commitments which they (more or less) accept. It does require an empirically realistic view of the capacities and capabilities agents have, of ways in which they are vulnerable to others, and of ways in which existing institutions may be either resilient or fragile. This is the context within which the construction of more robust and reliable institutions which can secure justice even for the relatively weak must be undertaken.

PART I

*Philosophical bounds of justice*

# CHAPTER I

# Four models of practical reasoning[1]

Any convincing account of justice builds upon some conception of reason: yet the more self-consciously we think about reason, the less confident we become that we know what reason requires, or what authority those requirements have. In the daily fray of life, science and politics few of us hesitate to appeal to reason, or to comment adversely on others' lack of reasons for what they say or do. We appeal to reason as an authoritative arbiter of disputes. But when we are asked to vindicate this confidence, it ebbs. This is hardly surprising. If reason is the basis of all vindication, how can we vindicate it? Will not each attempt end in defeat – if we invoke anything unreasoned – or in circularity – if we offer only reasons?

Despite this venerable dilemma, I believe that there is much to be said about the vindication of reason. Here I am mainly concerned with the sorts of reasoning that we attempt in contexts of action, and shall have little to say about theoretical reasoning. I hope that this will not limit the inquiry as much might be surmised. For I shall assume neither that theoretical reason provides the foundations for practical reason nor that theoretical reasoning itself needs no vindication. I suspect that, on the contrary, any adequate vindication of theoretical reasoning requires a vindication of practical reasoning; but this too is more than I can make plausible here.[2] For present purposes I shall simply bracket issues that are specific to theoretical reason, and shall consider what can be done to vindicate practical reason.

---

[1] An earlier version of this essay appeared under the title 'Vier Modelle der praktischen Vernunft', in Hans Friedrich Fulda and Rolf-Peter Horstmann, eds., *Vernunftbegriffe in der Moderne* (Stuttgart: Klett-Cotta, 1994), 586–606.

[2] Some reasons why a vindication of theoretical reason may build on rather than ground practical reason are sketched in Onora O'Neill, 'Reason and Autonomy in *Grundlegung III*', in *Constructions of Reason: Explorations of Kant's Practical Philosophy* (Cambridge: Cambridge University Press, 1989), 51–65 and 'Vindicating Reason', in Paul Guyer, ed., *The Cambridge Companion to Kant* (Cambridge: Cambridge University Press, 1992), 280–308.

I shall organize my thoughts around a consideration of four conceptions of practical reason, each of which has a long history and many var-
iants, as well as many contemporary advocates and detractors. As I do
so, I shall draw on a certain intuitive understanding of what we might
hope that reason can provide either for practice or for theory. I begin by
characterizing this understanding. This hope is not one that those who
are sceptical whether anything can count as (practical) reason are likely
to object to: their scepticism is, after all, a claim that nothing meets standards of reason. Sceptics about reason are not without views about what
reason would provide; they simply hold that it cannot be provided.[3]

Reasoners and sceptics probably agree on two points. They hold, in
the first place, that anything that could count as reasoned would make
no arbitrary moves: when we reason we neither introduce assumptions
arbitrarily nor move from one point to another arbitrarily. This formulation eschews the thought that reason must provide some non-arbitrary
foundation on which all reasoned thought and action builds – perhaps
it does so, but all that is presented in this initial thought is the demand
that the moves made in reasoned stretches and aspects of thought and
action avoid arbitrariness. In the second place both reasoners and sceptics expect anything reasoned to have a certain authority in guiding
thinking and acting, which is quite generally discernible, and so does not
presuppose any views – or prejudices – which are not, or might not
be, generally shared. Ultimately these two considerations – non-
arbitrariness and accessible authority – are not really separable: any
sequence of thought or action based on principles that are not generally
accessible and authoritative would seem arbitrary from some points of
view, and any arbitrary move in thinking or acting will be vindicable only
to those who share some arbitrary assumption or other, and hence would
lack generally accessible authority. However, for expository purposes it
can be useful to distinguish arbitrariness from lack of accessible authority.

It is hard to articulate these expectations more fully at this stage, but
I hope that they can be made clearer and more plausible by considering
four conceptions of practical reason, each of which would be presumed
by its advocates to meet at least these meagre standards. I shall first consider those *teleological accounts of practical reason* which see reason as guiding
action by connecting it to the ends of action, and then move on to more

---

[3] Contemporary sceptics are in the main post-modernists of one sort or another, whose dis-
appointment with what others take for reasoning is evidently based not on lack of views
on what reason *should* provide, but rather on conviction that it is not available.

strictly *action-based accounts of practical reason* which take a more direct approach to guiding action. All the accounts I shall offer are schematic; even when linked with the names of particular philosophers they are not to be taken as textually accurate, but only as useful stereotypes.

## TELEOLOGICAL CONCEPTIONS OF PRACTICAL REASON I: REASONED ACTION AIMS AT THE OBJECTIVELY GOOD

One ancient and formidable account of practical reason unites it with theoretical reason and identifies both with apprehension of the Good. A clear knowledge of the Good can orient both knowledge and action with authority; both thought and action will be disoriented and more or less arbitrary where this vision is lacking or blurred. Reasoned action is action informed by reason's knowledge of its end and guided by its striving for that end. This conception of practical reasoning is most famously associated with Plato, but paler versions are to be found in many later writers.

The serious difficulty with this vision of reason as simultaneously theoretical and practical, *logos* and *eros*, arises from its ambitious metaphysical claims about the ends of action and the congruent claims about human beings, whose knowing and doing are both drawn to these ends. The metaphysical, cognitive and motivational claims of the Platonist vision and of its many descendants are hugely ambitious. Although they are deeply attractive to many people, they are also deeply unconvincing (often unconvincing even to those who find them so attractive). For those not convinced by the metaphysics of some version of Platonism and by a congruent account of moral knowledge and motivation, conceptions of practical reason which appeal to the Good as the arbiter of reasoned action invoke an arbitrary and illusory authority;[4] they purport to find

---

[4] The term 'practical reason' is more readily associated with Aristotle than with Plato, yet no single model of practical reasoning captures the full Aristotelian picture. Aristotle's reputation is so high that protagonists of various accounts of reason try, with some plausibility, to claim Aristotle as their own. Some see Aristotle's account as close to Plato's: practical reasoning is teleological since it bears on ends rather than on acts, moreover on objective ends. The differences are that for Aristotle the good is neither unitary nor separable from particular cases nor closely linked to theoretical knowledge. Others go some way to identifying Aristotle's account of *eudaimonia* with subjective ends, and so begin to elide his account of practical reasoning with instrumental reasoning. Yet others construe Aristotle's view of practical reason as bearing directly on action, which should be guided by the judgements of particular acts made by the *phronimos*: the Good is not seen as orienting but as constituted by such judgements. Yet others identify the *phronimos* with historically determinate figures, and so arrive at the norm-based, relativized accounts of practical reason, favoured by Hegelianizing readers of Aristotle.

objective ends where there are none. It follows that the supposed guidance offered by such conceptions of practical reason is equally illusory.

Long before Hume scoffed that "tis not contrary to reason to prefer the destruction of the whole world to the scratching of my finger'[5] and concluded "tis in vain to pretend, that morality is discover'd only by a deduction of reason',[6] it proved notoriously hard to show that any ends are intrinsically reasoned or reasonable, or indeed intrinsically motivating, let alone to establish which ends these are. Those who scoff often think that all that remains of reason's pretension to guide practice is a subordinate role, and that in Hume's words again 'Reason is, and ought only to be the slave of the passions, and can never pretend any other office than to serve and obey them.'[7] Hume's arguments in these celebrated passages invoke no general scepticism about reason. They leave room for an account of cognitive and so of instrumental rationality; they merely reject the claim that practical reason provides either knowledge of the ends of reasoned action or motives for acting reasonably.

## TELEOLOGICAL CONCEPTIONS OF PRACTICAL REASON II: SUBJECTIVE ENDS AND INSTRUMENTAL REASONING

Hume's scoffing provides a canonical text for a reduced account of practical reason that is still widely accepted (mainly by writers who ignore Hume's broader naturalism about reason), and deeply despised by others. It is worth considering why instrumental rationality is still both the most admired and the most criticized conception of practical reason.

The admiration is evident in the enormous role this account of reason retains in philosophical writing on ethics, in certain social sciences (particularly economics and political science) and in daily life. The achievement of an instrumental conception of practical reason is that it retains the teleological structure of the older 'Platonist' vision, ostensibly links justification to motivation, sheds the metaphysical commitment to provide an account of the Good, yet claims to guide action with some precision. Practical reasoning is integrated into an empiricist conception of action and motivation, which appears to allow for a fruitful and measurable way of thinking about both individual and collective action, but rejects as illusory the idea that reason has ends of its own. If no account of objective ends is available, this is an appealing strategy. For what more

---

[5] David Hume, *A Treatise of Human Nature*, ed. P. H. Nidditch, 2nd edn (Oxford: Clarendon Press, 1978), II.iii.3; 416.    [6] Ibid., III.i.1; 457.    [7] Ibid., II.iii.3; 415.

could we then demand by way of justification than the choice of action which is an efficient and effective instrument for achieving subjective ends? Since we are in any case motivated to seek subjective ends, justification and motivation will then be closely linked. The price to be paid for the fact that no objective ends are discernible is only that this link is less immediate than it was in the Platonist conception: justification will attach to means, and motivation will flow from subjective ends. In this picture the notion of practical reason has in a way been dismantled: where Plato thought of reason as erotic, Hume sees it as inert; in less vivid, Kantian terms, Hume denies that reason is of itself practical.

Once we accept this account of practical reason, much of the contemporary agenda for ethics and the social sciences is fixed. First, the ambitions of practical reasoning to guide action and policy can strive to match the ambitions of the sciences in establishing causal connections. Second, if ends are subjective, reasoned action by different agents need not converge, so egoism, economic rationality and competition will be paradigms of reasoned action. Ethics and social science are thereby set the tasks of defusing or reducing or coordinating the Hobbesian implications of a conception of reason which is hostage to individuals' desires or preferences, and their beliefs, which seems the inevitable corollary of an empiricist and anti-metaphysical outlook.[8]

Other more critical approaches dispute the claim that instrumental rationality provides a full account of practical reason. The most standard criticism is the rather obvious complaint that on this account all that is reasoned is the choice of actions as instruments to intrinsically arbitrary ends, but that nothing shows why efficient or effective pursuit of such ends is reasoned. Although many approaches in ethics and in the social sciences speak of subjective ends as *values* or *valuable*, this merely asserts or stipulates the value of satisfying either actual or hypothetical preferences. Whenever the content of preferences is vile or reviled, doubt can be cast on the presumption that securing or pursuing those subjective ends is rational.

[8] There have been many distinguished attempts to derive moral theory from theories of rational choice, where rational choice is seen as guided by preferences, beliefs and instrumental rationality. For example, John Rawls, *A Theory of Justice* (Cambridge, Mass.: Harvard University Press, 1971); John Harsanyi, 'Morality and the Theory of Rational Behaviour', in A. Sen and B. Williams, eds., *Utilitarianism and Beyond* (Cambridge: Cambridge University Press, 1982); David Gauthier, *Morals by Agreement* (Oxford: Oxford University Press, 1986). In his later writing Rawls concluded that moral conclusions could not be reached by way of a conception of rational choice: see *Political Liberalism* (New York: Columbia University Press, 1993), 53, n. 7.

The only arguments offered by the defenders of the varied empiricist conceptions of practical reason to show that preferences are not wholly arbitrary consist of quite limited claims about the rational *structure* of preference orderings: this structure is said to be reasoned if preferences are, for example, transitive, connected and commensurable. However, demands for coherence of these sorts among preferences cannot show that their pursuit (however efficient or effective) is intrinsically reasoned. The challenge that ends are in themselves arbitrary, so that the conditional claims which instrumental reason can reach lack authority for those whose ends differ, is one that those who identify practical reason with instrumental reasoning alone cannot rebut. They may show that omelette makers cannot reasonably refuse to break eggs, but they cannot show whether making omelettes is reasonable.

If this were all that could be said about instrumental conceptions of practical reason we would, in a way, have no more than a stand-off between its admirers and its detractors. The admirers would concede that the detractors were quite right that no ends were shown reasoned; the detractors would counter that this was not enough; the admirers would retort that no more is available. However, there are other troubling features of a merely instrumental account of practical reasoning. Two in particular seem deeply perturbing, in that they query the very empiricist model of action and motivation which is the background to this account of practical reasoning.

The first of these is that the accounts of the structure of subjective ends elaborated in models of rational choice are fictitious. In particular, the status of claims that agents' preferences are, for example, connected, transitive and commensurable is disputable. Here much is obscured by the fact that two rival and incompatible models of rational behaviour, which view desires and preferences quite differently, are often simultaneously deployed and not adequately distinguished.[9]

One view takes a realist view of preferences, which are seen as real states of agents at particular times. On this view the attribution of connected, transitive and measurable preferences to each individual is certainly speculative; in so far as we have information, it is false. On the second view, preferences and their structure are not understood as empirically ascertainable properties of agents, but are ascribed to agents on the basis of their choices *on the assumption that their preferences are*

---

[9] Theses are hardly new worries; for discussion of the issues sketched in the next paragraphs see Amartya Sen, 'Rational Fools: A Critique of the Behavioural Foundations of Economic Theory', *Philosophy and Public Affairs*, 6 (1977), 317–44 and Chapter 2 below.

*systematically structured, for example, that they are connected, transitive and com-
mensurable.* Under the second 'revealed' interpretation, the structural
and metric properties usually ascribed to rational preference orderings
*must* hold, since they are assumed in order to infer preferences from
choices. On this model of preference-based action, agents cannot, by
definition, act counter-preferentially: mistakes apart, whatever they
actually do must be taken to identify what they most prefer in that situation, assuming the coherence of their preferences. By the same token,
agents cannot on this model act counter-rationally: mistakes apart,
whatever they actually do must be taken to disclose their judgement
about efficient and effective pursuit of their preferred ends in that situation, assuming the coherence of their preferences. Action can then be
criticized as irrational only when based on mistaken belief or calculation.

Neither interpretation of preferences shows that their efficient and
effective pursuit has any unconditional claim to be viewed as reasoned.
Strictly speaking, no *authority* is assigned to preferences in what passes
for preference-based practical reasoning. A realist view of preferences
might, at least in principle, be supplemented with arguments to show
that there are good reasons for satisfying whatever preferences people
actually have: Utilitarians and others have looked for such arguments,
which have proved elusive. The 'revealed' or interpretive view of preferences cannot make this move. Rather it undercuts the basis for thinking that the satisfaction of preferences has either moral weight or social
importance, by reading the aim of optimal preference satisfaction into
all action. Once we infer preferences from choices on the assumption
that preferences must have the stipulated structural and metric properties, and that their satisfaction is efficiently pursued in the light of
whatever beliefs are held, we shall indeed and trivially discover that
whatever is done counts as instrumentally rational attempted preference satisfaction – and if something other had been done, it too would
have had to count as instrumentally rational attempted preference
satisfaction.

Serious as these considerations are, they have not yet put in question
work in the social sciences and in ethics which treats instrumental reason
as the whole of practical reason. However, a second problem shows
more signs of undermining this view. This is the fact that all real-world
instrumental reasoning has to begin from some listing of the 'available'
options, whose outcomes are to be reckoned so that their contribution to
the satisfaction of preferences can be evaluated. Given that we cannot

individuate and list each possible act,[10] lists of options must be lists of act-types, specified by act-descriptions; typically they are short-lists of practical principles or of social norms, which incorporate a few salient act-descriptions. Instrumental reasoners cannot then begin by surveying all possible acts; rather they begin from some listing of act-descriptions. Typically these incorporate the socially accepted and prized categories of action which participants view as the 'real' options for a given situation. The weighing of preferences will be limited by this initial listing of options, which itself precedes, and so derives no vindication from, instrumental reasoning.[11]

In commercial or public-policy reasoning it may be appropriate to look only at options that take for granted the relevant established social framework, and privilege its norms and categories. However, instrumental reasoning that is premised on a short-list of 'established' options lacks warrant in less circumscribed contexts, and in particular in ethical reasoning. At most such reasoning could reach conditional conclusions of the form: given these norms, principles or commitments, the following action would be instrumentally rational. The reasoning will assume rather than support those norms, principles or commitments, which will escape critical appraisal and reasoned assessment. However, once actual norms and salient options are taken to provide the basis of practical reasoning, the instrumental aspects of reasoning are subordinate. The core of practical reasoning is no longer seen as result-oriented instrumental reasoning, but as the action-based and frequently norm-directed patterns of practical reasoning used in daily life and in institutional settings.

### ACTION-BASED ACCOUNTS OF PRACTICAL REASON I: SHARED NORMS AND PERSONAL COMMITMENTS

For some advocates of instrumental rationality it may seem a discovery that instrumental reasoning presupposes action-based and often enough norm-directed reasoning. Others will view this sense of discovery as belated, having long held that practical reasoning can only deal with the

---

[10] A physicalist account of action might provide ways of listing the available actions in a given situation exhaustively, by reference to spaces and times filled by each act token.

[11] For various lines of argument suggesting that preference-based reasoning presupposes norm-based, and hence action-based forms of reasoning see Sen, 'Rational Fools', n. 5; Martin Hollis, *The Cunning of Reason* (Cambridge: Cambridge University Press, 1987); Onora O'Neill, *Faces of Hunger: An Essay on Poverty, Development and Justice* (London: George Allen & Unwin, 1986), ch. 4; Jon Elster, *The Cement of Society: A Study of Social Order* (London: Routledge, 1989), ch. 3.

link between action and its ends if it has some way of grasping or engaging with action. They will also point to the enormous part that action-based reasoning plays in daily life, in social practices such as law and administration, in social and theoretical inquiries within sociology, anthropology and jurisprudence and in philosophical work by historicists, communitarians and Wittgensteinians as well as by those more traditional Kantians who have not been seduced by empiricist accounts of self, action and rationality.[12]

One of the attractions of thinking of practical reasoning as directed basically at action is that it links very readily with all these familiar practices in which action is chosen under descriptions, which may form the content either of social norms and practices or of more personal commitments or projects. Action-based reasoning breaks away from viewing preferences, whether actual or hypothetical, as justifying action; it allows that there may be good reasons not to satisfy certain preferences. In place of preferences it starts with the thought that some types of action are justifiable not as instruments for achieving either objective or subjective ends but simply because they are actions of a certain sort. In doing so it construes practical reason as directly focussed on action, rather than seeing action merely as the instrument for producing results. In making this move we break away from the thought that practical reasoning must have an intrinsically teleological pattern.

The central question to be raised about any action-based conception of practical reason must, of course, be how it can distinguish rationally justified types of action from others that are thought unreasoned and unjustifiable.

A common line of thought here is that the types of action that we can justify are those which express the fundamental norms of a given time or place, or the fundamental commitments or projects of a given person's life or identity. In this way action-based conceptions of practical reasoning may be said to make explicit what is done covertly by those whose practical reasoning is ostensibly merely instrumental. The more social, norm-directed versions of this view are mainly associated with 'Hegelian' writers, and in particular today with communitarians, who see the deepest practices and norms of a tradition or community as a bed-rock on which justification must build, and which cannot itself be put into question. The more individual versions of this view are

---

[12] The picture is confused because many contemporary writers on justice are spoken of as Kantians, but in fact rely in some part on preference-based conceptions of practical reasoning.

particularly associated with more Wittgensteinian writers, who see the
integrity, commitments and attachments and other personal projects of
particular lives as providing a comparable bed-rock which cannot itself
be put into question,[13] and with the work of Bernard Williams, who sees
personal projects and commitments as a framework beyond which our
reasoning cannot pass.

There is in fact much overlap between the more collective and the
more individualist versions of action-based reasoning. In both cases the
thought is that certain norms or commitments or projects are not ones
which we can regard otherwise than as reasons for action, because they
constitute, as it were, part of our community's identity or of our own
individual identity. Practical reasoning takes as its premises those features of our lives which we cannot 'go behind' or assume away without
undercutting our very sense of self, community or identity. In thinking
of an act as required by public attachments and loyalties, or as wrong
because it is cruel, or required if we are not to harm one we love, we do
not (it is claimed) simply invoke some arbitrary principle, but one that is
constitutive of a shared or individual sense of identity, and so part and
parcel of what we are. It is not that we think our way towards such
matters or that we decide on them, but that they are part of the framework of our lives. There are no more basic norms, commitments or
values in terms of which these could be vindicated. Bernard Williams
expresses the thought that 'I must deliberate from what I am' with a
telling instance of the perversity of seeking to deliberate about one's
most basic commitments: in a shipwreck the husband who seeks a reason
to rescue his wife rather than an equally drowning stranger has 'one
thought too many'.[14] Practical reasoning starts from the norms and
attachments that are constitutive of our identity. It is not arbitrary, given
what we are; if it is accessible to others, their access will be conditional
on their understanding what our deepest commitments and attachments
are. Since their understanding will be premised on these, any 'external'
criticism of our commitments or projects will be stymied.

One of the attractions of this account of practical reasoning is that,
like the other two considered, it links accounts of justification and of

---

[13] More Hegelian positions have been put forward by Alasdair MacIntyre and Charles
Taylor; more Wittgensteinian views in the work of Peter Winch and John McDowell.
Elements of both positions are combined by Bernard Williams, especially in *Ethics and the
Limits of Philosophy* (London: Fontana, 1985).

[14] Ibid., 200; 'Persons, Character and Morality', in his *Moral Luck: Philosophical Papers 1973–80*
(Cambridge: Cambridge University Press, 1981), 1–19; 18.

motivation. Both the accepted norms and ways of life of a given society and the deepest commitments and projects of individual lives determine a sense of identity and will be deeply internalized. When they provide reasons for action, the reasons will be inward for those for whom they are reasons.

Of course, the well-internalized reasons invoked both by *norm-based* and by *commitment-based* accounts of practical reason will not invariably be reflected in action. There can be sharp divergences between what is done and what reasoning based on established norms or personal commitments enjoins. In some situations the various norms to which agents are bound by their tradition may come into conflict: Antigone's predicament has many parallels. Equally, in some situations an agent's deepest commitments may conflict with public norms or with other personal commitments: the figure of the conscientious objector epitomizes one such possibility. More prosaically, those whose action is guided by public norms or by personal commitments, or by both, may have desires and preferences that pull in quite other directions. The point is not that norms and commitments are invariably honoured, but that they are acknowledged, and that their flouting will be a source often of guilt and at the least of regret, remorse and other remainders.

On a standard, empiricist conception of action as based on, or at least revelatory of, preferences it can be obscure how norms or commitments could either motivate or justify. However, once we have appreciated the impossibility of specifying options except in term of act-descriptions, preference-based accounts of practical reasoning must lose their claim to provide a comprehensive account of motivation, while their claim to provide an adequate conception of vindication has never been strong.

Yet there is also a fair degree of mystery in the claim that action that expresses either established norms or deep personal commitments is reasoned. Does not practical reasoning that starts either from norms or from personal commitments itself introduce an arbitrary element? How can it have any generally accessible authority? In particular, it is often said that norm-based reasoning is intrinsically conservative and ethnocentric. Commitment-based reasoning might be thought conservative and self-centred for analogous reasons. Both types of reasoning argue unashamedly from what is actually respected or internalized to what ought to be respected or internalized. Both lack authority for those who do not begin by accepting the pertinent norms, who dispute the accepted categories or who abhor others' basic projects. Both privilege an intrinsically insider's view of what counts as reasoned vindication. For outsiders norm-based or commitment-based practical reasoning is quite simply arbitrary, and its authority fades where norms and commitments are not understood or are not found acceptable.

The criticism of conservatism is one that can and has been answered by many proponents of norm-based conceptions of practical reasoning. Once we remember that the norms of a community will underdetermine action, that they will be open to interpretation and reinterpretation, we can see them in a historical perspective, as open to revision and reinterpretation. We shall then see that the norms of a society, and indeed the identity of its members, constitute a revisable basis for reasoning rather than a set of fixed and timeless conclusions. We may come to revise our norms and our beliefs. Norms and principles in their real historical contexts enable open-ended traditions of debate, and may allow for critical and revisionary practical reasoning.[15]

Norm-based practical reasoning is not, then, unavoidably conservative. However, the charge that it is ethnocentric is harder to dispel. Any set of norms or commitments which supposedly provides the framework of justification and the source of motivation will be those of a particular tradition, community or sense of identity. They may not be shared by outsiders. If norm-based reasoning is unavoidably insider's reasoning, it can be followed by outsiders only when they tacitly supply as premisses the norms or commitments which they do not themselves share.

This matters in two ways. In the first place, it matters for insiders. Once we become aware of the diversity and fecundity of traditions and identities, it is harder to maintain the conviction that only the traditions or identities 'we' have ourselves internalized have authority. Indeed, where many have internalized multiple traditions – Christian with liberal, Scots with European, British with Jewish and countless other groupings – the view that practical reason can rest on the achieved norms or loyalties of a tradition becomes suspect.

In the second place, the ethnocentrism of norm-based reasoning matters for relations between insiders and outsiders. Once upon a time it might not have mattered if those who lived in homogeneous but isolated societies reasoned in ways that could not have been accessible to hypothetical others with whom they had no connection. But today societies, cultures and traditions are not bounded or impervious. So it matters when reasoning is based on principles that are internal to some tradition yet not even accessible to outsiders. Ethnocentric reasoning will

[15] This view is held by many communitarians, and was put eloquently in Alasdair MacIntyre's *After Virtue* (London: Duckworth, 1981).

fail or falter for those who attempt communication across boundaries; it will lack authority – and may prove inaccessible to others. Norm-based conceptions of reason will not suffice in a pluralist world. If any ways of organizing either thinking or action are to have quite general authority, they cannot presuppose the norms and opinions of a particular time and place.

Analogous points might be made about more individualistic, commitment-based conceptions of practical reason. These too need not be intrinsically conservative, since we can revise and change our commitments and projects across our lives. However, such reasoning, although not necessarily selfish, will unavoidably be self-centred: it argues from *my* commitments, *my* life-projects and *my* attachments. My commitments, projects and attachments may not be selfish, but equally they may not be noble: there are those who are moved to rescue their wives from drowning, and those who are not. There are even those whose commitments are selfish, who may be moved to drown their wives when opportunity arises. Even when a project is deeply internalized, its vindication may be meagre. Yet it is not clear what opening is left either for vindication or for criticism within a view that construes actual commitments, actual attachments and actual personal projects as the bed-rock of practical reasoning. These commitments will no doubt prove motivating, but it does not follow that it is rational to live lives that express whatever commitments happen to have been internalized. Can there not be reasons for revising or even for ditching rather than expressing certain commitments, for shelving rather than achieving certain projects, however much we have made them our own? Is it not intrinsically arbitrary to view existing commitments, and their internal revisions, as intrinsically justifying?

## ACTION-BASED ACCOUNTS OF PRACTICAL REASON II: CRITICAL REVISION OF NORMS OR COMMITMENTS

The main advantage of both norm-based and commitment-based accounts of practical reasoning is that they provide a more direct way of grasping action than the teleological approaches which take either objective or subjective ends as the basis of reasoned action. The main disadvantage is that the privilege claimed for specific social norms or personal commitments may seem arbitrary from any other point of view. How might this arbitrariness be overcome? In the absence of a metaphysical framework, how could we envisage a reasoned critique of those deep norms and practices, those commitments and projects which frame communities and lives?

We may begin be reconsidering the initial sketch of the standards all ways of structuring thought and action have to meet if they are to count as reasoned. Reasoning about action needs, I suggested, in the first place to be accessible to others. Another way of looking at this thought is that reasons must be the sort of things we can present to others – we offer and accept reasons, criticize, reject and discard them. Any way of organizing thought or action along lines which others *cannot in principle follow* will fail to meet this condition, and so cannot count as reasoned. However, if accessibility is *required*, this requirement constitutes at least a minimal claim to authority. What will have authority is not each particular way of securing accessibility to others, but the demand that accessibility be maintained. The standard that *must* be met by any structure of thought or action that is to count as reasoned is simply that it *must* be such that others *can* follow it. In this very minimal explication of the authority of reason we can recognize a more general version of the Kantian conception of reason as doubly modal: as the *necessity* to adopt principles which we think it *possible* for others to follow. The best-known formulation of this conception of practical reason is, of course, 'act only in accordance with that maxim through which you can at the same time will that it be a universal law'.[16]

In the present context my concern is neither with Kantian texts nor with the distinctive features of theoretical uses of reason. However, some further clarification of the sense in which reasoned thought and action must be followable is needed. When we are concerned with theoretical reasoning, the structures of thought, discourse and communication must presumably be such that others can follow them in thought or conversation. They must be intelligible. With others who share many specific beliefs the requirement is readily met. But where they do not, it will be demanding. Reasoning across social and ideological boundaries will often achieve conditional rationality. What both can follow will have a conditional structure, although it may be that only those of one persuasion are willing to affirm the antecedent of the conditionals which both find intelligible.

---

[16] Immanuel Kant, *Groundwork of the Metaphysics of Morals*, IV:387–460; 421, in Immanuel Kant, *Practical Philosophy*, tr. and ed. Mary Gregor (Cambridge: Cambridge University Press, 1996), Here and elsewhere references to Kant's work cite the standard volume and page numbers of the Prussian Academy edition and the title of a translation. A further page number is included only if the translation does not include this standard pagination.

Practical reasoning, by contrast, aims not just at intelligibility but at guidance – for oneself, for shared activities and for others. Here the requirement that reasoning conform to what is judged followable by others cannot be merely a requirement of intelligibility, of sticking to principles which others can follow in thought. Practical reasoners must find ways of acting that they judge can be recommended to others; they can offer reasons only for principles which they believe those whom they address could adopt as principles of action (whether or not others could act successfully on these principles in any particular situation is a further question). Using an old Kantian metaphor, we may say that practical reasoning must adhere to principles which have 'the form of law', which could be principles for all, and that any attempt to persuade others to principles which do not meet this condition must lack authority. Since in our world reasoning must reach beyond the like-minded, our practical reasoning must often be based on principles that are widely accessible; its authority will vanish if we duck the requirement to keep to such structures. Where we attempt to base practical reasoning on principles that do not meet this requirement, at least some others will find that we put forward principles that they cannot share, and will understandably judge our proposals arbitrary and lacking in authority – in short, unreasoned.

This stripped-down Kantian conception of practical reasoning shares the focus of norm-based and commitment-based conceptions of practical reason: it is directed at action, or rather at the norms and commitments, the practices and projects, by which we collectively or individually organize our lives. It is directed at actions as specified by certain act-descriptions, rather than at acts considered as instruments for producing results. Where it differs from norm-based or commitment-based conceptions of practical reasoning is in its view of the *scope of reasoning*, of the *fixity of identities* and of the *mutual accessibility of traditions*. It allows for the thought that what might seem a reason for me or for the insiders of some tradition, even a reason that is burnt into souls, may not be any sort of reason for others. Insiders' reasoning – Kant spoke of a *private use of reason*[17] – cannot reach outsiders except by linking it with other reasoning which they can follow. Where this is achieved, practical reasoning may be able to link those who are outsiders to one another's traditions and offer reasons for changes in deep commitments, even in sense of identity.

[17] Immanuel Kant, *An Answer to the Question: What is Enlightenment?*, VIII:35–42, in Immanuel Kant, *Practical Philosophy*, tr. and ed. Mary Gregor (Cambridge: Cambridge University Press, 1996).

The critical account of practical reason sketched here neither permits arbitrary moves nor lacks accessible authority. Its vindication is simply that it meets these two meagre requirements, and that the other conceptions of practical reason considered do not. This is not, of course, to say that either instrumental or norm- or commitment-based reasoning can be discarded if we adopt a critical account of practical reasoning: rather both will be *aufgehoben* in a critical account of practical reason. What a critical conception of reasoning provides is the beginnings of an answer to the question whether particular norms and commitments, from which daily practical reasoning starts, can survive critical scrutiny or are merely arbitrary. It offers a framework for instrumental reasoning which discards the assumption that actual or idealized preferences have an automatic justificatory role, and provides some means for distinguishing those which can justifiably be pursued from others which cannot.

The various differences between these models of practical reason can now be summarized. Like norm- and commitment-based accounts of practical reasoning, a critical conception does not take the efficient pursuit either of actual or of ascribed preferences as intrinsically rational. Unlike these conceptions of reason, a critical conception does not take the expression of the basic norms of a community or of one's own personal commitments as intrinsically rational. Like Platonist conceptions of reason, critical accounts take it that reason affords a critical view of actual preferences, norms and commitments; unlike Platonist conceptions of reason, a critical conception takes it that the substance of reason's demand is not given to us but has to be constructed without arbitrarily taking elements of self and community as premises.

Many further questions could be raised about the form and implications of any critical conception of practical reason; I shall try to anticipate three of them.

The first is the matter of motivation. All the other conceptions of practical reasoning discussed link rationality and motivation very closely. This is not surprising, for in each case what it is reasonable for me to do is defined in terms of something that is very central to what I am: the sovereignty of the Good over my real self, my actual or inferred desires and preferences, my internalizations of shared norms or of personal commitments. However, it should be noted that these claims are more honoured in theory than they are felt in practice. The ideal sovereignty of the Good may well be eroded and replaced by empirical desires in actual lives; the motivating power of preferences is decently obscured by the disputes between realist and revealed conceptions of preference; the norms of community and the commitments of individuals are both matters of struggle rather than automatically motivating.

The gap between justification and motivation is more explicitly thematized in critical conceptions of practical reasoning. This gap is such a commonplace of human existence that we may not notice that instrumental, norm-based and commitment-based accounts of practical reason ascribe it to quite particular circumstances – to the divergence between the preferences of different individuals, or to the clash between social norms or fracturing of personal commitments or projects. However, this phenomenon may, for all we can discern, be less local than any of these diagnoses suggest. There is no general reason to expect that motivation will emerge to endorse vindication *unless we have subscribed to an account of vindication which builds in the elements of motivation.* Critical accounts of practical reason are compatible with the assumption that preferences and identities often help motivate us to act in ways that are rationally vindicable, but leave no basis for thinking that motivation will automatically buttress justification. On this account motivation must be fostered rather than found. The locus of a critical account of practical reason is a strong conception of human freedom.[18]

The second question that I shall try to anticipate to a small degree concerns the implications of accepting a critical account of practical reasoning. Some at least will contend, and with long precedent, that they see nothing wrong in the criterion of accessible authority except its total emptiness. To regard reasoned recommendations as confined to those principles of action which all can follow – which are universalizable – has at least some implications. Others will have the converse worry that universalizability, far from being empty, is regimenting. Yet a moment's reflection shows that this too is an illusion. No constraint on principles of action can overcome the indeterminacy of principles, or supersede the need for judgement. Many constraints are in fact rather weak, and

---

[18] I shall say nothing about this here. Discussion of a critical conception of practical reason is rare, indeed overlooked in much would-be Kantian writing; at present the issues are explored most thoroughly in the secondary literature on Kant's writings. See recently, for example, Henry E. Allison, *Kant's Theory of Freedom* (Cambridge: Cambridge University Press, 1990); Richard Velkley, *Freedom and the End of Reason: On the Moral Foundation of Kant's Critical Philosophy* (Chicago: University of Chicago Press, 1990). Kant's approach to freedom is distinguished from most current approaches because he does not seek to establish theoretical reason and its causal claims, only to find human freedom threatened and in need of rescue. Rather he views practical reason as part of the framework within which the authority of theoretical reason and so of causal claims can be established. See also the references for n. 2.

do not require that very specific types of acts be uniformly done or even universally done, but only that those who seek to reason propose basic principles which they think others too could adopt.

The requirement of acting only on principles which are taken to be accessible to others is not empty. For example, principles which enjoin destruction or coercion or deceit *could not* be recommended to all; among mutually vulnerable beings a principle of mutual indifference *could not* be recommended as accessible to all. In every case the widening adoption of such principles would create victims who were disabled – by others' action on these very principles – from adopting the same principles. Of course, this is only a gesture towards the detailed arguments that would be needed to show just how much guidance can be derived from a critical conception of practical reason. These sample practical principles are formulated at the highest level of generality. Much further consideration would be required to show which institutions, which practices and which ways of life could best embody principles such as those of rejecting destruction, coercion, deceit and indifference for a given time and place.

The third question that I shall briefly address is how far a critical conception of practical reason differs from a discursive conception. Once again, I shall not refer to texts, but rather to tendencies. In so far as a discursive conception of reason is anchored in *actual* discursive practice, it amounts to a form of norm-based reasoning. It may be reasoned relative to those norms; but cannot provide reasons for those norms. In so far as a discursive conception of reason is anchored in certain supposed ideals – for example, an ideal speech situation – it invokes a transcendent vantage point, and its vindication will incur the problems faced by other metaphysical theories. In so far as it is understood as a matter of sticking to practical, including discursive, principles that are accessible to all – that can be followed by all – then we are dealing with a critical account of discursive rationality.

CHAPTER 2

# *Agency and autonomy*[1]

Reasoning about action is for agents: if there are no agents, there will be no useful practical reasoning, let alone reasoning about justice. Work in political philosophy and ethics often takes it that a central feature of agents is that they can be, are, or at least should be autonomous; yet there is a spectacular amount of disagreement both about what autonomy is and about its moral significance. Writers on autonomy usually claim that it is either some form of *independence* in acts and agents or some form of *coherence* or *rationality* in acts and agents: this division runs deep.

Those who depict autonomy as some sort of independence tend to think of it as relational and graduated: independence is *from* something or other and may be *more or less complete*. Autonomy is seen as a hard-won and (usually) desirable psychological trait that may be manifested, for example, in independence of judgement, inner-directedness, self-control, adherence to principle and self-sufficiency.[2]

Those who depict autonomy as some sort of coherence or rationality usually think that it is *not relational*, and *not graduated*. Sometimes they view autonomy, or at least the capacity for autonomy, as an inherent feature of all human beings, even as the basis of human worth or dignity, and not as something which the more self-sufficient or successful or independent have developed to greater degree than the rest of us, or that could be confined to one area of life.

Many versions of these and similar views of autonomy can be found. In 1988 Gerald Dworkin surveyed numerous discussions of autonomy and found that it has been equated with liberty, self-rule, sovereignty,

---

[1] An earlier but very different version of this essay appeared as 'Autonomy, Coherence and Independence', in David Milligan and William Watts Miller, eds., *Liberalism, Citizenship and Autonomy* (Aldershot: Avebury Press, 1992), 209–29.

[2] See Thomas E. Hill, Jnr, 'The Kantian Conception of Autonomy', in his *Dignity and Practical Reason in Kant's Moral Theory* (Ithaca, N.Y.: Cornell University Press, 1992), 76–96, esp. the section titled 'What Kantian Autonomy is Not', 77–82.

freedom of the will, dignity, integrity, individuality, independence, responsibility, self-knowledge, self-assertion, critical reflection, freedom from obligation and absence of external causation. He concluded – whether in despair or with mild sarcasm – that 'About the only features held constant from one author to another are that autonomy is a feature of persons and that it is a desirable quality to have.'[3]

In fact, it is not generally agreed even that autonomy is a feature of persons or that it is desirable. Plenty of accounts of human action deny that persons can be, and *a fortiori* that they are or should be, autonomous (behaviourism; structuralism; some Marxisms); plenty of ethical and political views dispute the value of autonomy. Although a lot of writers on justice, rights and applied ethics admire autonomy, others dispute or deny its value. For example, many virtue ethicists and communitarians, and some religious believers and feminists, who variously praise and admire solidarity, mutuality, interdependence, relationship, care, tradition (and in a few cases even dependence and obedience) criticize autonomy as inimical to these values.[4] Unsurprisingly, accounts of the value of autonomy are pulled in different directions depending on the relative emphasis placed on independence, on rationality or coherence, or on other interpretations.

Attempts to depict autonomy as solely a matter of independence raise many problems. I was made vividly aware of some of them by a former student in New York. When spring finally arrived one year in the now-distant 1970s, some male undergraduates stripped off their clothes and bounded across Broadway to invite female undergraduates to join them. My student was the only woman to join in the fun, and was duly photographed gambolling naked across Broadway with many male companions. When I asked her why she had responded to the invitation, she told

---

[3] Gerald Dworkin, *The Theory and Practice of Autonomy* (Cambridge: Cambridge University Press, 1988), 6. Thomas Hill's work on autonomy also documents a huge range of varied interpretations: see n. 2 above and also 'The Importance of Autonomy', in his *Autonomy and Self-Respect* (Cambridge: Cambridge University Press, 1991), 43–51.

[4] At a certain point, perhaps in the sixties or seventies, there may have been a consensus that autonomy is always of value. But since at least the eighties the idea has been widely challenged. The dates of publication of some of the most-cited and earliest challenges are closely clustered: Lawrence Blum, *Friendship, Altruism and Morality* (London: Routledge & Kegan Paul, 1980); Carol Gilligan, *In a Different Voice: Psychological Theory and Women's Development* (Cambridge, Mass.: Harvard University Press, 1982; 2nd edn, 1993); Michael J. Sandel, *Liberalism and the Limits of Justice* (Cambridge: Cambridge University Press, 1982; 2nd edn, 1996). In their wake a truly enormous literature on community, care, virtue, and the role of emotions in morality has developed. This literature is relentlessly critical of autonomy, but not very clear about the nature of that which it criticizes.

me that it was the only way in which she could establish that she was free, and that she now knew that she was autonomous. I owe her a lot, because her comments started me wondering. Of course, the problem was not that I did not see what she might have had in mind. She may have been thinking that she had now shown her independence from conventions of respectability or from her parents. But had she not also shown herself highly dependent on male initiative? Did she think her fellow-streakers also counted as autonomous? Or did she see them as non-autonomous because they only dared streak in a group? Her act, like many others, was surely dependent in some respects and independent in others – and did not seem to draw any special value from the ways in which it was independent.

More generally, can just any independent or unconventional action, including deviant and criminal activity, count as autonomous? If so, the value of autonomy is highly questionable. While distinctions among specific types of independence and dependence can often be morally important, independence *per se* does not seem to be either necessary or sufficient for an act to be morally valuable or an agent to be excellent.

On the other hand, an interpretation of autonomy that sees it as some form of rationality or coherence, and which brackets all issues of dependence and independence, also seems unpromising. Can acts of deference, obedience and dependence, which can be wholly rational and coherent in contexts of power or threat, ever count as autonomous? Interpretations of autonomy that stress independence obscure its supposed value; interpretations that stress rationality or coherence may suggest (at least vaguely) that it is to be valued, but do not show what makes it distinctive, or whether it is in any way linked to agency, freedom and independence.

An appealing way of dealing with these problems would be to seek an account of autonomy that *combines* notions of independence and of coherence. Yet this is harder than one might suppose, particularly within the confines of a broadly empiricist view of action and motivation. I shall explore this possibility and conclude that it offers scant prospects. In search of a more convincing way of linking independence to rationality or coherence I shall turn to the source through which the notion of autonomy acquired its contemporary resonance, and outline an interpretation of Kant's account of autonomy. Although I shall not argue that this interpretation of Kant's approach provides either the sole or the best account of autonomy, I shall argue that it meets three important criteria. First, unlike currently popular views, it provides an integrated account of the roles of independence and coherence or rationality in autonomy. Second, it allows for an interesting and weighty account of the ethical significance of autonomy. Third, it provides a framework for judging when and why specific sorts of independence are valuable, and for criticizing some but not other relations of power and dependence: Kantian autonomy, as I understand it, neither mindlessly endorses ideals of self-sufficiency nor devalues all forms of dependence and interdependence.

I  AUTONOMY IN EMPIRICIST VIEWS OF HUMAN ACTION

Many of the political philosophers who now lay most store by autonomy speak of themselves as 'Kantians'. By this they sometimes mean no more than that they are not Utilitarians: they do not judge actions right because they maximize the good, or specifically because they maximize happiness; their fundamental ethical category is that of the right, and often specifically that of rights. Their views of right(s) and of autonomy are often closely linked: autonomy is important because it is required for the exercise of rights; rights are important because they protect autonomous action. Violations of others' rights and of their autonomy are both morally suspect; respecting their rights fosters both the capacity for autonomy and its exercise.

The conceptions of action and motivation relied on by most contemporary proponents of 'Kantian' ethics (many of them advocates of liberal theories of justice), like those favoured by the Utilitarians whom they oppose, often construe reasoned action in broadly empiricist terms as a matter of choosing between ways of pursuing an agent's preferences (desires, motivations, inclinations).[5] Rawls in his supposedly Kantian account of justice in *A Theory of Justice* is not unusual in taking a broadly empiricist view of action, choice and rationality, but only in being more explicit than many other liberal theorists of justice in articulating his views of action and choice.[6] In some other writing on justice and on

---

[5] For brevity I shall generally use the more abstract, relational term 'preference' even where it might be more natural to speak of *desires, motivations* or *inclinations*; in speaking of Kant's position I shall indicate some of his psychological vocabulary in parentheses.

[6] John Rawls, *A Theory of Justice* (Cambridge, Mass.: Harvard University Press, 1971), pictures agents as having complex preferences (desires, interests) which they pursue by instrumentally rational action, 14–15, 143. In *Political Liberalism* (New York: Columbia University Press, 1993), he defends a different conception of action, speaks of 'the obvious non-Humean character of this account of motivation' and claims that 'the class of motives is wide open'; see 48–54; 85–6.

autonomy it is harder to be sure which theory of action is espoused: seemingly empirical claims about preferences and desires, together with beliefs, determining all action can be found side by side with claims about the roles of interests, of the will and of reflection in determining action, any of which could be read as claims that agents can act counter-preferentially and as repudiating or questioning certain empiricist views in the theory of action.[7] It may be that the contrast between some 'Kantians' and the Utilitarians they oppose lies only in their normative claims, and not in their conception of human agency.

In any case 'Kantian' and Utilitarian views of the importance of autonomy are not as distant as one might imagine. While Utilitarians must view autonomy as a subordinate value, few of them now think it unimportant, and most argue energetically that paternalism and violations of rights do not maximize utility. Some with Millian affiliations aspire to take rights and autonomy almost as seriously as contemporary 'Kantians' take them. Like 'Kantians', Millian Utilitarians need an account of action that leaves room for the conception of autonomy by which they set such store. It would be useful both for Utilitarians and for certain 'Kantian' theorists of justice and autonomy if it were possible to show straightforwardly how the independence which autonomy seems to require can be fitted into an empiricist account of action.

Empiricist views of human action can be presented either in theoretical or in normative terms. In either case they regard rationality as linking actions to preferences and other states of agents, but as unable to pick out specific preferences as rational: for empiricists there are no ends of reason. Empiricist theories of action aim to explain action as caused by the preferences and beliefs and other inner states of particular agents; empiricist normative theories aim to guide agents by showing how instrumental reasoning can point those with a specific configuration of preferences and beliefs to specific actions. The difference between theoretical and normative approaches is not fundamental, since the causal connections that the former emphasize are recapitulated by the instrumental reasoning stressed in the latter.

The problem for an account of autonomy that starts with an empiricist model of action is to show why some but not all instrumentally

---

[7] For example, Robert Young, *Personal Autonomy: Beyond Negative and Positive Liberty* (London: Croom Helm, 1986), begins by seeing 'the choices of an autonomous person as expressive of his or her own preferences', 8, but also introduces notions of willing and reflection which may undercut this initial position. See also Richard Lindley, *Autonomy* (Basingstoke: Macmillan, 1986); Dworkin, *The Theory and Practice of Autonomy*, 20.

rational ways of pursuing given preferences in the light of given beliefs should count as autonomous. This is often done at a surface level by suggesting that certain acts are independent and coherent in the relevant, 'autonomous' way because they reflect the self or agency or freedom of the agent in peculiar measure. Yet an account along these lines is problematic for many empiricist acounts of action and motivation. Those who view the self as nothing but a set of mental states, agency as nothing but the pursuit of preference, freedom as nothing but the absence of constraint, have difficulty explaining how some acts can be more central than others to the self, freedom, identity or integrity of an agent. There have nevertheless been various proposals for fitting an account of autonomy into an empiricist framework; I have not yet met a convincing one. Some examples will indicate the sorts of difficulties that arise.

Some proposals suggest that acts expressing or implementing preferences with a specific sort of *content* should count as autonomous. For example, Mill insists that there are certain 'higher pleasures', whose pursuit more truly reflects the self or person. He takes as the hallmark of a pleasure being 'higher' that the experts (who know both sorts of pleasure) prefer it.[8] This demarcation was meant to serve as a moral criterion, and has often been criticized as such and also for dispersing the conceptual rigour and economy of a bolder Utilitarianism. However, from the point of view of an account of autonomy, the deficiencies are more basic. In simple terms, it is unclear why the pursuit of *any* category of pleasures should be thought of as escaping from the fundamental picture of pleasures, and the preferences directed at and satisfied by those pleasures, as states of affairs which befall some but not other choosers. The criticism is, so to speak, not that we have not been shown that poetry is better than pushpin, but that we have not been shown whether or why a preference for poetry is other than one of life's happy accidents, susceptible of causal explanation, but not in itself evidence of liberty, self-rule, sovereignty, freedom of the will, dignity, integrity, individuality, independence, responsibility, self-knowledge, self-assertion, critical reflection, or freedom from obligation, let alone of absence of external causation. Why is happening to prefer poetry (or other 'higher' affairs) evidence of independence, coherence or any other conception of autonomy?

Others try to fit autonomy into empiricist approaches to action by identifying it not with the *content* but with the *structure* of certain prefer-

---

[8] J. S. Mill, *Utilitarianism*, in Mary Warnock, ed., *Utilitarianism; On Liberty; Essay on Bentham etc.* (London: Fontana, 1985), 258–62.

ences. Autonomous action is still pursuit of preference, but is distinguished by the fact that it is guided by *second-order preferences*.[9] On such views, common-or-garden eating, which aims only at enjoyment and satisfaction of hunger, is not autonomous, but witting eating, which not merely satisfies hunger and taste but also fulfils a preference for having, or for being a person who has, these or those attitudes to food – for example, for being a gourmet, an ascetic, a vegetarian – is autonomous action.

Attempts to pick out what makes actions autonomous by reference to the structure of systems of preferences do not on reflection seem convincing. Second-order preferences are sometimes described as *endorsing*, or *reflectively endorsing*, first-order preferences. The metaphor of 'endorsement' sounds duly judicious and an appropriate source of autonomy. However, if 'endorsement' is not covertly backed by some conception of a unified or substantial self, or of free will, or of practical reason (all of them suspect for empiricists) which endorses some but not other preferences, the idea of *endorsing* will have to be interpreted entirely formally.[10]

If preferences can endorse one another only in the sense that one may refer to another (of the same individual), and so be a second-order preference, little is gained. The interlocking structure of human preferences will guarantee that an enormous amount of human action, including most trivial action, receives second-order endorsement. Most trivial preferences are not merely congruent with but linked to or components of more broadly described preferences, thereby becoming the objects of second-order preferences.

---

[9] The idea has Millian origins, and was developed for rather different purposes in a still influential paper by Harry Frankfurt, 'Freedom of the Will and the Concept of a Person', *Journal of Philosophy*, 68 (1971), 5–20. Frankfurt intended to offer an account not of autonomy but of personhood. He focussed on an example of compulsive, first-order preferences which might be the object of varying second-order preferences, to show why second-order preferences are important. Where a first-order preference (for example, for drugs) is compulsive, we can distinguish those addicts (whom Frankfurt calls *wantons*) who also prefer to remain addicted and others (whom he calls *persons*) who prefer the fix but not the addiction. Although Frankfurt's focus on second-order preferences has been thought helpful for an account of autonomy, I do not believe that it can be adapted to this use without adding the very notions of self or free will that empiricists hope to do without.

[10] Of course, some authors who use the idea of second-order endorsement are happy to step outside an empiricist framework. For example, Charles Taylor's conception of *strong evaluation*, although he connects it to the idea of second-order preferences, deploys more than the formal notion of a second-order endorsement, and cannot be fitted into an empiricist account of action. See Charles Taylor, 'What is Human Agency?', in his *Human Agency and Language: Philosophical Papers 1* (Cambridge: Cambridge University Press, 1985), 15–44.

So there is no general reason to think that action which receives second-order endorsement is autonomous. A teenager may dress to defy parental demands. The preference for clothes that irritate the parents but which conform to some youth fashion is itself preferred, since the teenager wants to be a person who rejects parental demands. A patient who develops a dependent relationship with a doctor may have a preference not only for taking prescribed medicines conscientiously, but for doing whatever the doctor orders; and the latter preference will refer to the former. Yet there is no particular reason to think that teenagers who follow youth fashion or dependent patients manifest any distinctive independence, rationality or coherence, or should be seen as distinctively autonomous. Second-orderedness is just too commonplace to guarantee any distinctive, ethically significant coherence or any sort of independence; it is not a likely basis for autonomy.

None of this shows that second-orderedness is unimportant. Individuals bereft of all second-order preferences could hardly form coherent plans. The more general case of second-orderedness in the preference structure of a group, rather than of a single individual, has been and remains of immense importance for political philosophy. Debates about altruism, competition, positional goods and struggles for recognition all make claims about the cross-referring structure of the preferences of distinct individuals, and often go on to discuss ways in which an individual's sense of identity depends on others' recognition and so derives from membership of groups. However, these debates simply *presuppose* uncontentious second-orderedness within the preference structure of any given individual, and do not treat it as a matter of distinctive moral or social significance.

## 2 REVEALED PREFERENCES

It is tempting to look for a way out of these impasses by abandoning a straightforwardly naturalistic version of empiricist views of preferences and beliefs as states (or events) that cause acts, and interpreting them rather as inferences from acts that are done and from other observables (context, avowals, gestures). Once preferences are interpreted as revealed in action, they are seen as conceptually rather than causally connected to action. This move abandons, or at any rate brackets, naturalism in the theory of action, even if not empiricism of wider sorts, in favour of an interpretive approach to action. However, although revealed preference approaches need not view preferences or beliefs as real states of agents, they remain broadly empiricist in their view of practical reasoning as guided by making instrumental links between (ascribed) preferences and action.

Unfortunately the revealed preference approach to recasting an empiricist view of action does not simplify the task of giving an account of autonomy in terms either of independence or of coherence. Revealed preference accounts of action make the connection between outward action and imputed preferences so close that it becomes hard – unless some further account of freedom, will, person or the like can be introduced – to see how anything could be singled out as satisfying an interpretation of autonomy that points to a deep form of independence, such as liberty, self-rule, sovereignty, freedom of the will, independence or self-assertion. Since revealed preference theories construe all action as expressive of, and so adapted to, agents' preferences and beliefs, the only sort of independence for which they leave room is a specific independence from one or another particular contingency of life: the very sorts of independence that are not always morally desirable.

On the other hand, it seems that revealed preference versions of empiricist accounts of action must require the ascription of coherence to almost any pattern of action. How could acts that must *necessarily* reflect a whole web of coherently linked ascribed preferences avoid satisfying those interpretations of autonomy that appeal to rationality or coherence? If we ascribe consistent, transitive and connected preferences to all action, we should not be surprised if all action meets these standards of coherence or rationality.

In short, revealed preference accounts of action are hard-pressed to explain why some human acts count as autonomous and others do not. They preclude interpretations of action as revealing deep forms of independence, and they require us to view action as revealing (a measure of) internal coherence. An account of autonomy seems to be impossible, empty, or at best trivial once we adopt a revealed preference account of action.

If autonomy is identified with independence, and the link between acts and states of agents is regarded as conceptual, we shall have ensured that no act can break loose from the preferences and beliefs it is interpreted as manifesting, and that no account of autonomy that stresses independence that is more than contextual will be satisfied. What we might commonsensically distinguish as heroic independence and craven deference will both manifest whatever preferences and beliefs are rationally and coherently attributable to an agent. The only basis for calling the courage and independence shown by Sakharov and Havel autonomy, but not calling the caution and deference shown by some others autonomy would go no deeper than the thought that preferences differ.

Equally, if autonomy is viewed as some form of rationality or coherence, it will be guaranteed by the coherence of the preference structure that revealed preference theories impute. Both the action of those with superbly articulated life-plans and the action of those who defer to others, muddle through and follow the whims of the moment will manifest coherent sets of preferences and beliefs, and so will count as equally autonomous.[11]

### 3 MERE, SHEER CHOICE

A tempting way to avoid these impasses is to set aside empiricist accounts of preferences and beliefs as causes of action, and to view action as manifesting mere, sheer choice. Autonomy is then simply capacity for and manifestation of free will, understood in a metaphysically more robust sense than can be incorporated within an empiricist approach to action. Iris Murdoch portrayed this existentialist conception of human autonomy (which she oddly imputes to Kant) in a wonderful passage:

We are still living in the age of the Kantian man, or Kantian man-god. Kant's conclusive exposure of the so-called proofs of the existence of God, his analysis of the limitations of speculative reason, together with his eloquent portrayal of the dignity of rational man, has had results which might possibly dismay him. How recognizable, how familiar to us, is the man so beautifully portrayed in the *Grundlegung*, who confronted even with Christ turns away to consider the judgement of his own conscience and to hear the voice of his own reason. Stripped of the exiguous metaphysical background which Kant was prepared to allow him, this man is with us still, free, independent, lonely, powerful, rational, responsible, brave, the hero of so many novels and books of moral philosophy . . . He is the ideal citizen of the liberal state, a warning held up to tyrants. He has the virtue which the age requires and admires, courage. It is not such a very long step from Kant to Nietzsche, and from Nietzsche to existentialism and the Anglo-Saxon ethical doctrines which in some ways closely resemble it. In fact Kant's man had already received a glorious incarnation nearly a century earlier in the work of Milton: his proper name is Lucifer.[12]

---

[11] There are many other reasons for having reservations about revealed preference interpretations of rational choice. See Amartya K. Sen, 'Behaviour and the Concept of Preference', *Economica*, 40 (1973), 241–59; 'Rational Fools: A Critique of the Behavioural Foundations of Economic Theory', *Philosophy and Public Affairs*, 6 (1973), 317–44. Both are reprinted in his *Choice, Welfare and Measurement* (Oxford: Blackwell, 1982).

[12] Iris Murdoch, *The Sovereignty of Good* (London: Routledge & Kegan Paul, 1970), 80.

As Murdoch indicates, this radical conception of autonomy lurks even within many broadly empiricist discussions of autonomy. It can be seen in persistent attempts to discern some form of independence that is more than contingent independence from particular powers or authorities, and is of fundamental moral value. However, the underlying assumption of empiricist theories of action is that acts and agents are either causally or conceptually bound to – so dependent on – preferences and beliefs, or other inner states. There is no room here for the more radical existentialist view of human autonomy.

The conception of autonomy as mere, sheer choice has most often been criticized for its unclear or excessive metaphysical claims. For present purposes these deeper issues can be set aside, since a simpler problem renders this approach problematic for discussions of autonomy. Contemporary discussions, whatever else they dispute, all insist that autonomy is of moral value. This is why they balk at any simple identification of autonomy with independence, or with independence from agents' preferences or other inner states. The moral importance of autonomy would vanish if it were manifest only in *actes gratuites*. If autonomy is of value, this can hardly be because it is a matter of arbitrary wilfulness; it can be valuable and admirable only if it manifests some deeper coherence or structure. The entire basis for admiring autonomy is swept away if it is construed simply as mere, sheer independent choice: when decision becomes king there is little left to admire in its majesty.[13] Yet it is profoundly unclear how coherence or rationality, of whatever sort, could be elements of a conception of autonomy that insists on the radical independence of autonomous action.

## 4 ARE INDEPENDENCE AND COHERENCE EVEN COMPATIBLE?

These considerations may lead to scepticism about the ethical importance of autonomy. If autonomy were only a matter of independence, then it would sometimes be valuable, sometimes unimportant, and sometimes to be avoided. There is no reason to admire action merely because it is independent of something else. By contrast, while there might be reasons for admiring or valuing action that is rational and

---

[13] It is worth remembering that Sartre in his famous essay 'Existentialism is Humanism' did not construe autonomy – authentic choice – as mere, sheer choice, but as a quasi-Kantian matter of choosing for everybody. Cf. 'Existentialism is Humanism', in Robert C. Solomon, ed., *Existentialism* (New York: Modern Library, 1974). Other versions of existentialist choice are more radical.

coherent, there is no very clear reason for thinking that such action is invariably autonomous. Yet, as we have seen, there are considerable problems, at least for those who take a broadly empiricist view of action, in thinking that a given act could be *both* reasoned and coherent *and* independent in some fundamental way.

It may then seem as if the idea of autonomy is only a mirage, an illusory ideal patched together by combining an exaggerated image of action as independent not merely of specific external constraints and influences but also in deeper ways, and a moral vision which demands modes of coherence and rationality which (if we rely on an instrumental view of practical rationality) can be found only in action which is through and through dependent on whatever agents happen to prefer. Faced with this thought we might retreat from the task of explicating or vindicating a conception of autonomy and wonder only how we came by so problematic an ideal and why it has become so well entrenched in current ethical and political debates. However, a brief look at that historical question suggests that scepticism may not be the only remaining position.

The history of the notion of autonomy before its contemporary proliferation of interpretations is remarkably specific.[14] The term was used in Greek political discussion in a sense very close to its etymology, to characterize independence from tyranny or foreign rule: autonomous polities are those that make their own laws, and to be contrasted with those polities whose laws are given them by a mother city. Autonomy acquired a wider prominence in political discussion via early modern jurisprudence, and retains a sense close to its original one in international relations and constitutional law, and a related usage in child and personality psychology.

The extended use of the term 'autonomy' to describe a fundamental capacity of rational agents is attributable to Kant. His choice of this term can be connected historically with traditions of political theory, in that he uses the term to characterize an extended conception of what Rousseau called *liberté morale*.[15] However, it is in Kant's writing that we first meet the idea that human agents, or quite specifically the human will, rather than polities, are the primary locus of autonomy.[16] In Kant's

---

[14] See *Historisches Wörterbuch der Philosophie*, vol. 1 (Basle: Schwabe, 1971); J. B. Schneewind, *The Invention of Autonomy: A History of Modern Moral Philosophy* (Cambridge: Cambridge University Press, 1998).

[15] See Andrew Levine, *The Politics of Autonomy: A Kantian Reading of Rousseau's 'Social Contract'* (Amherst: University of Massachusetts Press, 1976), 58; Rawls, *Theory of Justice*, 256.

[16] Hill, 'The Kantian Conception of Autonomy', 84.

work autonomy is for the first time treated as pivotal for human freedom and for morality. So it is not surprising that it is from his writings that we inherit the idea that autonomy is a matter not just of independence (which may or may not be of value) but of rationality or coherence, even of morality.

Kant's conception of action differs both from the broadly empiricist conceptions of action, in which so many have tried to embed a conception of autonomy, and from the existentialist conceptions. It may offer a way of avoiding the incoherence that threatens attempts to show how autonomy combines independence with rationality and coherence within these approaches.

Since Kant's writing on autonomy is extensive, scattered and forms part of the core of his critical enterprise, I shall discuss it very selectively. I shall try mainly to characterize his conception of autonomy and its place in his accounts of freedom and morality. Although this is strenuous enough, it avoids the most basic of Kant's arguments, which (in my view) are those which seek to ground the authority of theoretical and practical modes of reasoning by depicting them respectively as the conditions of autonomy for a plurality of agents who think or act.[17]

Since I shall neither give an exhaustive account of Kantian autonomy nor deal with any positions that are neither broadly empiricist nor existentialist nor Kantian, I cannot show that Kant provides the *only* coherent account of autonomy. The conclusion I shall reach is more restricted. It is that there is at least one consistent account of autonomy that combines notions of independence and of rationality or coherence, but that this account requires a distinctive, non-empiricist view of action. More specifically, I shall suggest, we probably have to choose between a moral vision that makes much of autonomy and a theoretical

---

[17] This is a contentious matter. Among the significant Kantian texts are the *Doctrine of Method* of the *Critique of Pure Reason*, tr. and ed. Paul Guyer and Allen Wood (Cambridge: Cambridge University Press, 1998); *An Answer to the Question: 'What is Enlightenment?'*, VII:35–43, in Immanuel Kant, *Practical Philosophy*, tr. and ed. Mary Gregor (Cambridge: Cambridge University Press, 1996); and *What does it Mean to Orient Oneself in Thinking?*, tr. Allen W. Wood, in Immanuel Kant, *Religion and Rational Theology*, VII:133–46, ed. Allen W. Wood and George di Giovanni (Cambridge: Cambridge University Press, 1996). These two essays present Kant's conception of autonomy in action and in thinking as the basis of the theoretical and practical uses of reason. For interpretive suggestions see Onora O'Neill, 'Enlightenment as Autonomy: Kant's Vindication of Reason', in Peter Hulme and Ludmilla Jordanova, eds., *Enlightenment and its Shadows* (London: Routledge & Kegan Paul, 1990), 184–99, and 'Vindicating Reason', in Paul Guyer, ed., *The Cambridge Companion to Kant* (Cambridge: Cambridge University Press, 1992), 280–308.

picture that extends empiricism into our conception of our own acting. This, I believe, is a substantial challenge to much contemporary thinking about ethics and about liberal conceptions of justice.

### 5  KANTIAN AUTONOMY AND ITS CRITICS: RATIONALITY AND COHERENCE

Kant's best-known discussion of autonomy is in the second and third chapters of his *Groundwork of the Metaphysic of Morals*. In Chapter III he analyses the connections between freedom and morality, and argues that we can provide no theoretical proof but only a 'deduction' (i.e. *vindication*) or 'defence' of human freedom.[18] His account sees *negative freedom* or *freedom of the will* as a capacity 'to work independently of determination by alien causes' and *positive freedom* or *autonomy* as a specific, coherent and reasoned way of using negative freedom. It is the capacity for positive freedom which Kant equates with autonomy. [19]

'Negative' freedom *by itself* would not, Kant insists, involve any form of coherence or rationality; it is only a presupposition of rational and coherent action. For example, random action or action that reflects mere, sheer choice would show a capacity to work independently of 'alien' causes, and so be negatively free: but only negatively free. Kant characterizes such action as 'lawless' (literally: not law-like),[20] and regards it as antithetical to morality. He rejects the view that there is any merit in mere, sheer choice: there is only independence but neither rationality nor coherence.

If we are to use capacities to act freely in ways that exhibit not only negative but positive freedom, we must work not by subordinating ourselves to something 'alien' or external, but by adopting a 'self-imposed law'. The term 'autonomy', which originally characterized cities that made their own laws, is evidently an appropriate one for such 'positive freedom'. 'What else', Kant asks, 'can freedom of the will be but autonomy – that is, the property which will has of being a law to itself?'[21] Even

---

[18] Immanuel Kant, *Groundwork of the Metaphysics of Morals*, IV:447, 459, in Kant, *Practical Philosophy*, tr. and ed. Mary Gregor (Cambridge: Cambridge University Press, 1996). For an account of Kant's understanding of the notion of a deduction see Dieter Henrich, 'Kant's Notion of a Deduction and the Methodological Background of the First *Critique*', in Eckhart Förster, ed., *Kant's Transcendental Deductions: The Three Critiques and the Opus Postumum* (Stanford, Calif.: Stanford University Press, 1989), 29–46.

[19] Kant, *Groundwork of the Metaphysics of Morals*, IV:446.

[20] Ibid., IV:446; *What does it Mean to Orient Oneself in Thinking?*, VIII:144–6.

[21] Kant, *Groundwork of the Metaphysics of Morals*, IV:447.

more starkly he asserts: 'on the presupposition that the will of an intelligence is free there follows necessarily its autonomy as the formal condition under which alone it can be determined'.[22]

The classical and the deepest criticism of Kant's account of autonomy is that he builds on an unacceptable, indeed metaphysically preposterous, account of negative freedom as an ability to work in *independence* 'from alien causes'. More limited conceptions of autonomy as ability to act independently of this or that particular event or power are thought plausible; Kant's more radical conception is not. I shall return to this fundamental criticism in section 6; in this section I shall say a bit more about the conceptions of rationality and coherence which Kant introduces in his account of positive freedom.

A lesser but still very important criticism of Kant's account of autonomy has been that he does not in the end introduce any idea of rationality or coherence, that he does not explain what the merit of autonomy is. This line of criticism is more easily addressed. A little thought shows that the notion of *lawlikeness* itself amounts to a strong requirement of coherence. To put the point – the point that Murdoch misses in assimilating Kant to a radical existentialist position – in terms of the political origins of the notion of autonomy, Kant holds that autonomy is a matter not merely of *self-imposed law*, but specifically of *self-imposed law*.

When Kantian autonomy is misread – as by Murdoch – as emphasizing mere sheer choice or independence, to the exclusion of any form of reason or coherence, the constraints it requires have simply been overlooked. They can best be grasped by noting that the heart of the notion of 'self-imposed law' is not an appeal to a transcendent self that does the imposing, or to some other panicky metaphysics, but a modal, reflexive constraint. Kant is interested in the *capacity* to adopt principles that could be adopted by all: principles that could be self-imposed by a plurality must have 'the form of law'. Kantian autonomy is the capacity to adopt principles that *can* be universally adopted, because they are *law-like*, and more significantly the rejection of principles that *cannot* be universally adopted; the exercise of this capacity is the core of Kantian ethics.[23]

Unlike contemporary proponents of 'Kantian' ethics, who rely on preference-based models of action, Kant is not interested in principles because they are (likely to be) universally or widely accepted or adopted: that focus would reintroduce a dependence on actual preferences and

---

[22] Ibid, IV:461.
[23] Here I pass over wider arguments to show why Kant views law-likeness as the core of practical reason; but see Chapter 1 above.

beliefs, and so in his opinion a view that action works by one sort of 'alien' cause. The capacity for acting on self-imposable laws – the capacity for autonomy – is no more than the capacity to live by principles that a plurality *can* adopt. Kant therefore holds that this demand for action only on universalizable maxims which constitutes the Categorical Imperative for human action can also be termed the 'principle of autonomy':[24] the exercise of autonomy on his account just is a matter of acting freely on principles that all can adopt. Hence his initially surprising, but crucial, claim that the capacities for positive freedom and for morality, and hence (since capacities for freedom of the two sorts go together) for any freedom and for morality, are the same: 'thus a free will and a will under moral laws are one and the same'.[25] (In saying this Kant claims only that a free will is a will *capable* of moral action, and not that all free action is *actually* morally acceptable: a will capable of moral action is also capable of immoral action.)

## 6 KANTIAN AUTONOMY AND ITS CRITICS: INDEPENDENCE AND FREEDOM

I have left until last a consideration of the conception of independence, of negative freedom, on which Kantian autonomy is built. This is by far the most controversial aspect of his account of human action, indeed probably the most controversial aspect of his entire philosophy. And the stakes are high: if Kant cannot provide arguments for negative freedom, his account of autonomy, and so his account of morality, will fail. He will be left claiming that autonomous action *if possible* would be law-like, and hence coherent, but not have shown that it is possible.

The claim that negatively free action, and thereby also positively free or autonomous action, is a matter of agents working independently of 'alien' causes is the centre of the difficulty. Acts are events in the world, and so subject to causality, and so surely cannot have 'independence from alien causes' if those 'alien' causes are construed to include preferences, desires, inclinations or other states of the agent. Such freedom, it is held, assumes a metaphysically extravagant if not incoherent conception of the self as (in part) outside the causal order. Kant's critics object that the notion of self-legislation that is independent of 'alien' causes presupposes negative freedom that could be enjoyed only by a particular sort of agent, a 'noumenal self', who is independent of the empiri-

---

[24] Kant, *Groundwork of the Metaphysics of Morals*, IV:420, 440.     [25] Ibid., IV:447.

cal world and so of all causality. Reluctance to credit human agents with noumenal freedom lies behind Rawls's reluctance to go the whole way with Kant,[26] and Sandel's polemic against something that he calls the 'deontological self' and attributes to Kant and to contemporary 'Kantians'.[27] Many other commentators think that Kant's account of negative freedom, and hence his account of autonomy, is not only intrinsically implausible, but flies in the face of his own critique of transcendent metaphysics, by introducing and building on notions of a 'noumenal' or 'intelligible' self and world. Kant's claim that human action, and so autonomous action, is independent of 'alien causes' is subject to perennial accusations of metaphysical hubris and inconsistency with the core of his own philosophy.

These are serious criticisms. However, in reading the problem as one of metaphysical extravagance, critics overlook the wider framework within which Kant defends his conceptions of negative and positive freedom. This framework rejects not the possibility, or indeed the necessity, but the sufficiency of an empiricist approach to human action. In the third chapter of *Groundwork* Kant repeatedly insists that human beings *must* take two standpoints, a theoretical standpoint from which they seek to know the world and its causal orderings, and a practical standpoint from which they deliberate about action. He sees these two standpoints not merely as jointly indispensable but as mutually irreducible. Probably the easiest way to show why he thinks that the practical standpoint is not dispensable, or subordinate to the theoretical standpoint, is to note that he insists that we must take ourselves to be agents if we are to judge and deliberate, reason and argue, including reasoning and arguing about the world we know: only beings who can own and control their action can adopt the theoretical standpoint, which opens the road to causal explanation. Equally, only beings who can own and control their action can adopt the moral standpoint, by seeking to impose the demands of positive freedom or autonomy on their action. If we try to eliminate our own agency by viewing the theoretical standpoint and its cognitive stance as comprehensive, we shall undercut the possibility not only of morality but of knowledge.

In taking it that we must adopt two entirely different stances, Kant rejects the empiricist view that normative and theoretical approaches to action differ only in the uses to which they put a single, encompassing theoretical model of action. It does not follow that Kant rejects an

---

[26] Rawls, *A Theory of Justice*, 256–7.    [27] Sandel, *Liberalism and the Limits of Justice*.

empiricist view of knowledge of action, or claims to know that we can act counter-causally. On the contrary, he insists that some causal account can be given of any event, and so of any act. But he claims that we can reach this view *only* by taking it that we are agents with capacities for both negative and positive freedom. He denies only the ambitious claim that empiricism provides an all-encompassing conceptual framework for action as well as knowledge.[28]

Kant offers no proofs for these claims. Nor, as he makes explicit, could he consistently do so. The notion of proof is itself part of a theoretical stance, and its use would imply a view that the theoretical standpoint is comprehensive and the practical standpoint subordinate. In the early part of the third chapter of *Groundwork* he had noted that an 'analysis of freedom' leads us only into a circle,[29] and proposes that the only exit from this circle is via a critique of reason, which offers reasons why freedom is not to be denied, but no proof of freedom.

The strategy of argument that Kant uses to argue for freedom in the 'critical' sections in chapter III of the *Groundwork*[30] can be understood as a way of throwing doubt not on the merits, but on the scope and sufficiency of any empiricist approach in which acts are seen as naturally caused by states of agents. He does not thereby deny that we can look at action from a theoretical standpoint: human action forms part of a natural order whose causal structure Kant regards as exceptionless. The 'empirical character' of human action is entirely within the scope of causal inquiry.[31] What he denies is that we could conceive of action solely in this way. The practical standpoint is ineliminable.

Despite the difficulty of these fundamental thoughts, the terms in which Kant offers his practical account of action are unsurprisingly more familiar than those to be found in theoretical accounts of action, whether philosophical or psychological. From a practical point of view, when action is an object of deliberation and decision rather than cognition, we are not dealing with individual acts: these have yet to be performed. Rather we consider the propositional content of action that might be undertaken: we consider possible act-descriptions and consider the feasibility, the implications, the desirability and the morality of

---

[28] For closer textual suggestions and reasons for preferring a two-standpoint to a metaphysically more startling two-world reading of Kant on agency, see Onora O'Neill, 'Reason and Autonomy in *Grundlegung* III', in *Constructions of Reason: Explorations of Kant's Practical Philosophy* (Cambridge: Cambridge University Press, 1989), 51–65.

[29] Kant, *Groundwork of the Metaphysics of Morals*, IV:450.  [30] Ibid., IV:452 onwards.

[31] Kant, *Critique of Pure Reason*, A539/B567ff.

action that might be done under these descriptions. In particular, Kant thinks, we consider what it might be to act on certain maxims, or fundamental principles, incorporating various act-descriptions. If we are aiming at positively as well as negatively free action, we ask whether these maxims are ones that could be adopted by all.

The activity of deliberation is not an exercise in introspection. Since Kant holds that agents are opaque to themselves – as to others – they may often be unsure whether a given principle is 'really' their maxim on a given occasion.[32] But this is less important than may appear: even where knowledge fails, practice has a footing. Agents can aim to work out what they would have to do and what would come about if they were to act on a certain maxim in a given situation. For practical purposes we do not need to answer the question 'What is my "real" maxim?', but rather the question 'What can or should I do to express or enact this maxim (or, specifically, this maxim on which I ought to act)?' For the practical problem is not to achieve some startling feat of depth psychology which penetrates to my 'real' maxim (a task that assumes a theoretical standpoint with a more penetrating insight than Kant thinks is available to us), but to identify and seek to express certain maxims, including maxims of duty. On Kant's view, the principle of autonomy states the fundamental criterion by which agents can identify maxims of duty, which requires only the rejection of maxims of action which could not be adopted by all. In rejecting maxims that cannot be universally adopted, we adopt laws that are self-imposable for a plurality, and when we act on these laws we may achieve morally acceptable action and exemplify Kantian autonomy.

The role of preferences in this practical account of action is quite different from their role in typical empiricist theories of action, in that preferences and desires are seen not as (some of) the invariable *causes* of action, but as potentially part of the *content* of maxims of action. Kant is notorious for having written in some passages as though maxims that refer to preferences (for Kant: desires or inclinations) are invariably regrettable, if not morally reprehensible.[33] However, this is clearly not his overall position. Although Kant often speaks of lives which *systematically* give maxims of satisfying preferences priority over maxims of rejecting non-universalizable principles as dominated by a fundamental

---

[32] For more detailed discussion of Kant's conception of action see Onora O'Neill, 'Kant's Virtues', in Roger Crisp, ed., *How Should One Live? Essays on the Virtues* (Oxford: Clarendon Press, 1996), 77–97.

[33] See the endlessly studied passages at the end of chapter I and beginning of chapter II of the *Groundwork of the Metaphysics of Morals*.

maxim of self-love, and based on the rejection of morality,[34] a little reflection shows that he regards it as entirely normal and acceptable to act on particular maxims whose content is shaped by preferences (desires, inclinations). His basic distinction between action done *in conformity with duty* and action done *out of duty* would otherwise make no sense. Innumerable acts that are fully in accord with duty are done for a variety of reasons, and often to satisfy preferences, and hence not, or not only, in order to act dutifully. Moral failure arises where duty is subordinated to self-love, that is to what is desired or preferred.

So Kant's conception of negative freedom from 'alien' causes does not endorse puritanism or self-sufficiency or detachment from others. Although there are much-quoted passages where Kant depicts preferences (desires or inclinations) as in themselves morally suspect,[35] there are also passages where he insists that they are good. He writes, for example, 'Natural inclinations, considered in themselves, are good, that is, not a matter of reproach, and it is not only futile to want to extirpate them but to do so would also be harmful and blameworthy.'[36] The most plausible reading of Kant's position is not (as often alleged) that desires and inclinations are bad, and hence to be opposed by reason and morality, but that their relation to action may not be that of empirical cause to effect. Although we can at any time adopt the theoretical standpoint and seek the natural causes of particular acts, in acting we must take the practical standpoint. The sense in which preferences can determine action is that agents who choose to act on maxims that refer to their preferences thereby adopt maxims of a determinate propositional content. In acting on our preferences we make them part of the formal, intelligible rather than of the efficient, natural causes of action. Whether they are also, seen from another standpoint, part of the efficient cause of action is a matter for theoretical inquiry.

### 7 SOME CONCLUSIONS

Kant's conception of action and freedom provides the basis for an account of autonomy that links independence to coherence and rationality; it also leaves many questions open. Do we have to embrace the view that human life is lived from two mutually irreducible yet indispens-

---

[34] For example, Immanuel Kant, *Religion within the Boundaries of Mere Reason*, VI: 3–202; 36, tr. George di Giovanni, in Immanuel Kant, *Religion and Rational Theology*, ed. Allen Wood and George di Giovanni (Cambridge: Cambridge University Press, 1996).

[35] For example, *Groundwork of the Metaphysics of Morals*, IV:406–8.

[36] Kant, *Religion within the Boundaries of Mere Reason*, VI:51.

able standpoints? Could some simpler account of action and freedom also support a strong account of autonomy as combining independence with coherence and rationality? Are those social sciences (above all politics and economics) which have built on empiricist views of action and self compatible with a Kantian view of agency and autonomy?

These demanding and complex issues are not, however, the immediate ones for public policy and an account of justice. Rather public policy and ethical debate can – and if Kant is right, they must – engage with a practical account of agency and autonomy: they must deploy and presuppose capacities for agency and autonomy, for negative and positive freedom, of normal agents. Ethics and politics are not spectator sports.

Kant offers linked accounts of agency, autonomy and morality which provide a framework for evaluating specific sorts of principles, policies, practices and institutions. More specifically he provides a framework within which to evaluate the innumerable specific types of dependence and independence which human lives and practices may produce, and for judging which are valuable or admirable and which are not. On Kantian views it will be important to devise institutions and practices that secure and sustain basic capacities for agency and autonomy for all, under specific and varying circumstances; this is unlikely to be fostered by any idolization of self-sufficiency or of mere sheer independence. A Kantian starting point may show that some specific forms of dependence and interdependence are morally valuable, even a source or precondition of developing strong abilities to act and to act autonomously.[37]

Many current debates, on matters ranging from work and education to medical ethics and civil rights, advocate forms of independence which are viewed as indispensable for autonomous action. Yet these debates all too often obscure the moral significance of the very independence they advocate, by conflating autonomy and its moral value with independence *sans phrase*. This conflation may have lead to an over-valuing of mere independence and (supposedly) independent lives, and to failure to see the deeper reasons for valuing autonomy. Once we have an account of those deeper reasons, we may find reasons to value both specific forms of dependence and specific forms of independence.

---

[37] For contemporary writing that looks at ways in which Kant's and 'Kantian' ethics might view specific sorts of dependence, relationships, attachments, emotions see Barbara Herman, *The Practice of Moral Judgement* (Cambridge, Mass.: Harvard University Press, 1993); Marcia Baron, *Kantian Ethics almost without Apology* (Ithaca, N.Y.: Cornell University Press, 1995); Jane Kneller and Sidney Axinn, eds., *Autonomy and Community: Readings in Contemporary Kantian Social Philosophy* (Albany N.Y.: State University of New York Press, 1998).

CHAPTER 3

# Principles, practical judgement and institutions[1]

Contemporary writing in ethics and political philosophy is deeply divided about the importance of principles and rules. Most philosophical writing on justice seeks to establish principles of justice. These are thought of as stating standards to which just societies, institutions and actions are to conform – or at least aspire. However, many other writers on ethics suspect that practical principles or rules are corrupting, stifling or even illusory, and *a fortiori* that they are ethically disastrous. They maintain that ethical concern should focus on virtues and community, on care and commitment and on other distinctive excellences, and assert that none of these can be adequately specified or captured by principles or rules.[2] The partisans of justice and of virtue often speak past one another. Theorists of justice concentrate on justifying universal principles, and are often rather uncommunicative about the implications of principles for particular cases. The sponsors of virtue care about sensitive discrimination and articulation of particular cases, but are often cavalier about questions of justice and justification.

It is worth reconsidering some of the criticisms that are brought against theories of justice, and more broadly against ethics of principle. I shall do so by offering an account of practical principles, and considering whether it falls foul of objections made by those who are suspicious of principles. I shall try to show that a commitment to practical principles is not only coherent but practical: when linked to a plausible account of practical

[1] An ancestor of this essay appeared as 'Principles, Judgement, Institutions', in John Tasioulas, ed., *Law, Values and Social Practices: William Galbraith Miller Centenary Lectures in Jurisprudence* (Aldershot: Dartmouth Publishing Company, 1997), 59–73.

[2] The opponents of principles and rules are more heterogeneous than this may suggest. Some, including communitarians and those interested in ethical pluralism, object only to 'abstract' and 'universal' principles and rules, and base their own accounts of ethics on the more determinate norms of communities, that is on socially embodied principles. Others have more radical objections, and hold that ethical judgement must be wholly particularist, dealing with each case as it arises. See n. 7 below.

judgement, principles can guide action. Although I shall say nothing about the justification of principles of any specific sort, I take it that certain practical (including ethical) principles can be justified; this is a good reason for thinking seriously about the ways in which principles can guide action.

## I PRACTICAL PRINCIPLES

Principles of action – practical principles – refer to *types of action*. Every practical principle embodies some description of a possible action, which may be as stark as that used in the principle 'take an eye for an eye', or as complex as that embodied in a statute that incorporates much technical detail and specifies many exceptions.

However, practical principles do more than *state* act-descriptions. In the first place, they take up a *position* or *stance* with respect to action falling under the description they contain. They may, for example, prescribe or forbid, recommend or warn against action falling under that description. Those principles which formulate requirements (prohibitions, obligations, permissions, exceptions etc.) can quite naturally be thought of as *rules*; those which formulate recommendations or warnings cannot. I shall therefore try to keep the term 'rule' specifically for practical principles which incorporate one or another deontic notion. The distinction between rules and recommendations (or warnings) applies not only to ethical principles but to practical principles of every type. Practical principles (whether ethical or legal, prudential or social) may state *requirements*, or they may recommend *excellences* and warn against *failures* (again, whether ethical or legal, prudential or social).

Second, practical principles usually specify the *domain of agents* for whom they are to be regarded as relevant. Some are formulated as universal principles for all agents: they are seen as principles for mankind at large. Others are formulated for and addressed to restricted ranges of agents, for example, for cyclists or for pensioners. Frequently the domain of agents for whom a principle is proposed is left rather vague. Principles such as 'exercise due care and attention'; 'gratuitous violence is wrong'; 'love your neighbour'; 'waste not, want not'; 'dry food is good for man'; 'it is inadvisable to drink stagnant water' do not explicitly state that they are principles for all agents. By contrast, use of explicit *agent descriptions* is typical when principles are intended for restricted ranges of agents. Principles such as 'parents may not neglect their children'; 'children should be seen and not heard'; 'travellers in south-east Asia are recommended to take anti-malarial drugs'; 'customers are warned that pickpockets have been active' reveal quite clearly for whom they are intended.

Those practical principles which state requirements – rules – are distinctive in having (a degree of) deontic structure. This is not always apparent on the surface. Although some rules are stated using deontic terms ('ought', 'may', 'should'), others use imperatives to convey the notion of requirement: 'thou shalt not kill', 'keep your promises', 'insure your car', 'to make an omelette you will have to break eggs' all state requirements. Principles which formulate requirements are systematically linked in two respects. First, the rights and obligations, permissions and prohibitions pertaining to a given individual are systematically linked: for example, action that is required of some agent (whether ethically, legally, socially, prudentially) will also be permissible, and its omission forbidden for that agent. Second, the rights and obligations, permissions and prohibitions of two or more agents may be systematically linked: A can be entitled to B's action or forbearance only if B is obliged so to do or to forbear. Rules are linked in *systems* of deontic requirements.

Those practical principles which do not state requirements may recommend or exhort, warn or advise, point out what it would be good or excellent or virtuous to do or to be, and what it would be bad or vicious to do or to be. Once again the specification of the range of agents for whom a principle is intended may be left vague: 'don't push your luck', 'smoking can harm your health', 'honesty is the best policy', 'to thine own self be true', 'beware the Ides of March' are stated in open form, as advice or warning to the world at large. Other recommendations and warnings may be directed to specified ranges of agents. Like requirements, recommendations and warnings may be ethical or legal, prudential or social; unlike requirements they are not interlinked by any deontic structure. Omitting recommended action need be neither bad nor vicious; performance of virtuous and excellent action need not be claimable by others.

Although the distinctions between requirements and recommendations, and correspondingly between prohibitions and warnings, are clear enough, many practical principles are not readily classifiable and seem to carry both roles. Advice may be formulated as if it were a matter of requirement. We commonly say even of action not strictly required that it ought to be done, and of action that we are merely warned against that it ought to be avoided.[3]

---

[3] Part of this overlap may arise from the fact that what is required may itself be excellent: some requirements prescribe action that is also recommended or advisable; there can be duties of virtue. Part may arise from the fact that we commonly elide the prudential and technical assumptions that form the background of many practical principles, so obscuring the sources of supposed requirements. Part may reflect imprecision of language.

## 2 RIGOURISM AND ABSTRACTION

A recurrent objection against principles, and above all against rules, has been that they demand uniform enactment: an ethic of rules must lead to ethical rigourism and will be insensitive to differences between cases. Even if principles or rules are elaborated to incorporate many exceptions, this problem will remain because there is a limit to the amount of detail that can be incorporated.

This objection is generally irrelevant for the sorts of principles or rules that have been thought important for justice, and for other ethical principles, or more generally for ethics, and often irrelevant for legal, social and prudential rules and principles. For these practical principles are generally rather abstract and indeterminate: consider, for example, time-honoured principles such as 'injure no man', 'do as you would be done by', '*caveat emptor*' and 'neither a borrower nor a lender be'. Each of these practical principles enjoins action that can take many different forms; only some aspects of action are specified; much is left open. We would know very little about a person's life by discovering that she lived with scrupulous adherence to the principles of 'looking before leaping' and 'taking a stitch in time', or that she heeded warnings against smoking and recommendations to let mercy temper justice.

Fears that principles, and especially rules, must regiment those who live by them are misplaced, for the only principles that are equipped to regiment are algorithms of a peculiarly deadening and redundant sort that require uniform action regardless of varying situations. Yet rules that are close to being algorithms of this sort generally regulate only very minor aspects of life, and even these they do not totally regiment. The postal service prescribes a precise minimum value of stamps for letters whose weight lies within a precise range. This constrains the preparation of envelopes, but it does not regiment letter posting, let alone correspondence, let alone lives.[4]

Practical principles of the sort that interest us are indeterminate rather than algorithmic; they prescribe constraints rather than regiment action; they recommend types of action, policy and attitude rather than providing detailed instructions for living. They usually specify no more than an aspect of action, and this often quite vaguely. To be sure, there

---

[4] Strictly speaking postal regulations too do not state practical algorithms: even in this well-regulated domain we may lick and stick in various ways. True algorithms belong in formal systems which abstract from everything which they do not determine. In matters of action we find no more than quasi-algorithms.

can be practical rules or principles that are thought to require or to recommend too much uniformity in certain activities. Examples are easy: the poll tax (as opposed to taxation based on ability to pay) was thought by many to require too great a uniformity in one aspect of life; traditional conceptions of good mothers are often thought to recommend too rigid a conception of familial roles and domestic virtue. Yet even here, when we think about matters, we see that living by these principles does not fully regiment lives, or even aspects of lives: those who paid the poll tax lived varied lives; so did those who refused to pay; the lives of traditional good mothers have varied in many ways. How great a degree of uniformity or differentiation is to be prescribed for different aspects of life is surely a substantive question. It is not a *general* objection to principles, or even to rules, that some leave too little discretion, although there may be sound objections to specific principles and rules that do so.

Once we have noted that practical principles do not necessarily prescribe or recommend uniformity, we must also accept that they do not offer complete guidance. Curiously enough, opponents of principles and rules, and of those conceptions of ethics and of justice which propose principles and rules, have often combined their objection to demands for uniformity with complaints about lack of guidance (principles, including rules, cannot fail in both ways: if they regiment they won't be empty, and *vice versa*). Perhaps, then, the serious charge against an ethic of principles is not that it regiments but on the contrary that it cannot guide action.

Yet what is the alternative? The thought behind this second objection is presumably that in the end an action has to be quite particular and determinate, so that an adequate account of practical reasoning should provide total guidance that identifies the particular act to be performed. This thought seems to me wholly implausible. Perhaps the only way of thinking about ethics which holds out a seeming promise of practical reasoning that yields total guidance is classical Utilitarianism. However, its supposed completeness as a way of reasoning about action depends on false assumptions about the availability and precision of data (in particular about knowledge of causal connections and the availability of a metric for value). Classical Utilitarianism offers a merely notional practical algorithm: although this algorithm ostensibly prescribes with differentiated precision (and so escapes the regimentation objection), unfortunately it cannot be followed. Ordinary, watered-down Utilitarian reasoning offers much less than an algorithm, and provides guidance that may be no more complete than that offered by many ethics of principle. There are no reasons to suppose that there are genuinely practical algorithms which can wholly direct lives.

### 3 PRINCIPLES AND PRACTICAL JUDGEMENT

Practical principles (and rules) never provide complete guidance. The thought that there are complete rules for the application of rules leads only into an infinite regress. On this point both Kant and Wittgenstein are right, although some Wittgensteinians and communitarians rather oddly imagine that Kant and Kantians are on the other side of this fence.[5] However, if principles and rules cannot fully guide action, they must be complemented by judgement. The conclusion that principles are not enough is, of course, one which opponents of principles in ethical reasoning will welcome; and they are surely right to do so. However, some of them will insist that principles are nevertheless pointless, because judgement not merely *supplements* but *supplants* principles.

Certainly, so long as we hold onto the idea that something is awry in an account of practical reasoning if it cannot provide total guidance, principles must seem intrinsically inadequate. There will be a gulf between a necessarily indeterminate principle which requires or recommends an act type and particular acts. Yet to say that the gap must be 'filled by judgement', which can engage with (or at least reach towards) the particular, is little help unless we understand what judgement does. And here there is much murk. The thought that judgement is either necessary or sufficient for practical deliberation can only be made plausible if we can see more clearly what capacities to judge contribute to deliberation, and specifically what *practical judgement* contributes.

Many discussions of judgement in ethics view it as a form of cognitive judgement: judgement is to focus on cases that are to hand, for example, by determining whether a case at hand falls under some description (*subsumptive* or *determinant* judgement) or by finding a description that is apt for a case at hand (what Kant called *reflective* judgement).[6]

---

[5] The *locus classicus* is Immanuel Kant, *Critique of Pure Reason*, tr. and ed. Paul Guyer and Allen Wood (Cambridge: Cambridge University Press, 1998), A133/B172, where Kant argues that there cannot be complete rules for the application of rules. For an example of attribution of the contrary view to Kant see Charles Larmore, 'Moral Judgment', *Review of Metaphysics*, 35 (1981), 275–96; 278.

[6] This terminology was introduced by Kant, who wrote: 'If the universal (the rule, principle or law) is given, then the judgement which subsumes the particular is *determinant* . . . If, however, only the particular is given and the universal has to be found for it, then the judgement is simply *reflective*', in the *Critique of Judgement*, tr. James Creed Meredith (Oxford: Clarendon Press, 1973), 18/179.

However, it is quite obscure how practical judgement could follow either of these patterns *because it has to be undertaken when there is no case to hand*. Practical judgement does not focus on particulars, but on types, on possible action (policies, attitudes); it is undertaken *on the way* to enacting a particular act, not in order to grasp a particular act that has already been done. Practical judgement is neither subsumptive (determinant) nor reflective. It strives towards *specificity*, with a view to action; it does not and cannot grasp pre-existing particulars.[7]

Those who think that ethical judgement can be achieved without appeal to principles have put forward two views; but strangely neither view offers an account of practical judgement. Some writers – broadly speaking they are ethical particularists – take a more or less *intuitionist* view of ethical judgement, which they see as reasonably like Kant's conception of reflective judging (the particular is given, and the task is to find the appropriate 'universal' or description). This task is variously described as a matter of intuiting, perceiving, appreciating or appraising the salient characteristics, including any salient ethical characteristics, of particular situations.[8] This account of moral judgement as a capacity to judge actual cases is puzzling in two respects. First, particularists depict capacities to judge as quasi-perceptual, yet there are many disanalogies between ethical and perceptual judgement, particularly when it comes to resolution of disagreement. Second, and more perplexingly, the assimilation of practical to perceptual judgement seemingly overlooks the fact that practical judgement *does not have the matter that it judges to hand*.

The other common way of conceiving of capacities to judge cases without appeal to principles is (roughly speaking) tradition-based: prac-

[7] The exception may seem to be the case of ethical judgement of action already performed, which deals with particulars, or at least with descriptions of particulars. Part of a judge's task is retrospective. However, another part is prospective, and here practical judgement cannot be avoided. Deliberation, as Aristotle famously said, is about the possible.

[8] For thoughtful versions of particularism see David Wiggins, 'Deliberation and Practical Reason', in his *Needs, Values, Truth: Essays on the Philosophy of Value*, Aristotelian Society, 6 (Oxford: Blackwell, 1987); Jonathan Dancy, 'Ethical Particularism and Morally Relevant Properties', *Mind*, 92 (1983), 530–47; John McDowell, 'Deliberation and Moral Development', in Stephen Engstrom and Jennifer Whiting, eds., *Aristotle, Kant and the Stoics* (Cambridge: Cambridge University Press, 1996), 19–35. Attempts to depict reflective judgement as central to morality can also be found in some recent Kantian work: see Rudolf Makkreel, 'Differentiating, Regulative, and Reflective Approaches to History', in Hoke Robinson, ed., *Proceedings of the Eighth International Kant Congress*, vol. I, pt I, 123–37; G. Felicitas Munzel, *Kant's Conception of Moral Character: The 'Critical' Link of Morality, Anthropology and Reflective Judgement* (Chicago: University of Chicago Press, 1999).

tical judgement is seen as guided by the precedents of those who judge well within a given tradition. Legal decisions appeal to precedents established by good judges; ethical deliberation, for example, to the teachings of Jesus or of the Buddha, to the judgement of the *phronimos* or of other exemplars, which are to provide a pattern or template for judging other cases. This conception of ethical judgement is favoured by many communitarians and virtue ethicists.[9]

If a version of intuitionism could be made epistemologically plausible we would, perhaps, have an account of ethical judgement of a sort that could pass judgement on particular cases of action already performed without relying on principles. However, we would still have no account of practical judgement that could be used for practical purposes, that is in moving towards acting.

If, on the other hand, the authority of certain supposedly exemplary traditional figures could be shown canonical for making ethical judgements, we would once again have no account of practical judgement that could be used in the absence of principles. Appeals to cases that are already to hand, or known through tradition or literary sources, are mute in the absence of principles. For appealing to the past judgements of authorities is not enough: their judgement has to be known or shown to be relevant to some actual case – which inevitably differs in various respects. In generalizing from one case to another, differing case deliberators have to appeal to general claims that certain characteristics are ethically significant resemblances while others are not: in short, to principles. The principles relied on may use act-descriptions which are particular to a certain legal tradition or way of life; they may be the principles of an entire society or of a narrow community: they are principles none the less. Whether they are superior or more authoritative principles than the less socially determinate principles proposed by most theorists of justice and other writers on ethics is not to the point here. What is to the point is that (intuitionists apart) both those who advocate practical principles and those who criticize them *in fact* depict judgement as working in tandem with principles.

---

[9] A well-known account of ethical judgement along these lines can be found in Alasdair MacIntyre, *After Virtue* (London: Duckworth, 1981). The view is widespread among hermeneutic and communitarian writers.

### 4  MULTIPLE PRINCIPLES AND MORAL CONFLICT

It is sometimes said by those who are wary of principles that, even if it were possible to augment principles with judgement, still some principles, and above all rules, will lead ethical reasoning into disaster, not because they are either 'too rigid' or 'too abstract', but because any agent committed to multiple obligations will find from time to time that these conflict. Life and literature abound with cases of conflict, often of conflicts between ethical requirements: 'to save a friend from murder, a lie must be told' (Kant's example); 'to save a life, a doctor must be kidnapped' (Mill's example); 'to feed the hungry, the Sabbath must be breached' (Christ's example). Other recurrent conflicts pit ethical requirements against other practical principles: 'to save a life will cost a fortune' (an NHS predicament); 'to feed ambition, lives must be taken' (Macbeth's predicament).

Such problems can arise even when no plurality of requirements is under consideration, since a single rule can seemingly demand two incompatible acts. In so-called Buridan moral dilemmas (named for a famous donkey's predicament), as discussed by Ruth Barcan Marcus and others, agents are described as having to choose between two indiscernibly differing requirements, such as 'rescuing one of two drowning twins', when rescuing both is impossible.[10] Seemingly, if 'ought' implies 'can', if two rescues cannot be managed, and if nothing differentiates the two cases, it cannot be the case that both rescues are obligatory: since they are (by hypothesis) indiscernible and not compossible, neither can be obligatory. Others, in particular Bernard Williams, have discussed examples of conflicts between obligations which are not quite Buridan cases, since the two incompatible actions are discernibly different, although they appear to fall under a single principle, for example, the dilemma posed by a choice between 'rescuing one's drowning wife' and 'rescuing an equally drowning stranger'. Williams concludes that any ethic centred on rules or obligation is morally flawed: it would commit one to a relentless impartiality, and so preclude taking cognizance of personal attachments, bonds or commitments, or rescuing one's wife rather than the stranger.[11]

In considering conflicts between rules or obligations it helps to distin-

---

[10]  Ruth Barcan Marcus, 'Moral Dilemmas and Consistency', *Journal of Philosophy*, 77 (1980), 121–36; see esp. 125 and the discussion of the requirements for ethical consistency.

[11]  Bernard Williams, 'Persons, Character and Morality', in *Moral Luck* (Cambridge: Cambridge University Press, 1981), 17–18.

guish two quite different cases. Some pairs or larger sets of principles are *intrinsically* not jointly satisfiable, because they enjoin mutually exclusive types of action, policy or life. Nobody can accept an obligation both to give away all worldly goods and to make a fortune. Nobody can regard it as obligatory to be open and to be secretive with all. Nobody can view both revenge and forgiveness as obligatory wherever wrong has been suffered. Nobody can accept rules whose enactment is intrinsically incompatible.

However, the practically significant cases of conflict arise where principles are *not intrinsically but contingently incompatible*: they are jointly satisfiable in some cases but (as it appears) not jointly satisfiable in a given context. I may commit myself both to honest dealing and to concern for my friends, and find the commitments compatible until a situation arises where my honesty will harm my friends. When such situations arise, at least one commitment must fail. Peter was committed to acknowledging Christ, but also to self-protection: when it proved prudent to conceal his identity he denied knowing Christ. Does the evident possibility of contingent conflicts between principles tell against the coherence or the usefulness of practical principles, and in particular of ethical principles?

If we suppose that principles provide total guidance, then (it seems to me) even contingent conflicts between them will entail that nobody can coherently adopt multiple principles; indeed, since contingent conflicts can arise in the application of a single principle, it will follow that *any* use of practical principles, let alone *any* ethic of principles, must lead to incoherence. However, we have already seen that there are no good reasons for supposing that principles are algorithms rather than indeterminate, and so none for expecting them to provide total guidance to agents. Contingent conflicts between principles to which an agent is committed set a task, often a demanding task; but they do not show that principles and commitments to principles are impossible.[12]

When the various principles to which an agent is committed may conflict, even contingently, acute problems can arise. If I have to lie to save a friend, or steal to save a life, or betray one person unless I betray another, or murder if I am to attain my ambition, I may face sharp, perhaps agonizing, dilemmas. Yet the solution to the dilemma cannot be that we should stop thinking in terms of principles: to be sure, the dilemma would then vanish, since the types of action which principles

---

[12] See Barbara Herman, 'Obligation and Performance', in her *The Practice of Moral Judgement* (Cambridge, Mass.: Harvard University Press, 1993), 159–83 for arguments for viewing deliberation as a task.

prescribe or proscribe, recommend or abjure, would no longer make their claims. The solution, and it can only be a partial solution, must rather lie in the ways in which we cope with and forestall possible and actual contingent conflicts of principle. The resolution of contingent conflicts, I shall suggest, may draw on several different deliberative strategies. The most central of these is practical judgement, by which action that satisfies multiple principles is sought. A second and longer-term strategy is the development and reform of institutions and characters in ways that reduce the likelihood of recurrent contingent conflict between principles. A third deliberative strategy handles moral and other failure by dealing with the 'remainders' with which unmet obligations and requirements leave us.

## 5 PRACTICAL JUDGEMENT AND MULTIPLE PRINCIPLES

Agents usually bring multiple commitments and principles, and multiple goals, to any deliberative task. The first part of their task is to judge whether there are ways of acting that satisfy the claims of all significant principles (and do not obstruct other goals), so avoiding both (moral) conflict and (moral) failure. For example, we may regard principles of order, liberty and democracy as requirements of justice, while knowing that they can easily come into tension with one another. In running a business we may view it as a requirement to secure new investment, stable labour relations and high profitability, while knowing that they are often in tension. In running a university or a university department we may view fostering good research and good teaching (and other less edifying performance indicators) as requirements, while knowing that they are often in tension. Parents may think that they ought to bring up a child to be honest and kind, while knowing that these objectives are often in tension. However, the response which legislators, business leaders, academics and parents make to these possibilities of conflict between their various obligations is not to conclude that there was something awry about commitment to a plurality of obligations, or to principles as such, but to search for ways of acting which meet the constraints of all the principles (and the varied goals) which they see as important. This need not be problematic in itself, given that each principle is relatively indeterminate; however, like many tasks, it cannot always be fully achieved.

Still something must be said about how the task is achieved, or the process of practical judgement will remain a mystery. Clearly we cannot expect to find a complete account of the moves to be made: that could be given only if there were complete rules for judging, providing a practical algorithm. In the absence of a practical algorithm, practical judging simply seeks to identify *some* act or pattern of action that adequately meets the several requirements of the case.

Such a process of practical judgement has considerable analogies with solving a design problem. In designing a stove, for example, numerous distinct constraints must be met. The stove must be made of available materials; the heat it yields must be accurately controllable; its energy consumption and waste must be held down; safety standards must be met; the stove must be affordable and attractive to those who are envisaged as purchasers. These design criteria constitute a set of constraints and standards which cannot all be met perfectly, but which also cannot always or perhaps generally be traded off against one another: the stove that does not heat fails even if it is very, very safe.

Practical judgement too is a matter of identifying some way of meeting a plurality of requirements and recommendations of various types. And as with design problems, the task is not best conceived as that of balancing different principles, or different obligations. Complete success in living up to one obligation may go no way to compensate for deficiency in meeting another: killing others is a very effective strategy for avoiding coercing them, but quite beside the point. Killers do not 'balance' their misdeeds by pointing out how perfectly they avoided other injustices to their victims. The difficulty of judging how to satisfy a plurality of obligations is not eased by invoking an illusory metric by which observance of various principles can supposedly be balanced and traded off: the real task of practical judgement is simply to seek ways of acting that respect multiple obligations. Although there is no algorithm to be followed, the process of practical judging may be better or worse, and may improve or deteriorate. Those who regularly violate many requirements, or who fail to identify obvious lines of action which respect all requirements, do not show good practical judgement.

## 6 INSTITUTIONS AND CHARACTERS

Practical judgement is the crucial but not the only component of deliberation framed by principles. A second aspect of deliberation investigates ways in which possible contingent conflicts between principles can be forestalled, so easing the task of practical judgement. Potential collisions between enactments of principles form familiar patterns, and by reforming or adjusting institutions, practices, ways of life and traits of character to lessen the likelihood of these patterns, people can avert or minimize contingent conflicts.[13]

Some examples can make the point. Commitment to principles of liberty and of democracy are quite likely to lead to conflicting demands. However, by exempting basic civil rights from direct democratic procedures, it may prove possible to construct a better institutionalization of democracy, as well as of liberty and of order, than could be built by exposing all aspects of life directly to democratic process. Or again, if commitments to democratic governance and civil rights alone left members of minority cultures and religions over-exposed to the assumptions and assimilation of a majority culture, this might be eased by specific measures to protect cultural diversity and the varying identities of citizens.[14]

Institutional changes that accommodate and minimize conflict are not, of course, confined to the political arena. Business practice may face conflicting demands to achieve new capital investment, good labour relations and high profitability: the likelihood of conflict may be reducible across the long haul not by seeking to maximize all three objectives but by compromises that limit action in pursuit of any one objective. Practices of child rearing may seek to educate each child into kindness, honesty and prudence, and find that the best approach is not to seek constant perfection in all three (that way hypocrisy lies) but to lead children into routines of life and thought within which stark conflict between these principles is less likely while shielding them from difficult conflicts until both principles and the web of ways in which conflict can be averted or mitigated are better understood.

## 7  PRACTICAL JUDGEMENT AND REMAINDERS

Judgement is indeed, as Kant said, a 'peculiar talent'.[15] It is a talent in that it follows no algorithm: there are no complete rules for the application of rules. It is not a matter of deducing comprehensive instructions for action from relatively indeterminate principles. Rather it is a question of finding ways of meeting multiple constraints and recommendations set by a plu-

---

[13] See Marcus, 'Moral Dilemmas and Consistency': 'we ought to conduct our lives and arrange our institutions so as to minimize predicaments of moral conflict', 121. While I doubt that the aim of *minimizing* makes strict sense, her stress on the role of institutions and character in averting conflict is highly convincing.

[14] See James Tully, *Strange Multiplicity: Constitutionalism in an Age of Diversity* (Cambridge: Cambridge University Press, 1995).    [15] Kant, *Critique of Pure Reason*, A133/B172.

rality of principles. Although no recipe for judging can be set out, the constraints it imposes often allow agents to distinguish better from worse judgement, by noting how well the various relevant principles are respected. Like other talents, judgement can be better or worse developed.

Even the best-developed capacity for practical judgement and the most energetic attempts at institutional reform and cultural development cannot avert all conflicts. In thinking about the possibility of conflicts between principles it is pointless to assume that institutional or cultural reform will always be on the cards, or that if successful it will eventually wholly avert contingent conflicts of principle. In real-time deliberation, agents will always find certain institutions and practices, certain habits and customs, certain virtues and certain faults, already in place, which may variously help or hinder their attempts to live up to their multiple principles. In daily reasoning about action it will often be pointless or misleading to assume away these institutional structures and ways of life.

If conflict is not wholly avoidable, some account must be given of ways of dealing with moral failure, when agents cannot or do not respect all the principles to which they are committed. Often they may think that had institutions been better, or had they themselves made better decisions in the past, no contingent conflict would have arisen. But they will realize that in the world as it is, they cannot avoid a degree of moral failure. What, then, are they to do?

Where existing institutions and characters force hard choices, and agents can find no ways of living up to all the principles – ethical and legal, prudential and social – which they take seriously, they may still recognize the claims of unmet, indeed contingently unmeetable, commitments and obligations, standards and recommendations. It is widely agreed that the fact that an obligation or commitment has proved contingently unmeetable does not exempt an agent from its claims. The unmeetable obligation has 'remainders': the fact of moral failure may be recognized, for example, in expressions and attitudes of regret, apology or remorse. There are also other, more active, approaches to moral and practical failure, which may be more important than the attitudinal responses which have been so much emphasized in discussions of 'remainders'. More active responses might include expressions of apology, attempts at reform, offers of compensation, forms of restitution and the like.[16]

---

[16] See Barbara Herman, 'Obligation and Performance', in her *The Practice of Moral Judgement* (Cambridge, Mass.: Harvard University Press, 1993), 159–83; Onora O'Neill, 'Instituting Principles: Between Duty and Action', in Mark Timmins, ed., *Kant's Metaphysics of Morals* (Oxford: Oxford University Press, forthcoming).

The importance of remainders in the moral life, like the importance of institutions and characters, shows not that principles are dispensable, but that taking them seriously is hard and demanding. Taking principles seriously, far from pointing those who do so to 'a system of rules by which to spare themselves some of the agony of thinking and all the torment of feeling that is actually involved in reasoned deliberation', requires us to take practical judgement and the construction of institutions and characters which ease its task seriously.[17] Principles without institutions and characters may be empty, but institutions and characters without principles may be not merely blind but corrupt.

[17] Wiggins, 'Deliberation and Practical Reason', 237.

# CHAPTER 4

# Kant's justice and Kantian justice

Much contemporary work on justice is seen, both by protagonists and by critics, as Kantian. Evidently not all its conclusions accord with Kant's views on obligations, rights or justice; but this in itself is not surprising since its aim is to develop Kant's basic insights, even to improve on his conclusions.

The improved conclusions are plain enough. No contemporary writer has endorsed Kant's lack of concern with democracy, or his exclusion of women and of workers from active citizenship, and most aim to offer an account of economic justice that is more than an account of just property rights. On the other hand, nearly all contemporary writers on justice endorse Kant's liberal, republican conception of justice, his concern for respect for persons and for rights, and many see his writings on international justice as having a distinctive importance in the post Cold War world, in that he queries both the statism assumed by 'realist' writers on international relations and the merely abstract cosmopolitanism favoured both by some 'idealist' writers on international relations and by many advocates of human rights.[1]

The reasons for preferring some contemporary version of Kantian justice to Kant's account of justice may seem overwhelming; at any rate I shall not dispute their merits. And yet, I believe, there is much more to be said. The deeper and more significant differences between Kant's work and contemporary Kantianism lie not, I shall argue, in the specific conclusions about justice or about morality that each body of work offers, but in the background conceptions of action, freedom and reason on which each relies.

The agenda of reaching more or less Kantian conclusions while starting from more acceptable premisses, and in particular more acceptable

---

[1] In this essay I largely neglect the excellent work on Kant's political philosophy which has been appearing since the late 1980s. My concern is mainly with the underlying assumptions that distinguish Kant's from Kantian work on justice, rather than with Kant's texts.

conceptions of reason, freedom and action, has been fundamental in late twentieth-century Kantian approaches to justice. It was made quite explicit by Rawls, himself a serious student of Kant, in his earlier writings. Rawls describes his work as presenting 'a conception of justice which carries to a higher level of abstraction the familiar theory of the social contract as found, say, in Locke, Rousseau and Kant',[2] and he states that his 'principles of justice are also categorical imperatives in Kant's sense'.[3] However, Rawls was crystal clear in his rejection of Kant's starting points. The point is put succinctly in 'The Basic Structure as Subject', where he writes

The problem is this: to develop a viable Kantian conception of justice the force and content of Kant's doctrine must be detached from its background in transcendental idealism and given a procedural interpretation by means of the construction of the original position[4]

and that

The procedural interpretation of Kant's view not only satisfies the canons of a reasonable empiricism, but . . . At the same time it proceeds from a suitably individualistic basis.[5]

Although few have been as explicit as Rawls in stating the objectives of contemporary Kantian work on justice, I believe that nearly all of its exponents have taken from him the aim of reaching more or less Kantian conclusions from more or less empiricist views of reason, action and freedom. If the enterprise is to succeed, the empiricist conceptions which are to form the starting point must be free of the types of difficulties which Rawls and many others have seen in Kant's starting points.

If these are the ambitions of contemporary Kantian work on justice, it is rather surprising that it has constantly been targeted by critics of many differing persuasions with the very criticisms that they level against Kant.[6] In the eyes of many critics, contemporary Kantians fail in the very ways in which (they believe) Kant failed. This is in some ways discouraging for the proponents of revisionary forms of Kantianism.

---

[2] John Rawls, *A Theory of Justice* (Cambridge, Mass.: Harvard University Press, 1971), 11.

[3] Ibid., 253.

[4] Rawls, 'The Basic Structure as Subject', *American Philosophical Quarterly*, 14 (1977), 159–65; 165. See also *A Theory of Justice*, 251–6.        [5] Rawls, 'The Basic Structure as Subject', 165.

[6] These criticisms – some of them dating back to Hegel and Marx – can be found in the writings of socialists (now rather silent), Utilitarians, communitarians, virtue ethicists and certain feminists.

Either their critics are persistently mistaken, or they have been less successful in detaching themselves from Kant's difficulties than they had hoped.

## I CRITICISMS OF KANTIANISM

Both Kant's accounts of morality and justice and contemporary Kantian writing are repeatedly accused of three failings.

The first group of criticisms is directed at the presumed premisses of such work, which are said to be *abstract* or *too abstract*, designed for *abstract individuals*, so leading to abstract conclusions that are irrelevant to *real* people who lead *real* lives.

The second group of criticisms targets the normative claims of both positions, which are said to consist of *universal principles* or *rules* that mandate relentlessly *uniform* treatment of diverse cases, and so ignore all the sensitivities and responsiveness to differences which many opponents of Kantian ethics admire and think morally significant. In the area of justice the corresponding criticism is that universal rules require us to overlook and so neglect the fragility, mutual vulnerability, social embeddedness and constitutive loyalties of real people.

The second type of objection is readily linked to a third, which alleges that neither Kant nor contemporary Kantian approaches offer a convincing account of *judgement or deliberation*, because both seek to base normative conclusions on abstract, universal principles, or rules, and in doing so neglect the diversity and complexity of the moral life.

In my view, each of these criticisms blurs important distinctions. Abstraction in itself is both innocuous and unavoidable. We abstract whenever we make claims or decisions or follow policies or react to persons on a basis that *brackets* some predicates, that is indifferent as to their satisfaction or non-satisfaction. All normative principles and standards, including principles of justice, are always, inevitably and properly abstract.

Abstracting is not a bad habit peculiar to Kant or Kantians. Any normative reasoning that uses act-descriptions, in principles of any type (whether of narrow or wide scope, or of culturally specific or non-specific content, whether consisting of rules that state requirements, or of principles that merely propose standards or recommend excellences), is abstract. Act-descriptions are necessarily indeterminate. Even those who aim to be deeply attentive to the particularities of cases will have to abstract from – bracket – nearly all the features of any case to which they attend (attention, as its admirers often remind us, is selective!).

Abstraction does not make ethical reasoning (or, more specifically, reasoning about justice) either irrelevant or impossible or objectionable, although there is plenty of room for considering and reconsidering which abstractions are important for specific aspects of justice, as can be seen in countless discussions of the claims of equality and discrimination.

However, reasoning which, rather than *bracketing* certain predicates that obtain, either *denies* those predicates (asserts their absence) or *asserts* that absent predicates obtain is another matter. When this happens, reasoning may be based on false, *idealized* conceptions, of reason and action, of persons and situations. The objections that contemporary Kantian writers themselves had to Kant's starting points could be described as claiming that his conceptions of the autonomous will and of the noumenal self are idealizations, and false of real people leading real lives.

Evidently it is not easy to avoid idealizations. The critics of contemporary Kantian work on justice may have a point (which they misleadingly speak of as an objection to abstraction) in that 'the canons of a reasonable empiricism' too may harbour idealized conceptions of reason, freedom or action. I shall return to this point.

The second group of criticisms levelled against Kant and Kantian work charges that any position which argues for *universal* principles renders it ethically deficient. Universality may be understood in various ways. Minimally, a principle is *formally universal* if it applies to all cases within its scope – whether that scope be large or small. More ambitiously, a principle may be said to be *universal in scope* if its domain is very large – for example, cosmopolitan. However, the feature that has generally worried critics of Kant and of Kantian ethics is neither of these sorts of universality, but rather the thought that any (universal) principle mandates *uniform treatment*, thereby overlooking all the differences between cases, and requiring inflexible similarity of treatment. However, if universal principles are abstract they will underdetermine action, and so will not prescribe uniform action. Neither universal form nor wide scope entails uniform requirement.

It is not therefore in the least surprising that many of the universal principles advocated by Kant and by proponents of Kantian conceptions of justice patently do not require uniform treatment. For example, social justice liberals think that justice requires economic arrangements that assist the poor: they are committed to institutions will treat the rich and the poor differently. By contrast, advocates of libertarian conceptions of justice think that economic justice requires only enforcement of property rights: they are committed to institutions which will treat the propertied and the unpropertied differently. More generally, proponents of Kantian justice have all been concerned with – some of their critics think obsessed with – rights, but rights (as socialist critics of liberal justice long complained) do not secure uniform treatment, but only treatment that is uniform in some perhaps quite minor respect or aspect. Any commitment to an abstract principle is commitment to a principle that requires uniformity only in some respect, and is likely to require different rather than uniform treatment of differing cases.

Those who (mistakenly) object that Kantian principles require uniform treatment have often expressed their objection as one against *moral rules*. Perhaps the suspect and objectionable type of principles are those that state *requirements*, that formulate *prohibitions* and *obligations*, that declare *rights* or *entitlements*. There may indeed be much to be said against the assumption that rules are the *only* principles important to the moral life, and for being aware of the other types of principle of action that may be important in real lives: obligations and rights are not the whole of the moral life.[7] Yet there is little doubt that principles which formulate requirements will be important in any account of justice, and of the working of institutions. Rules have their role. However, since rules are principles they too do not prescribe uniform action: they too incorporate act-descriptions that are necessarily indeterminate.

The common criticism that Kant and Kantian accounts of justice require uniform action fails. No doubt one or another position held by Kant, or by contemporary Kantians, has endorsed various specific principles that are unacceptably rigid, that prescribe too much regimentation: if so, there may be serious criticisms to be made of those specific proposals. But the criticism cannot be generalized to all Kantian thought about justice: principles underdetermine what is done by those who follow them, and so not merely *may* but *must* leave wide scope for non-uniform treatment.[8]

Those critics who accuse Kant and contemporary Kantian work on justice alike of requiring uniform treatment often then go on to claim that both fail to give proper place to the *judgement of particular cases*, and even that they leave no room for judgement. In a way this criticism

---

[7] See in particular the work of Bernard Williams, especially his *Ethics and the Limits of Philosophy* (London: Fontana, 1985), ch. 10, where he accuses Kant and Kantians of exaggerated and possibly incoherent views of the importance of obligation.

[8] See Chapter 3 above for further discussion of the possibility of algorithmic practical principles.

follows easily from the previous ones. If Kantian approaches did require uniform treatment of cases, then there would be seemingly nothing, or much less, for judgement to do.

In fact, neither principles nor judgement are redundant in Kantian work. Judgement is evidently not redundant in any Kantian conception of ethics or of judgement, since principles, including those that state requirements, are indeterminate. Principles do not and cannot determine which particular act an agent is to do. With this we are entirely familiar in daily life, and it is odd that anyone should imagine that Kant or Kantians, who think principles important for ethics and specifically for justice, expect them to do more.[9] The voluminous discussions of legal interpretation by Kantianly inclined philosophers of law and of topics in applied ethics by Kantianly inclined writers are sound evidence that there aren't many proponents of Kantian accounts of justice – or more generally of Kantian ethical positions – who think that principles alone will guide action.

Principles are not redundant because an ability to make practical judgements needs the supporting structure of a process of reasoning about action: there is no magical ability to pick right acts, or appropriate acts. Judgement is possible precisely because act-descriptions and principles of action provide its matrix.[10]

## 2 AVOIDING IDEALIZATIONS

Of all the criticisms that have been so plentifully levelled both against Kant's ethics and against Kantian work on justice, the most serious, it seems to me, is the allegation that these approaches build on unsustainable idealizations. The charges against Kant are well known, indeed were the reason behind the enterprise we now think of as Kantian theories of justice. What is less easy to see is whether the latter work has avoided unacceptable idealizations.

There are *prima facie* reasons for thinking that it may be hard to avoid idealizations. First, if it were *easy* to reach more or less Kantian conclu-

---

[9] Kant perhaps wrote more on judgement than any other philosopher has yet done. Everything that he wrote is set within the context of his famous observation that rules (indeed all principles, including all practical principles adopted as maxims) are necessarily incomplete or indeterminate and must be joined with capacities for judgement. Immanuel Kant, *Critique of Pure Reason*, tr. and ed. Paul Guyer and Allen Wood (Cambridge: Cambridge University Press, 1998), A133–5/B172–4.

[10] See Chapter 3 above.

sions without complex idealizations, Kant too might have offered a simple set of abstract starting points. He was, after all, a powerful critic of traditional metaphysics and of unwarranted assumptions. Second, the hope that staying within 'the canons of a reasonable empiricism' will avoid unacceptable idealizations is rather optimistic. The thought is, after all, not that only empirical truths will be used as premisses, but that a form of empiricism that involves no idealizations will be found and used to build Kantian conclusions. I think that we may take Rawls's work across more than twenty-five years, in which the more or less Kantian conclusions about justice have remained constant but the underlying set of assumptions has been considerably revised, as evidence that this is by no means easy.

For it will not meet the original purposes of revisionary Kantianism about justice simply to accept some empiricist model of man that provides sufficiently strong assumptions about the structure of reason, freedom and action. These models too are based on idealizations of the sorts of ability to reason and to act that real people have. Nobody actually enjoys the capacities of Rational Economic Man, or is equipped with fully consistent, transitive and connected preferences. (What is more, if people were like this, it is a reasonable bet that Utilitarians would have a head start over Kantians in providing a convincing account of justice.)

The proper question to address is therefore not whether the whole range of Kantian approaches to justice prescribe abstract principles (they do), or prescribe uniform treatment (they do not) or overlook the contribution of judgement (they do not). The serious question will be whether particular Kantian positions in fact rely on unjustified, perhaps unjustifiable, idealizations. However, this is a criticism which can only be raised of particular positions: theories of justice need not wear their idealizations on their sleeves, in the way that they display the abstract principles which are their conclusions. So finding out whether unacceptable idealizations are assumed is much more demanding than a blanket – but rather pointless – accusation of abstraction against all Kantian views of justice.

My own belief is that idealizations are common in the background assumptions of contemporary liberal, Kantian theories of justice, and that they are not always explicitly justified. I shall illustrate rather than document this by indicating some features of the work of John Rawls. This is a significant illustration because no other contemporary Kantian writer has been more concerned or careful about the deep assumptions of his or her theory.

In fact a number of unargued idealizations can be detected in the premisses for Rawls's arguments for his two fundamental principles of justice. In *A Theory of Justice*,[11] these range from adopting 'the concept of rationality standard in social theory',[12] to ruling out the motive of envy,[13] to ascribing desires for more rather than less of each of a short list of primary goods to each agent,[14] to thinking of agents as 'deputies for a kind of everlasting moral agent or institution',[15] to assuming that an account of justice can in the first instance be worked out for the case of a 'bounded society'. Some of these assumptions could perhaps be justified as no more than simplifications of – abstractions from – empirical truths; others probably could not. In any case, the strategy of working with a limited and minimal set of supposedly merely abstract claims about human agents is one that Rawls set aside in his later work.

For example, in his 1980 Dewey Lectures he explicitly used 'the Kantian ideal of the person' as one of the premises for constructing an account of justice.[16] Critics objected that he did not offer any argument that this idealized conception is 'the uniquely plausible ideal of the person'.[17] Yet once again Rawls was ahead of his critics, and argued in his 1985 article 'Justice as Fairness, Political not Metaphysical' that the justification for choosing one rather than another ideal of the person had to be political: the ideal of the person to which he appealed from the mid 1980s is that of the person as citizen of a modern democratic polity.[18] This 'political' vindication of principles of justice was deepened in Rawls's 1993 *Political Liberalism*, in which a conception of the democratic citizen is used to introduce a distinctive account of public reason,[19] thereby cutting loose from the instrumental account of rationality which

---

[11] I have set out some of these thoughts about idealizations in Rawls's earlier and later work respectively in 'Constructivisms in Ethics', in *Constructions of Reason: Explorations of Kant's Practical Philosophy* (Cambridge: Cambridge University Press, 1989), 206–18, and others about his later philosophy in 'Political Liberalism and Public Reason: A Critical Notice of John Rawls, *Political Liberalism*', *Philosophical Review*, 106 (1997), 411–28.

[12] John Rawls, *A Theory of Justice*, 143.    [13] Ibid., 143.    [14] Ibid., 62.    [15] Ibid., 128.

[16] John Rawls, 'Kantian Constructivism in Moral Theory', *Journal of Philosophy*, 77 (1980), 515–72.

[17] See David O. Brink, 'Rawlsian Constructivism in Moral Theory', *Canadian Journal of Philosophy*, 17 (1987), 71–90; 73.

[18] John Rawls, 'Justice as Fairness: Political not Metaphysical', *Philosophy and Public Affairs*, 14 (1985), 223–51.

[19] John Rawls, *Political Liberalism* (New York: Columbia University Press, 1993), 49–51. In developing a conception of 'public reason' Rawls uses a term that is also central to Kant's conception of reason. However, his account of public reason is more Rousseauian than

had been one of the cornerstones of *A Theory of Justice*. Inevitably there is much more to be said about the successive refinements and emendations of Rawls's theory of justice. However, I think that it is instructive that his own sustained concern has been not to alter the substantive conception of justice which he defended in his earlier work, but to find starting points for that theory of justice which met his own standards better. Across the years, one might say, Rawls has moved from optimism about the agenda of finding true, abstract starting points to the conclusion that the available starting points are socially determinate, and that they enable the construction of an account of justice based on and adapted to the reasoning that takes place among those who conceive of themselves as citizens of a bounded, liberal democratic society. Some aspirants to a Kantian conception of justice that sits on properly empiricist foundations have been disappointed by this development of Rawls's work.

Of course, Rawls's difficulties may have been avoided by other approaches to a contemporary Kantian theory of justice; although I think that unlikely. One of the many ways in which his work is admirable is in its sustained effort not to smuggle in idealizations that establish the desired conclusions unless he can offer reasons for choosing those specific premises rather than alternatives. Nor do I think it surprising that this has proved so difficult. The agenda of contemporary Kantian theories of justice is precisely to reach liberal conclusions that improve on Kant's without using his supposedly objectionable accounts of reason, freedom and action. *Prima facie*, would-be Kantians who attempt this are left only with the meagre starting points that they share with the Utilitarians to whose conclusions they object: an instrumental account of rationality and a preference-based conception of action which look ill chosen to develop a distinctively Kantian account of justice (Utilitarians have found it hard to base convincing accounts of respect for persons on these starting points). So it is not surprising if extra assumptions are needed to reach the desired Kantian conclusions, or if these assumptions are hard to justify.

Kantian, in that he sees it as the public reason of a particular people who are fellow-citizens in a bounded and closed society. By contrast, for Kant public reason must be able to reach 'the world at large' and so cannot presuppose the shared assumptions of community or polity.

### 3 BACK TO KANT?

Bearing in mind the sheer difficulty of evading unwarranted idealizations in constructing a Kantian account of justice on empiricist foundations, we might do worse than look back to Kant. Of course, if we were obliged to attribute to Kant an account of (practical) reason that emerges from nowhere, an account of freedom that invokes a picture of non-causal interaction between two worlds (one temporal and the other atemporal) and a conception of agents as flitting between these worlds, we would not look back for very long.

It would be foolish at this point, and without offering serious textual exegesis, to insist that Kant's texts *cannot* support an idealizing account of the human subject. In fact they clearly *can* be read, and often have been read, to support an idealized account of the subject. Yet it may be a good deal more interesting to see whether they *need* be read in that way, that is whether they are also open to an abstract but non-idealizing reading.

The idealization which Kant's critics most commonly charge him with is the claim that the human subject is an autonomous self (not a phrase Kant uses – he predicates autonomy of wills and of the principles or laws they adopt when exercising their capacity for autonomy)[20] that lacks social context and relations with others, and is bereft of emotions and life-projects. If Kant does need this idealization, what he has to say about justice and more generally about ethics may not be relevant to human life. Yet it is not easy to offer textual evidence which shows that Kant has to be read in this way.

I believe that the main source of idealizing readings of Kant lies in a certain strategy of interpretation that assimilates Kant to his rationalist predecessors, and so reads the entire Kantian corpus as doing covertly what the Rationalists had hoped to do flamboyantly. Yet Kant's philosophy centres on a formidable critique of rationalist conceptions of ontology, theology, self and reason. It would be an amazing failure if after those criticisms he then meekly returned to the Rationalist fold. Yet generations of critics have charged Kant with just such a return. For present purposes it seems to me that the most useful thing might be to point to *some* of the elements of Kant's work that seem to offer most foot-

---

[20] See Thomas E. Hill, Jnr. in 'The Kantian Conception of Autonomy', in his *Dignity and Practical Reason in Kant's Moral Theory* (Ithaca, N.Y.: Cornell University Press, 1992), 76–96, and see Chapter 2 above.

hold to an idealizing reading of his conceptions of self, freedom, reason and action, and to show that these can be taken in another way.

One of the most striking apparent idealizations in Kant's writings must surely be the notorious noumenal self, and indeed the whole noumenal world. How could Kant use terms that are weighed down by their Platonist and Leibnizian pasts without being led back to their two-worldly conceptions of ontology and of the self, and so to a practical philosophy that is wholly dependent on unvindicated idealizations? However, here we must pay very close attention to Kant's numerous comments on his understanding of these terms. The noumenal world, he insists, is 'only *a point of view*, which reason finds itself constrained to adopt';[21] he offers sustained arguments to show that we are dealing with two standpoints, that neither can be reduced to the other, that each is indispensable, that they are not inconsistent. A two-aspect rather than two-world reading of the noumenal–phenomenal distinction is, of course, nothing new.[22] However, the implications of this reading for an understanding of Kant's practical philosophy, including his approach to justice, may not be fully explored. Here is one route for exploration.

If Kant is not committed to a two-world conception of reality, or specifically of selves, then we cannot take it for granted that his conception of critique of reason takes a 'Cartesian' view of the matter, and does no more than insist dogmatically that reason 'exists whole and complete in each of us'.[23] On the contrary, without a realist metaphysics, with its pre-established coordination between knower and known and of knowers to one another, there may be *nothing* that has quite general authority either for thinking or for acting. Our predicament may therefore be not that we need to *discover* what reason commands, but that reason *gives* no commands, and hence no starting points for constructing a reasoned account of justice.

This bleak picture fits Kant's initial depiction of the predicaments of human reason in the *Critique of Pure Reason*. He starts with the fear that

[21] Immanuel Kant, *Groundwork of the Metaphysics of Morals*, IV:458, cf. IV:462, in Immanuel Kant, *Practical Philosophy*, tr. and ed. Mary Gregor (Cambridge: Cambridge University Press, 1996); also Kant, *Critique of Pure Reason*, A5/B9, A255/B310ff.

[22] See, for example, Lewis White Beck, *A Commentary on Kant's Critique of Practical Reason* (Chicago, Ill.: University of Chicago Press, 1960), 192ff.; Henry E. Allison, *Kant's Theory of Freedom* (Cambridge: Cambridge University Press, 1990); Onora O'Neill, 'Reason and Autonomy in *Grundlegung III*', in *Constructions of Reason*, 51–65.

[23] René Descartes, *Discourse on the Method of Rightly Conducting One's Reason and Seeking the Truth in the Sciences*, in *The Philosophical Writings of Descartes*, vol. I, tr. John Cottingham, Robert Stoothof and Dugald Murdoch (Cambridge: Cambridge University Press, 1969), 112.

what we take for reason fools and betrays us, and that there may be no reliable authority for thinking or for acting. The iterated use of the most daily ways of supposed reasoning – for example, causal reasoning – leads us to the cognitive shipwreck of the antinomies. This conception of finite rational beings is hardly one which idealizes their powers of reasoning. Nor is it one that idealizes the separateness of human beings. It is quite clear that the predicament of reason sketched in the prefaces of the first Critique is to be read as the *shared* predicament of human would-be reasoners. In two respects Kant's conception of human reasoners does not bear out fears that he adopts an idealized conception of the self: he exaggerates neither the antecedent powers of reason of human beings nor their separateness and self-sufficiency. It might be plausible to think that he takes too little rather than too much for granted.

The same rather abstract but quite prosaic view of the predicaments of human reasoners is the starting point for Kant's attempt to establish what reason is, which we find in most explicit form in the early parts of the *Doctrine of Method*.[24] His strategy of thought is as follows: if principles of reason are not inscribed in each of us, then their institution is a *task* rather than a *discovery*. We cannot even define the solution to the task in terms of any antecedently given standards. The only available restraint on the standards we adopt is then given by the fact that they must be standards that we *could* use – that a plurality *could* use. We can give others no reasons to adopt principles which they cannot adopt; hence if we hope to reason – to communicate with others in ways that have an authority which is not simply a reflection of force or power – we must reject principles which we take it that those others cannot adopt. This meagre constraint leaves it quite open which of countless followable principles are to be followed. Using a metaphor that Kant invokes, all we can say is that the plan of reason is that there be some plan.

At this point I think that we can see, in a quite intuitive way, why Kant insists so strongly on the priority of practical reason. If a principle were to have quite unrestricted authority, it would have to be one that *at least could be adopted by all* – i.e. it would have to be *universalizable*. To see whether a principle is followable by all, is not enough to formulate it as a formally universal principle, even as a formally universal principle with wide scope, but rather necessary to see whether it is a principle by which all those within some domain could live, that is whether it is willable as a universal principle. This thought is recognizable as a stripped-down

---

[24] Kant, *Critique of Pure Reason*, A606/B735ff., especially the earlier sections.

version of the principle that Kant calls the Categorical Imperative – and on occasion more pompously the Supreme Principle of Practical Reason. Although Kant presents this stripped-down version as relevant for the conduct of thought as well as action, for present limited purposes I shall take the narrower domain and with it brush up once again against some long-standing polemics against Kant, which are ancestors to current criticisms of Kantian theories of justice.

There are two deep problems here. The first is that of understanding why *universalizability* should count as having unrestricted authority. The second is that of showing whether a requirement that the underlying principles of thought or action be universalizable has any significant normative implications, and in particular implications for justice, or whether universalizability too does not lead beyond empty formalism.

Answers to the first of these problems are helped by articulating the modal claims. A requirement of universalizability is only a requirement to adopt principles which *can* be willed for all, and to reject those that *cannot* be willed for all. The basic requirement that *must* be accepted by all is only the second-order principle of rejecting principles that *cannot* be willed for all. Only this counts as the principle of practical reason. However, since the principle of practical reason requires rejection of principles that cannot be willed for all, it will, *if* there are any principles which *cannot* be willed for all, have at least some derivative implications.

Many have doubted that a strict modal interpretation of universalizability has any further implications. Are not virtually all principles universalizable in this weak sense? To see that this approach is not trivial, it is important to bear in mind that instrumental rationality is not rejected, but put in its place – *aufgehoben* – in Kant's account of practical reason. Rational agents must then will both *some means* to anything they will and the *foreseeable results* of whatever they will. Hence they can will as universal only principles where the foreseeable results of their universal adoption would not undermine necessary means for their enactment. Of course, universalizable principles that meet these constraints might not in fact be universally accepted, let alone universally liked or preferred. The requirement is only that they be capable of being willed for all.

## 4 FROM UNIVERSALIZABILITY TO JUSTICE

This sketch of a reading of Kant's account of practical reason by itself does nothing to rebut the classic charge that the Categorical Imperative

leads only to empty formalism. Perhaps the demand for universalizability
will draw no significant ethical distinctions, let alone help us to think about
justice. After all, the limited conception of practical reason just proposed
enjoins only the rejection of non-universalizable principles, on the
grounds that these are not even competent for general authority in guiding
thought or action. Kant's account of reason is only a second-order constraint on our adoption of principles for dealing with life and thought.

Here I can offer no more than the merest sketches to suggest why
there may be arguments from the demand of universalizability to
certain principles of obligation, some of them relevant to any public
domain, and so to justice.[25] The sketches do not stick to Kant's own way
of developing his practical philosophy, which is often designed around
rather awkwardly schematic illustrations designed to give instances that
fill out a set grid of *perfect* and *imperfect* duties to self and to others, of
which he thinks only perfect duties to others relevant to questions of
justice.[26]

If we take simply the idea that we can offer reasons for the adoption
only of those principles which (we take it) others on the receiving end of
reasoning could also adopt, then a range of types of action must be
rejected. We cannot offer reasons to all for adopting principles of deceit
(one of Kant's favourite examples), of injury or of coercion. For we
cannot coherently assume that all could adopt these principles: we know
that were they even widely adopted, those acting on them would meet
at least some success, and hence that at least some others would be the
victims of this success, so that contrary to hypothesis they could not be
universally adopted. The rejection of these principles provides a starting point for constructing a more detailed account of principles of
justice.

Of course, these are very indeterminate principles: but they are less
indeterminate than many of the principles of liberty and equality that
have recently been the preferred building blocks for theories of justice.
One of the interesting respects in which they are more determinate is
that they are evidently principles for finite, mutually vulnerable beings –

---

[25] A fuller development of the sketch might also explore why Kant, unlike contemporary
Kantian theorists, proposes an account of virtue as well as of justice. Here I note only that
since Kantian work is not committed to uniform prescriptions or to denying the role of
judgement, there is no reason why it must be unable to offer an account of virtue as principled *and* sensitive to particularities. Virtue is not, after all, a matter of undifferentiated
sensitivity or responsiveness – but of intelligent, principled responsiveness to cases.

[26] For an account of different uses to which this distinction has been put, see Thomas
Campbell, 'Perfect and Imperfect Duties', *The Modern Schoolman*, 102 (1975), 185–94.

for beings who might in principle suffer by being the victims of deceit, injury or coercion. Principles of equality and liberty are on the surface more abstract.

However, despite the fact that they leave so much open, these are significant constraints, since there are also many sorts of action and institution whose fundamental principles could *not* be followed by all – for example, principles based on deceit, injury or coercion.[27] Those who refuse to base lives or policies on injury or on deceit may have many options in most situations – and yet taken both individually and jointly, these constraints can be highly demanding.

## 5 CONCLUSIONS

In offering this sketch of the background assumptions of Kant's approach to justice I have said nothing about the texts within which he discusses the connections between basic principles and just institutions. His political philosophy, and in particular the *Doctrine of Right*,[28] contains many lines of thought, in particular a distinctive justification of state power. Kant reached many specific conclusions which look unconvincing after the passage of more than 200 years, some that many people find rebarbative and others which have become fundamental to contemporary political culture.

Here I have tried only to follow a series of linked criticisms that have been thought to hold against the underlying strategies of Kant's and contemporary Kantian work on ethics and more specifically on justice. Although some of these types of criticism seemed groundless, they did at least bear out the assumption that there are close structural connections between Kant's ethics and contemporary Kantian ethics. Both are ethics of universal principles; neither takes it that principles prescribe with rigid uniformity; both deny that principles are algorithms; neither assumes that decisions are entailed by principles.

However, on the third and most fundamental matter, the claim that contemporary Kantian ethics is based on unacceptable idealizations, there turned out to be deep differences between contemporary work and

---

[27] For indications of ways in which these starting points could serve as the beginnings of a theory of justice see Onora O'Neill, *Towards Justice and Virtue: A Constructive Account of Practical Reasoning* (Cambridge: Cambridge University Press, 1996).

[28] Immanuel Kant, *The Metaphysics of Morals*, in Immanuel Kant, *Practical Philosophy*, tr. and ed. Mary Gregor (Cambridge: Cambridge University Press, 1996); the *Doctrine of Right* is the first part of this work, VI:229–378.

Kant's approach. Much recent Kantian work has indeed been predicated on unvindicated idealizations, which undermine its applicability to human life. Kant's approach may be read in another sense, in which the finitude of human beings, of human rationality and the connectedness among human beings, is stressed rather than denied. If this reading of Kant's work can be sustained, the charges made by its contemporary opponents will, at the very least, need revision. If it cannot, then the challenge of constructing an account of ethics, and specifically of justice, whose premisses rely only on genuine abstraction without idealization remains open rather than shown impossible.

CHAPTER 5

# *Which are the offers **you** can't refuse?*[1]

Coercion matters to almost everybody, and almost everybody thinks it wrong. Yet few agree on what counts as coercion. Theoretical investigations of coercion have often proposed 'analyses' of the concept, which rival theorists have submitted to trial by counter-example and found wanting. But no analysis has been generally accepted as convincing.

Looking for necessary and sufficient conditions for an offer to count as coercive, which are then to be tested by appeal to cases, strikes me as a *reductio ad absurdum* of a way of doing philosophy. The assumption that 'our' intuitions about possible examples and counter-examples can be treated as data, by which we may test, refute or confirm proposed analyses of necessary and sufficient conditions for the application of concepts, is an unpromising method. Trial by counter-example cannot get going unless there is agreement on the classification of cases; it breaks down when examples and counter-examples cannot be reliably distinguished. In discussions of coercion there is no agreement about cases: the long-running dispute between liberals and socialists about whether the wage bargain under capitalism coerces is only one of countless examples of disagreement. Any 'intuitions' invoked by protagonists in this debate reflect no more than different assumptions about who 'we' are; they offer an argument from (supposed) authority in contemporary dress rather than the prospect of a definitive analysis of coercion. For this and other reasons, I intend to say *nothing* about the vast philosophical and theoretical 'literature' on coercion. Instead I shall consult the experts.

---

[1] The original version of this essay appeared in R. G. Frey and Christopher W. Morris, eds., *Violence, Terrorism and Justice* (Cambridge: Cambridge University Press, 1991), 170–95. I have made extensive revisions.

## I EXPERT COERCION AND EXPERT VIOLENCE

The theoreticians may have reached an impasse, but there is plenty of expertise to be found. The real experts in this matter are, I take it, neither political theorists and philosophers nor even the victims of coercion, but the practitioners of coercion. They don't seem to find theoretical uncertainty inhibiting, and we may be able to learn something from them. My title poses the questions the expert coercers address: they look for 'offers' *you* can't refuse, not for 'offers' we (some 'we') can't refuse, or for 'offers' that *nobody* can refuse. They see their victims as particular others, not necessarily one of 'us' and not just anyone.

Consulting the expert coercers is not easy. They are self-effacing, for the best of reasons. Since nearly all coercion is morally suspect and much of it legally punishable, successful coercers will not want to testify. They are not likely to come forward to tell us just what they have done, which possibilities they considered and why they settled upon a particular strategy of coercion. So I shall rely on proxies for these experts by drawing on our common knowledge of journalistic, fictitious and dramatized discussions of coercing. Even those of us who have not practised major coercion are familiar with court reports, thrillers, spy stories, accounts of terrorism, and many other detailed descriptions of the business of coercion. However, I shall not treat these case histories as decisive or uncontentious instances of coercion: they figure here not as *intuitions* but as *illustrations* of the tasks coercers face.

Experts in coercion are also often expert at inflicting violence; but the two sorts of expertise are distinct. The coercer's aim is specifically to get others to *do* or to *desist*. Coercion, to put it vaguely, operates on the will and not on the body. The coercer's problem is not intrinsically a problem of working out how to inflict violence, how to maim, torture or destroy others. Not all violent acts coerce, and not all coercion uses violence. Some acts of violence aim only at another's body: for example, acts done by those who have run amok, what we call 'mindless violence'. Violence can be mute and brute. It need not demand anything of its victims or of others; there may be no implied conditions that victims or others can meet in order to avert it. Coercion (including coercion that uses violence) is different: it has propositional content. Coercers have to communicate with those whom they coerce, and fail if they merely destroy agents whose compliance they seek. This is sometimes hard to see because victims of coercion may also be victims of violence inflicted by their coercers. For example, if a coercer tortures a child in order to get her to reveal where somebody can be found, the child is a victim both of coercion and of violence: violence is the means to her coercion. However, other examples show that victims of coercion and victims of violence undertaken to coerce may be distinct: if a coercer tortures a child in order to get her father to reveal somebody's whereabouts, of which the child knows nothing, then it is the father who is the victim of coercion, although violence is done to the child. It is the father who can comply or refuse to comply; the child can do neither. In yet other cases coercers inflict no violence. They may rely on threat, menace and gesture that suggest varied harms to achieve their ends. Expert coercers concentrate on securing compliance; violence is important to them only when it produces results more effectively than other approaches.

## 2 RISK AND RETICENCE

Others' compliance can often be achieved by gentler means than coercion. For example, their action or inaction may be secured by asking or paying them to do or desist, or by negotiating or manipulating. Since much may be risked by coercing, these ordinary and acceptable ways of getting others to do or desist will usually be preferred. Coercing is not usually a strategy of first resort.

Because coercion is a risky and costly strategy, those who use it will not only avoid describing what they do as coercion, but go to pains to present it as something quite different. This is evident in the famous Mafia description of protection rackets as 'offers you can't refuse'. On the surface this sounds innocent enough, on a par with all those irresistible bargains and once-in-a-lifetime opportunities that advertisers proclaim. In reality the reason why the mafioso's 'offer' cannot be refused is that it has coercive backing. Those who don't comply will meet harm. Often the harm is hinted at rather than specified. Reticence about their activities and plans can pay off handsomely for coercers. If they are skilful, their victims may not (fully) realize what is going on. Confused or unwitting victims may comply better and more quickly, and complain less or less effectively. (Coercion is unlike revenge, which may not be adequate unless its victims realize what has happened: the Mafia demands varied expertise of its members.)

A fuller description of the expertise which coercers deploy would therefore emphasize the aim of securing compliance while minimizing others', and especially their victims', awareness that this is what they are doing. Coercion is a skilled as well as a risky business, a matter of controlling rather than of destroying victims. To do this coercers must articulate their demands without revealing more than is necessary. Victims must be clear about *what* is demanded, and *that* it is demanded; but it is best if they grasp little more. Coercers have good reasons to be reticent about their activities, to redescribe and disown what they do, and good reason to use violence sparingly. When victims are to be made to *do*, it is evidently self-defeating to destroy or damage them in ways that disable compliance; when they are to be made to *desist*, coercers often want them to remain alive and in action. Even in those cases where a victim is first to comply and then to be 'put out of action', violence must be used with caution.

The difficulties coercers face in these complex tasks are clarified by considering how coercion can misfire. Coercers fail unless their intended victim grasps *what* is demanded, and *that it is demanded*. The intended victim who simply fails to realize what is demanded – who misreads the coercer's menaces as a joke – may be a figure of fun, or tragic, but is insulated from coercion by failure to grasp the coercer's meaning. Such intended victims can be exasperatingly uncoerceable, simpletons or saints who (whether they suffer at the hands of would-be coercers or elude their grasp) fail to comply because they do not understand *what* is demanded. Deaf victims frustrate coercion. On the other hand, the intended victim who grasps *what* is demanded, but not *that it is demanded*, seeing the demand as mere request or proposal to be taken up or left, is equally awkward for the coercer's purposes. Faced with such victims, coercers have to spell out the implications of non-compliance with their preferred option more explicitly, so risking exposure.

These commonplace practical problems of coercing show that we are unlikely to get far in classifying acts decisively into the coercive and the non-coercive. Most coercive acts have more acceptable faces, and expert and interested parties who will insist that the more acceptable descriptions should command our attention. This point alone provides sufficient reason for doubting that any definitive analysis of the concept of coercion could be provided or would have much practical use. There are also more general, philosophically and historically deeper, reasons for doubting whether we can sensibly aim for or find definitive analyses of *any* concepts outside formal systems.[2]

---

[2] For some philosophical reasons one might look to Wittgenstein or Quine's 'Two Dogmas of Empiricism', in his *From a Logical Point of View* (New York: Harper & Row, 1963), 20–46; for the implications of such views for the history of ideas see Quentin Skinner, especially 'Meaning and Understanding in the History of Ideas', *History and Theory*, 8 (1969), 3–53, reprinted in James Tully, ed., *Meaning and Context: Quentin Skinner and his Critics* (Cambridge: Polity Press, 1988), 231–88.

### 3 STRATEGIES OF COERCION

The search for effective, opaque and deniable communication, which is relatively risk-free, shapes the practice of would-be coercers. Suppose that in a racially or ethnically divided society some potential coercers want to keep 'outsiders' out of 'their' neighbourhood. (Perhaps they fear integration or think that it will lower house prices.) In some places no coercion is needed. For example, in South Africa while Apartheid lasted, state power secured residential segregation. Even where segregation is illegal, residents may sometimes rely on the 'discretion' of local estate agents not to show or sell houses in 'their' neighbourhood to potential purchasers from the 'wrong' background. But where discrimination in house sales is monitored and penalized, those who want to avoid integration may be tempted to coerce. They will seek to act in ways that can be 'read' as menacing by their intended victims, but for which they cannot easily be brought to book.

Many possible moves can be imagined. For example, coercers might intimidate those whom they want to keep out with a brick through a window. The damage will be slight, with no violence done to any person; but if victims interpret the thrown brick as a threat of further and worse harm, it may be effective. On the other hand, throwing bricks through windows is illegal and readily detected: the communication may be effective enough, but is rather too public. Better ways of coercing might be found. For example, telling a child of the family who hope to move no more than 'Tell your Mummy and Daddy that if they love you they should not move here' might be enough. What is said is open to multiple interpretations. It might, after all, be a friendly warning from somebody who observes but does not approve of the coercers' plan. The coercers' hope would be that tone, gesture and circumstances will lead the family to interpret these opaque words as threatening unspecified, perhaps terrible, harm to the child should they move. Of course, if uttering these words is risky (the child may identify the coercer), other strategies might be safer. Perhaps a more overt message might be sent in the form of an 'offer' including a valuable option, such as payment if the family do not move, in the hope that this too will be read as, but be hard to prove as, coercive.[3]

Similar opacities are commonplace in the coercion which terrorists attempt. A campaign of terror does not have to inflict exceptionally high

---

[3] This point suggests that looking for a definitive distinction between threats and offers, or between coercive threats and coercive offers, may be a fruitless task.

levels of violence. For example, the use of terror by IRA and 'loyalist' groups in Northern Ireland, although extensive, did not raise the rate of violent death to the level it has persistently reached in many US cities. The coercers of the inner city in the US typically seek compliance to limited demands from a limited range of victims, rather than from whole communities; but in many cases they have used a large amount of violence in pursuit of these limited aims.

The coercion terrorists seek is more broadly targeted, and often uses skilled judgement to convey various messages to various audiences without creating strong support for anti-terrorist measures. The victims of terror are not just the few on whom terrorists inflict violence, but the many who are intimidated or terrorized by these and other means.[4] Those who might otherwise either act against terrorism or refuse to aid or abet it are pointedly reminded what it may cost them to inform the police about crimes planned or committed, or to testify against those charged with terrorist crimes of various sorts, or to refuse to contribute to terrorist funds. Those who are willing to play along are reassured that the costs of tacit support for terrorism remain low: the ordinary, dues-paying, passive supporters of terrorism are given to understand that this is not random violence, that their own lives and livelihood are not endangered – unless they step out of line. Sophisticated terrorist organizations, like the IRA, have consciously conveyed different messages to different audiences, or to the same audience on different occasions.[5] The tandem policy of relying on 'armalite and the ballot box' was designed to mix terror with political persuasion. When too much reliance on 'armalite' – more specifically: bombings, shootings, burnings, beatings – provoked revulsion and opposition, even among tacit supporters, violence could be reduced and a more appealing emphasis on political grievance and objectives could be used to re-enlist support.

If coercers succeed in conveying their various messages to their various audiences, victims will grasp both *what* is demanded and *that* it is demanded, even when nobody has been publicly menaced, and when

[4] This crucial point is often missed in journalistic treatments of terrorism, and sometimes in theoretical discussions, in which those on whom terrorists inflict violence are depicted as victims, but those whom they intimidate and coerce are not, despite the fact that the latter are often the more numerous victims and more significant for the terrorists' purposes.

[5] Less sophisticated terrorists like the 'real' IRA get their messages muddled and fail to keep those whom they hope to have as supporters on board. The Omagh bomb of August 1998, which killed many children, including many Catholic children, undercut support for terror in sections of the republican movement that had condoned, indeed passively supported, more accurately and 'acceptably' targeted terror.

the coercers leave little hard evidence that anyone was coerced and guarantee that those who were coerced are unable to identify their coercers. Sometimes everything will hinge on the interpretation of opaque messages and ambiguous gestures, or on grasping the implications of unattributable and scattered acts of violence and carnage. Even when coercion is laced with violence, as it is in campaigns of terror, much of the significance of any particular act can be obscure. We have to work hard to decode the political messages conveyed by campaigns of terror undertaken by little-known groups and aimed at unfamiliar audiences. Our interest in well-crafted thrillers is heightened by the fact that coercion can wear the most bland, or the most elegant, garb. We understand a thriller when we can follow a text or film at more than one level, and see the multiple messages implicit not only in grotesque signs of threatened violence (the severed horse's head, the dead cockerel delivered to the next victim, the tarred and feathered collaborator) but in the superficially innocuous small talk of the master-coercers. We understand the politics of terror when we can work out how and why multiple, veiled messages can come to define the possibilities for action of those who are terrorized. When we think about political, criminal and fictitious instances of coercion, we realize all too clearly why serious coercers veil their demands and the implications of non-compliance, and why skilled coercion is a matter of communicating irresistible demands while appearing to do far less. It is typical of coercion that it can be presented as something more acceptable – as the business deal that nobody would turn down, as the warning that it would be foolish to neglect, as a reminder to mind one's own business, or to pay one's dues by taking part in innocuous social practices.

## 4 UNDESIRABLE OPTIONS AND UNREFUSABLE OFFERS

These brief reminders of familiar strategies of coercion may suggest that nothing of general, let alone philosophical, interest can be said about coercion. If so, large stretches of political philosophy need rethinking, since they identify coercion as a significant source of injustice. Anarchists of right and of left see state power itself as unjustifiable because coercive. Many liberals and socialists see slavery and serfdom as unjust because coercive; most think a (near) state monopoly of coercive use of force justifiable (with exceptions for coercive action done in self-defence or in opposition to unjust powers). Socialists think the wage bargain in capitalist economies coercive and so unjust; liberals do not;

liberals think property relations and labour allocation decisions in socialist economies coercive and so unjust; socialists do not. Political philosophy will, it seems, be hobbled without a plausible account of coercion.
Even if a definitive 'analysis' of coercion cannot be provided, some
account is surely needed.

One approach to coercion would set it in the context of a conception
of action as motivated by desires and beliefs, which together determine
agents' preferences. Coercers alter others' preferences by playing on
their desires and beliefs, so that options they would otherwise view as less
preferred come to be preferred. The family who want to move change
their preferences and shelve their plan when coercers convince them
that the move will bring danger to their children. Citizens who want to
be law-abiding deny knowledge of terrible crimes committed by terrorists, even aid and abet them, if terrorists lead them to prefer complicity
to civic duty.

The difficulty of moving from these clear instances of coercion to a
more general account of it is that *any* action that alters another's preferences by playing on desires and beliefs will be formally indistinguishable
from coercion in these respects. If a shopkeeper offers a special price,
some customers will find that, given their desires and beliefs, they now
prefer to make purchases they would not otherwise have made. If a bus
company raises ticket prices in the rush hour, some travellers will prefer
to wait to get the cheaper tickets. Yet nobody thinks that shoppers or
travellers who respond to routine commercial incentives and disincentives are coerced. The threats coercers use do indeed alter their victims'
preferences, but not every action that changes others' preferences
coerces.

This suggests that it may be hard to base an account of coercion on
the familiar account of motivation, by which action is determined by
beliefs and desires. Agents will indeed reliably change their preferences
when their expectation of the sequel to certain actions is altered. If costs
and penalties are attached to action previously preferred, agents may
cease to prefer it; if rewards and incentives are attached to action not
previously preferred, agents may come to prefer it.

These thoughts are commonsensical enough, but something more
must be said if we are to find an account of the way in which coercion
operates on the will. For otherwise we are just left with the rather trivial
point that various interventions will lead to certain options sliding either
up or down an agent's preference ranking. If motivation is only a matter
of beliefs and desires, choice and will must be seen as a matter of suc-

cumbing to the predominant, preferred desires of a given moment. It then becomes hard to see that there is anything distinctive or wrong about coercing others' choices.[6] Coerced action too will be no more than action that is most preferred in the circumstances; it will be obscure why some ways of altering others' preferences should be condemned as coercive and others deemed acceptable since non-coercive. This approach to motivation does not show why it is worse to alter preferences by coercing than by bargaining or persuading, by payment for services or by bribery, by request or flattery. In short, it is hard to see what is distinctive about coercion so long as we think of it only as a matter of making some option less preferred than it would otherwise have been. This perspective loses sight of the claim that coercion *operates on the will*, that it *has propositional content*, that it thereby *makes agents complicit in a way in which brute violence does not*.

Here I think the Mafia may be on surer ground. They do not lose sight of the fact that coercion operates on the will. They focus not just on the fact that an undesired option is to be made into a desired option, but specifically on the way this can be brought about by embedding the option with which they want compliance ('the compliant option') in an *unrefusable* '*offer*' whose other option(s) ('the residual option(s)') are deeply injurious. They impose an 'offer' on their victim with the aim of securing compliance with an option which they assume the victim would not otherwise choose. The crucial thing for coercers is the difference between a genuine offer, where choice of one or another option can be seen as an expression of agency (and can thereby provide the basis for promising, contracting and even for legitimating consent), and a bogus, unrefusable 'offer', where the exercise of choice is corrupted by the structure of the offer.

A genuine offer, however tempting, however strongly one of its

---

[6] Hobbes is unusual and consistent in arguing that if motivation is reduced to current desires and beliefs, then coercion will not be fundamentally wrong: the fact that the fears which lead us to act are caused by others does not make them suspect. See Thomas Hobbes, *Leviathan*, ed. Richard Tuck (Cambridge: Cambridge University Press, 1996), esp. chs. 6, 13 and 20. Hobbes rejects any conception of will which could resist the predominant passion of the moment: will is only 'the last Appetite in deliberating' (45); he argues that in a state of nature where all are dominated by 'continuall feare, and danger of violent death' (89), submission to coercing powers is not only rational but basic for political legitimation; he maintains that in a state of nature where infants are 'in the power of the Mother, so as she may either nourish, or expose it . . . if she nourish it . . . it is obliged to obey . . . because every man is supposed to promise obedience to him, in whose power it is to save, or destroy him' (140). For Hobbes, coercion is the basis of the civil order and legitimate exercise of power, rather than its negation.

options is preferred to another, can be refused. No penalty, other than that of foregoing what is on offer, attaches to refusal. We do not have to take up cheap travel offers, or buy bargains, or to accept every political, commercial or sexual proposal. But the 'offers' coercers make, when fully spelt out, are different. The racketeers' 'offer' to protect a business from raids and thefts looks superficially rather like the genuine offer of an insurance policy (you pay your fee, and we will keep ruffians away): but if the compliant option is refused, racketeers do not simply leave those who refuse it to take their chances with the (supposed) ruffians: they impose the residual option, by taking 'enforcing' action. Terrorists purportedly 'offer' their loyal if tacit supporters protection from the other side: but the bogus character of their 'offer' is manifest in that refusing the compliant option is met not (simply) by absence of protection but by 'enforcing' action, often by brutal enforcing action: there is no way of saying 'no deal'. In effect, coercers force a choice; they secure compliance by linking non-compliance to injury; unlike genuine offers, these are 'offers' which are not open to refusal, to a choice of 'no deal'.

Of course, coercers try to disguise the way in which they have corrupted the very idea of an offer: they misleadingly speak of their own 'enforcing' action as 'the consequences', as if it were a natural or necessary corollary of rejecting the compliant option. While they undermine others' agency less radically than those who use violence to overpower, coercers show profound lack of respect for others' agency. Their use of 'enforcing' action is quite inadequately described as 'altering others' preferences by adding incentives and disincentives'. It is far more sinister. Coercers do not simply seek to make compliant action preferable: they seek to make the residual non-compliant option(s) unsustainable for a particular agent. They link non-compliance to injury (whether to life or limb, friends or family, property or livelihood, identity or honour) which they judge a particular agent unable to live with, and then cloak this sinister threat in the familiar guise of an offer.

Of course, because coercers are reticent, it is not always easy to tell whether a genuine, refusable offer has been made, or whether it is, as the Mafia rather honestly put it, an *offer you can't refuse*. It may be quite obscure whether a 'no deal' option is included within certain offers, or whether all non-compliant, residual offers have been made unsustainable for the agent. When racketeers suggest that a small trader pay a 'subscription' for their services a good deal more background must be filled in before it is clear whether this offer excludes the possibility of 'no deal', and whether it is an unrefusable 'offer' because the non-compliant options are injurious. When sexual attentions are pressed hard, it may be unclear whether the recipient is free to reject them, or whether this 'offer' has been made unrefusable by linking non-compliance, for example, to rape, violence or humiliation.

## 5 INTEGRITY AND REFUSABILITY

None of this suggests that there is a general answer to the question 'What makes "offers" unrefusable?'. Unrefusable 'offers' work because they link choice of any but the compliant option to residual option(s) which the particular agent cannot survive or sustain. The coercers' skill is to identify how to tailor 'offers' to the incapacities of particular victims, how to make non-compliant action not merely less preferred but unsustainable, so that their victims are driven to compliance. An unrefusable 'offer' is not, indeed, one where non-compliance is made logically or physically impossible for all victims; it is one that a particular victim cannot refuse without deep damage to sense of self or identity.

Victims vary in what they can sustain. Martyrs, heroes, rebels and men and women of honour often refuse options with which their would-be coercers aim to have them comply. Sometimes coercers misjudge their victims: a Socrates or an Aung San Suu Chi may (at least partly) elude carefully constructed coercive 'offers' made by mighty powers. However, even their escape is incomplete: in refusing compliance Socrates was killed and Aung San Suu Chi finds her life deeply constrained and limited: their achievements make plain what it is to choose the residual option in an 'unrefusable offer'. Should we describe such heroism as amounting to 'refusing the unrefusable'? In a colloquial sense this might well be said; but there is no paradox here. What exceptional people refuse when coerced is compliance with the *option* that coercers want. They do not and cannot refuse the '*offer*', of which that option is one disjunct. The *mark of coercion is the unrefusable 'offer', not an unrefusable option*. The fact that coercion acts on the will is all too plain both to the compliant and to resisters, and adds to their pain. An 'offer' is not rendered uncoercive because some victims (perhaps to the surprise of those who would coerce them) refuse to comply and choose to take the 'consequences'. Defiant and heroic victims too have to stay within the framework of the unrefusable 'offer'.

Heroes and martyrs refuse compliance because, harsh as the 'consequences' of non-compliance have been made, they hold that compliance will destroy something they see as integral to their lives and sense of self.

Sometimes they will be able to weather the 'consequences' with which their coercer hoped to secure compliance; sometimes they cannot. The most complete and harshest forms of coercion ensure that both compliance and non-compliance destroy their victims. Every option leads either to breaking of lives and limbs or to destruction of psychological or moral integrity. For example, compliance with coercers may cost an individual, a group or a nation integrity and sense of identity, while the residual option of non-compliance may cost physical survival, and ultimately also aspects of integrity and identity. When Poland was invaded by the Nazis in 1939, the Poles could have complied with the Nazi ultimatum and collaborated in the occupation of the country; they chose to resist. The compliant option would have cost national and individual integrity; the residual option cost the physical integrity of the nation and the lives of many. Heroic refusers as well as craven collaborators, and those whose capacities lie between, are coerced when they are trapped in an 'offer' all of whose options will destroy, damage or transform who and what they are.

Of course, much coercion is on a smaller scale: but even when it is on a small scale it relies on the same corrupt type of 'offer'. When victims have meagre capabilities, slender resources and multiple commitments to others, it is easy to construct unrefusable 'offers'. Threats of exposure or harm that may seem sustainable to one person can spell deep humiliation or risk to another. School, household and work-place bullies find simple ways of structuring unrefusable 'offers' that overwhelm their victims. Media exposure to which public figures are hardened may spell destruction to vulnerable others. Paltry threats may be enough to blackmail the weakest.

The predicaments that coercers force on their victims are, I believe, trivialized when thought of merely as a matter of adjusting the relative 'costs' and 'incentives' attached to different options, leading victims to adjust their preferences in the light of their changed beliefs and desires. What is at stake is victims' survival and integrity, their sense of self, their ability to live with themselves. Unamuno put it with appropriate force when he noted that 'neither a man nor a people (in a certain sense a people is also a man) can be asked to make a change that will break the unity or continuity of the person'.[7] The coercer notes that such changes will be refused if merely *asked* for, but that they

---

[7] Miguel Unamuno, *The Tragic Sense of Life in Men and Nations*, tr. Anthony Kerrigan (Princeton, N.J.: Princeton University Press, 1972); 13. He exaggerates, in that such changes can be asked for, and sometimes even achieved by the agent, for example by those who convert or assimilate to differing ways of life and thought: but they should not be asked for.

can perhaps be secured by constructing an unrefusable 'offer'. *The victim finds that choosing the compliant option destroys integrity and sense of self (and perhaps more), while choosing the residual option forfeits whatever the coercer has chosen to construct the unrefusable 'offer': whether life or limb, friends and family, or again honour and integrity.*

Coercers do not, however, use or need any general formula for identifying unsustainable 'consequences' and constructing unrefusable 'offers'. They need only identify some option(s) that their intended victims cannot live with, and 'offer' a choice restricted to these and whatever option they seek to have their victim choose. Correspondingly, agents who seek not to coerce have to make sure that they do not inadvertently make unrefusable 'offers'. Any offers they make others must not link options either overtly or covertly to consequences with which those to whom they make the offer cannot live. Like coercers, they will therefore need to take account of others' strengths and weaknesses, of their *specific* vulnerabilities and of the *actual* limits of their capabilities. In particular, they will have to be alert to the ease with which the weak can be coerced.

The expert coercer, whether of the weak or of the strong, is not, then a technician who exploits some metric by which to decide how intense a pain, how severe a threat, or how potent a combination of 'sticks' and 'carrots' must be built into the options of an 'offer', to make the compliant option unrefusable for all victims in all circumstances. Expertise is a matter of finding a particular sort of pain, menace, disorientation, insecurity, humiliation, exposure or other injury by which to construct an 'offer' that is unrefusable for the intended victim, whose sense of self and integrity, capabilities for action and bonds to others have a determinate configuration. Although it is true that an unrefusable 'offer' often shifts a victim's preference from compliance to non-compliance – and so that coercion 'works' – an account of coercion that merely notes that it attaches incentives of greater magnitude to compliance is unhelpful. Rather, the claim that greater incentives are attached to compliance is inferred from the fact that the agent complies with an option that would not otherwise be chosen. What makes the coercer's move sufficient to its purpose is not that it leads to a compliant preference, but that it does so by making the non-compliant, residual option unsustainable for that particular victim.

## 6 POWER AND VULNERABILITY

Would-be coercers therefore need a keen eye for vulnerability. They don't merely assume that in general those whom they hope to coerce are agents who can choose, but whose choosing might be in part controlled by the construction of unrefusable 'offers'. They study the form. They look for the specific vulnerabilities around which they can structure an 'offer' that is unrefusable, not indeed for any agent whatsoever, but for the particular intended victims.

Only the most powerful, the boldest, or the least imaginative of coercers will rely solely on overt threats of physical damage or pain. Coercion that menaces only the body often has drawbacks. In making such threats coercers must expose themselves too much; in carrying them out they risk disabling victims' capacities to comply with their demands. If their power or willingness to deliver the violence they threaten is limited, they may find that many judge their 'offers' quite refusable, and see them as good reasons for retaliation. Even when coercers' power is not in question, they must reckon that some have the makings of martyrs, and that martyrs often inspire others. In executing their threats they also risk revenge and the attentions of the law. Threatened violence is simply too blunt an instrument for many of the purposes coercers may have.[8]

These familiar points reveal more about coercers' penchants for opaque and deceptive 'offers'. Coercers cloak their 'offers' not merely because they fear detection or resistance, but because the mask of persuasion is so valuable to them. The reason why it is unpromising to investigate coercion by distinguishing systematically between 'threats of harm' (to be condemned as coercion) and 'offers of benefit' or 'incentives' (to be condoned as non-coercive) can now be seen in a new light. The threatened transformations of political, national or personal integrity and sense of identity, which lead us to view certain 'offers' as unrefusable, can often be described equally plausibly *either* as threatening harm *or* as offering benefit. From the point of view of those on the receiving end of coercion, who are wedded to, indeed constituted by, their present sense of self, family, community and nation, what is proposed is threat indeed: the destruction of much or all that they hold dear and of their very selves. Those who propose the transformation may

---

[8] This is true even of presumably legitimate coercion, such as the use of state power to enforce laws. Laws may fail in their purpose unless paralleled by wider social disciplines and cultural norms that secure legitimation. The risk of provoking rebellion or secession by merely repressive policies can be large.

sometimes give a rosier account. They may claim to be offering others a chance to be part of the action, to take on a new and grander identity, to be part of the empire rather than barbarian outsiders, to embrace progress and development, even to be uplifted by the *mission civilisatrice*. Or again, a threat to destroy the liberation movement may be an offer to pacify the countryside and to restore law and order. A coercive proposal may sometimes be seen retrospectively as benefit by those whose integrity and sense of identity it once threatened, indeed destroyed. What appears in one perspective as threat of loss can often be depicted in another as promise of gain. Coercion cannot then be elucidated by invoking a supposedly sharp distinction between threats and offers.

In particular, the capitalist wage bargain may plausibly be either offer of benefit or threat of harm, and indeed may be coercive in some but not in other contexts. In one context a worker may have various options of choosing work which offers certain levels of pay and independence, and this can be a much better option than slavery or serfdom in return for subsistence and less independence: it appears a refusable offer, and its acceptance a freely entered, and so legitimate, contract. Set in a second context, the same wage bargain might be an option in a coercive 'offer': if there is no other work and no welfare state, those without other means must comply with the proffered wage bargain or face destitution. Vulnerable workers may have no choice but to comply with a pitiful wage bargain. In yet a third context, inadequate wage rates might be rejectable by workers with brighter or more varied prospects, fewer dependants, or a welfare state to fall back on. Various situations confront workers with differing offers. What would make a particular 'offer' unrefusable is not simply the level of the wage, or its legal form, or the propositional content of the wage bargain, but the fact that acceptance of specific work has been made the sole alternative to an unsustainable residual option, secured by the vulnerable life situation of those to whom the 'offer' is made.

In more general terms, we can see that what makes 'offers' unrefusable is the *relative* weakness of their intended victims. It is not their absolute lack of capabilities and resources that constitutes vulnerability to coercion; rather it is that they possess fewer capabilities, powers or resources than others, and specifically than their coercers. Agents become victims not just because they are poor, ignorant, unskilled or physically weak or emotionally fragile, but because they are confronted by others who are richer, more knowledgeable, more skilful or physically or emotionally stronger, and prepared to exploit these advantages.

Power depends on differentials. The prospects for making unrefusable 'offers' will always be numerous and varied, and more numerous and more varied where differentials of power are greater. The powerful can easily ensure that non-compliance with their favoured option is linked to residual option(s) that are unsustainable by their would-be victims.

This suggests that if we think that coercion is generally wrong, and to be prevented, two complementary approaches can be used. The first, and the more discussed, is to try to restrict the ways in which the relatively powerful misuse their advantage. A system of laws and regulations before which all are equal, enforcement of basic rights and democratic governance provide potent restraints on the relatively powerful, and so on their ability to make others unrefusable 'offers'. These institutional structures will themselves require some coercive backing as enforcement, which, however, will inflict less coercion than they prevent: so at least we are told by long traditions of political theory, which I shall not discuss here.

The second strategy for reducing coercion is to reduce not the misuse but the differentials of power, by reducing the relative weakness of those who would otherwise be most vulnerable, and so most open to coercion. No doubt it is impossible to eliminate all differentials in vulnerability; but many glaring differences have been eliminated. The abolition of slavery eliminated a set of social roles that ensured acute vulnerability for some and ease of coercion for others. The gradual reduction of the subjection of women in many parts of the world promises an even wider reduction of differentials of power and vulnerability, and the elimination of numerous contexts of easy coercion. Like the use of state power to enforce laws, the use of state and other powers to eliminate differentials of power may itself have coercive aspects. Nevertheless, here too we may find good reasons to judge that (on balance) such transformations reduce coercion by eliminating or circumscribing the contexts of vulnerability that provide coercers with opportunities to exploit.

CHAPTER 6

# Women's rights: whose obligations?[1]

Contemporary rhetoric about justice celebrates human rights, and justice for women is supposed to celebrate women's rights. Yet rights are mere pretence unless others have obligations to respect them. Why, then, do we now talk so relentlessly about rights, and so little about obligations? Does this show that we take rights seriously?

A Martian or a Venusian, listening to the public rhetoric of our day, just to the ordinary pronouncements of politicians and the ordinary reports of the media, might conclude that we take rights very seriously indeed, even that we are obsessed by them. She might even conclude that we take the rights of women very seriously indeed. Women's rights may have seemed shocking when Mary Wollstonecraft chose the title of *A Vindication of the Rights of Woman* in 1790; now they are part of the rhetoric both of the established order and of its critics. They elicit more yawns and inattention than hostility, although there is still a bit of that.

Taking the rhetoric seriously is one thing; taking the substance seriously another. One of the main uses of this rhetoric is to point out how often human rights, and with them women's rights, are violated. No doubt a gap between rhetoric and reality is unsurprising; but this gap is more than evidence of failure to practise what we preach. To put the matter starkly, if we think about justice primarily in terms of rights, we are more or less bound to find not only that we do not or cannot live up to it, but that we cannot work out what we are trying to live up to. The rhetoric of rights is not only deceptively easy to promulgate, but deeply evasive. Most of the difficulty of thinking about women's rights grows out of this general evasiveness of thought about rights, so it is to this pervasive difficulty rather than to battles about the rights women should have that I shall turn first.

[1] Originally published in Alison Jeffries, ed., *Women's Voices, Women's Rights: Oxford Amnesty Lectures* (Boulder, Colo.: Westview Press, 1999), 57–69.

## I RIGHTS AND OBLIGATIONS

In speaking of the rhetoric of rights as evasive I do not mean to suggest that human rights, or women's rights, are unimportant, or that securing them is an unimportant political goal. My concern is rather that talking as if rights were the *core* of justice, and rights for women the *core* of justice for women, is a lazy way of talking and of thinking, which systematically obscures what we would most need to think about and to do if we were to take rights seriously.

We often talk of *having* rights. This gives rights a nice substantial feel, as though they were bits of hardware that could be touched and traded, purloined or protected. This way of talking misleads. Talking of rights and talking of obligations are both ways of talking about action, not about items that can be possessed. Moreover, most important rights are intrinsically relational in that they are *claim rights*, which mirror certain sorts of obligation: both claim rights and the corresponding obligations are a matter of required types of action, or of omission.[2] When we talk of such rights we look at the required action from the perspective of the claimant or right-holder; when we talk of obligations we look at required action from the perspective of the obligation-bearer, of the one who is to act. So it is clear enough that there will be no claim rights unless others have obligations. If anyone is to have a right of free association, then everyone must have an obligation not to obstruct free association. If anyone is to have a right to information about family planning, then someone, or perhaps a number of people, must have an obligation to make that information available. If anyone is to have a right of access to children with whom they do not live, others must have obligations to allow that access and to ensure that it is not thwarted. If anyone is to have a right to a free or even to an affordable nursery place for her pre-school children, then somebody, and probably many people, must have obligations to contribute to providing that nursery place.

So far, so commonplace. In a way the fact that there are no claim rights without obligations is so obvious and well known that it is embarrassing to bring the matter up. Yet I believe that a great deal of

---

[2] The only exceptions are those unprotected rights sometimes spoken of as *mere liberties*. For example, I may have a right which is a mere liberty to pick up a coin from the pavement, and so may you. Neither of us will have an obligation to let the other exercise the right: finders keepers. This is quite different from my having a *claim right* to pick up the coin, which you have an obligation to respect – even if you find the coin first. The rights that are most important to justice are not mere liberties but claim rights with corresponding obligations.

discussion of rights, including of women's rights, continually mis-
states the ways in which and the extent to which rights and obligations correspond to one another, and hence fails to see how much it
matters whether discussion of justice emphasizes rights or obligations.

There are two very general reasons why starting with rights is a lop-
sided way of thinking about ethics, and even about justice. The first and
the more general, to which I shall return, is that while claim rights are
mirror images of obligations, not all obligations have mirror images. If
there are obligations without corresponding rights, it will evidently
impoverish moral thinking if one starts with the rights and leaves aside
those obligations not mirrored by any rights. This thought by itself is
reason enough to *begin* with obligations and not with rights. To do otherwise is about as sensible as trying to count the adult population of a
country by counting all the parents, and so overlooking all childless
persons. However, for the moment I shall leave aside this large reason
for starting with the obligations rather than the rights, and consider why
the rhetoric of rights has such great capacities to dash the very hopes of
justice that it raises.

The second very general reason why the rhetoric of rights creates
problems is not that it is blind to obligations without counterpart rights,
but that it obscures what is really at stake by focussing on the rights rather
than the obligations. The obscurity arises because it is easy to proclaim
rights without paying much attention to the obligations which are their
counterparts. This deceptive convenience is due, at least in large
measure, to the fact that it is so easy to slide between discussion of positive (institutional, customary) rights and of moral (natural, human)
rights. Everybody acknowledges that positive claim rights must have
well-defined corresponding obligations: to speak of them as *positive* is just
to speak of them as institutionalized, and we are evidently speaking of
one and the same set of institutionalized requirements for action (or forbearance) when we speak of positive claim rights and of their corresponding obligations. However, the point of appealing to human rights,
or to women's rights, is not to endorse the positive rights embedded in
existing institutions. The point is often to challenge existing positive
rights (or their absence) and, of course, existing positive obligations (or
their absence), or to justify different rights and different corollary obligations. What would be the point of appealing to human rights if they
were no more than the institutionalized rights of some social order, or
the various vestigially institutionalized 'manifesto rights' promulgated in

charters and declarations, however august?[3] The rhetoric of rights supposedly appeals to fundamental moral principles, and aspires to justify
or to condemn institutional and positive rights, and indeed to justify or
to condemn the claims of the grand declarations and charters, and so
cannot coherently presuppose them.

But once we start talking about moral (human, natural) rights, and
however we think that they are to be justified, it becomes easy to let questions about obligations drift out of sight. The Rights of Man have much
more immediate charm than the Duties of Man; and equally the Rights
of Women can have much more immediate charm than the Duties of
Women – let alone than the duties that correspond to the Rights of
Women.

It is easy to succumb to the charm of rights, and delightful to think
about claiming them. Claiming that one has a right, whether to certain
liberties or to security, or to goods or services, perhaps to welfare, can be
heady stuff. It is a matter of thinking about what one ought to get or to
have done for one, and about what others (but which others?) ought to
do or provide for one. Of course, claims are not likely to be effective
unless somebody ought to meet those claims, and often they will be
ineffective unless the claims are not merely allocated to some agent or
agency, but accepted and enforceable. But the actual claiming can go on
loudly and confidently, with panache and bravado, without establishing
who should deliver whatever is claimed. It is even possible to claim what
nobody can deliver as a right: I was once publicly admonished for asking
who holds the obligations that correspond to an alleged right to health
(not merely to a right to health care!) on the grounds that health is too
important to human beings not to be the object of a right.

Moreover, there can be political and rhetorical advantage as well as
charm in being vague about obligations. Claims about rights need only
assert what right-holders are entitled to; only the curmudgeonly will
object. Others may be animated and have their hopes raised. But claims
about obligations have to specify not only what is to be accorded, but
which obligation-bearers are going to have to do what for whom and at
what cost. This is a much less charming topic. Unsurprisingly the rhetoric of obligations and duties has an unsavoury reputation, and those on
whom burdens may fall often object.

---

[3] Manifesto rights can provide indicators for institution building. Too often, however, their
normative force is an illusion because they are neither principles of justice for which arguments are provided nor institutionally anchored normative requirements.

Yet strangely the rhetoric of rights is often praised for taking human agents and their dignity seriously. When we think of others as right-holders it is, of course, true that we no longer think of them as mere subjects, who plead abjectly for better treatment. We think of right-holders as full persons, as citizens or citizens-to-be. Yet when claimants point to others' duties (which others' duties?), they do not have to take much action, and may even wrap themselves passively in a cloak of grievance or of resentment. They do not need to work out who will have to do what for whom at what cost, let alone what they themselves will have to do at what costs to themselves. In short, the rhetoric of rights, although *more* active than a rhetoric of dependent pleading, of mere subjects, is still a rhetoric of recipience rather than of action. It still takes the perspective of the claimant rather than of the contributor, of the consumer rather than of the producer, of the passive rather than of the active citizen.

## 2 LIBERTY AND WELFARE

Of course, these points are hardly novel. They have surfaced repeatedly in the truly enormous contemporary literature on theories of justice. Much of this literature argues for rights and assumes that *if* claim rights can be established, then obligations will follow calmly in their wake. This theoretical literature may lack the full charm and bravado, let alone the political bite, of more public uses of the rhetoric of rights, but much of it shares the intellectual failings of claims to rights, in that it takes obligations less seriously than rights.

These failings cropped up repeatedly in the prolific disputes about justice throughout the last part of the twentieth century. The most enduring dispute has been between more and less libertarian thinkers and advocates of various conceptions of social justice. Libertarians have argued that all universal claim rights are liberty rights with corollary obligations not to interfere. The advocates of social justice have argued that there are also universal claim rights to certain goods or services, and in particular to welfare, with corollary obligations to deliver the goods.

All advocates of rights are agreed that *if* there are universal claim rights to liberty, then the corollary obligations must also be universal. For example, a right not to be raped, or a right to compete with others for employment, will be marred if it is a right against some but not against all others. If there were some others who have no obligation to refrain from raping, or no obligation to let others compete in the market place, then nobody would have an unrestricted right of either sort. Mere liberties apart, universal liberty rights require corresponding universal obligations.

Libertarian advocates of rights insist also that universal claim rights *must* be liberty rights, and that universal rights to goods or services, and hence to welfare, are incoherent. Goods and services have to be delivered at particular times and places, and hence by particular agents and agencies. They cannot be delivered by everybody rushing in everywhere and treading on one another's toes. There can be no universal obligations to provide goods and services that correspond to universal rights to goods and services *in the same way that universal obligations to respect others' liberties correspond to universal liberty rights.* It follows, they conclude, that there cannot be universal rights to goods and services, and hence that there can be no universal economic, social or cultural rights, and that the august charters and declarations make incoherent claims, which can indeed be put to rhetorical use, but can only disappoint those who take them seriously.

This libertarian line of thought is often extended with the claim that since there can be no universal rights to goods and services, any such rights must be not universal but 'special' rights, to which the 'special' obligations of specified parties correspond. In short, rights to goods and services and obligations to provide them are inevitably not moral or human rights at all. They are only the institutionalized or positive rights of a specific social order or reflections of a specific contractual arrangement or social role.

The implications of this line of thought can bite hard. For example, libertarians will agree that the staff of a maternity ward may have an obligation of care – a special obligation – to those patients who have been appropriately admitted, and those patients may have a special right to care from those staff. But they will deny that the staff have any more general obligations to provide care, or pregnant women a more general right to claim care. This line of thought accepts that all rights to goods and services are special rights, which presuppose the specific relationships that may be established, for example, by legislation or by contract, by custom or by practice. Which sorts of special rights to goods or services and which sorts of special obligations are to be established is left entirely open. Special obligations to provide and rights to receive medical care and attention from the staff of a maternity ward may be on a footing with special obligations to shackle women prisoners even when in labour and special rights to be protected from the threat of women in labour absconding.[4] On this account, rights to goods and services are not human or moral rights at all: they are no more than instances of the very sorts of institutional rights which the rhetoric of rights aspires to criticize.

But the argument is not sound. All that follows from the convincing thought that universal rights to goods and services cannot be matched by universally delivered obligations to provide at all relevant times and places is that *if* there are universal rights to goods and services, then aspects of the corresponding obligations which have to do with delivery will have to take a different form. There is no intrinsic problem here. While it is true that a right not to be raped, or a right to compete for employment, is marred unless the counterpart obligation is universally held, this is not true of rights to goods and services. If, for example, persons with dependent children have a right to adequate housing, then the right can be fully met if *somebody* – or *some body* – provides each such person who lacks housing with adequate housing. It is not necessary that everyone contribute to provision, and wholly counter-productive, not to say impossible, if everyone attempts to be the provider on all occasions. Or if women have a right to ante-natal medical care, then it will be enough if *some* medically qualified persons provide that care to each woman – and downright dangerous, not to mention exhausting, and ultimately impossible, if everybody medically qualified tries to do so for each or all women.

In short the obligations that correspond to rights to goods and services *must* differ in form from at least some of the obligations that correspond to liberty rights. Universal rights to goods and services are quite coherent,[5] provided that those aspects of the counterpart obligations which have to do with delivery are *distributed* or *allocated* to specific agents and agencies. On the other hand, those aspects of the counterpart obligations which have to do with *determining a scheme of delivery*, or with *refraining from obstructing delivery*, or with *contributing proportionally to costs* can quite well be universally held obligations.

Evidently, a universal right to some good or service is not taken seriously unless specific obligations to deliver the relevant good or service are established, so ensuring that the right is secured for each, and so for

---

[4] Regulations requiring prison staff in the UK to shackle pregnant prisoners when in labour were rescinded after public outcry during the winter of 1995–6.

[5] This argument to show that universal rights to goods or services are coherent is intended only to dispose of libertarian allegations that there cannot be such rights, and not to justify any specific rights to goods or services.

all, right-holders. We are quite familiar with the thought that universal rights can be met *distributively*, and can point to many cases where universal welfare rights have been established within the domain of certain states by distributing obligations to provide welfare to cover each, and hence all, right-holders. Those who established such welfare rights did not miraculously work out how everybody within those states could be omnipresent, forever fulfilling obligations to deliver food or medical care or housing to each and so to all, or even to all in need. What they did was hard enough, but it wasn't physically impossible.

There are then, as libertarians insist, certain clear disanalogies between universal liberty rights and universal rights to goods and services. However, the libertarian claim that universal rights to goods and services are incoherent has not been established. The disanalogy might be summarized as follows: the conclusion of libertarian arguments is a *political agenda* of securing a particular list of liberty rights and their corresponding universal obligations, but no rights to goods or services. The conclusion of a social-justice line of thought combines parts of the libertarian agenda – a rather more restricted set of liberty rights is to be secured – with an open *political debate* premised on the thought that there are obligations to support those in need, that a scheme for fulfilling these obligations must be established, and that once it is established all those in need will have acquired special obligations to specific goods and services. Universal rights to goods and services are to be secured by establishing any one of many possible schemes which distribute obligations to deliver those rights for each and so for all.

Social justice liberals have often queried this disanalogy.[6] They suggest that there are no serious differences between universal liberty rights and universal rights to goods and services. They point out, for example, that even impeccable liberty rights with well-defined counterpart obligations – a right not to be tortured, a right not to be raped – cannot be secured without complex institutions which will adjudicate cases and enforce rights. Liberty rights and their corresponding obligations may need police, courts and many other forms of accountability if they are to be enforced; institutions of enforcement too have to distribute obligations for specific aspects of enforcement according to one or another scheme. So liberty rights too are amorphous until one or another institutional scheme has been established, which determines who bears the counterpart obligations.

[6] An early and strongly argued version of the query can be found in Henry Shue in *Basic Rights: Subsistence, Affluence and U.S. Foreign Policy* (Princeton, N.J.: Princeton University Press, 1980).

However, there are deeper discrepancies between liberty rights and rights to goods and services than this attempt to yoke them allows. To be sure, the *enforcement* of liberty rights, or rather of their corresponding obligations, needs institutions: hardly news. However, the correspondence of universal liberty rights to universal obligations is relatively well defined even when institutions are missing or weak. For example, a violation of a right not to be raped or of a right not to be tortured may be clear enough, and the perpetrator may even be identifiable, even when institutions for enforcement are lamentably weak. But the correspondence of universal rights to goods and services to obligations to *provide or deliver* remains entirely amorphous when institutions are missing or weak. Somebody who receives no maternity care may no doubt *assert* that her rights have been violated, but unless obligations to deliver that care have been established and distributed, she will not know where to press her claim, and it will be systematically obscure whether there is any perpetrator, or who has neglected or violated her rights.

Rights to goods and services can be thought of only in the hazy way which the rhetoric of rights favours and allows until they are at least partly institutionalized. It may be possible to state *what* ought to be provided or delivered, but it will be impossible to state *who* ought to do the providing or delivering, and *who* can be called to account when deliveries are botched, or nothing is delivered, unless there are established institutions and well-defined special relationships. Rights to goods and services are easy to proclaim, but until there are effective institutions their proclamation may seem bitter mockery to those who most need them. Liberty rights, however, are different because far more is determined even when institutions are missing or weak: as soon as it is possible to state what ought to be provided – non-interference – it will also be possible to state who ought to provide: everyone and all institutions ought to do so. Institutions come into the picture subsequently for purposes of enforcement. By contrast, when we discuss obligations, of whatever sort, we immediately have to consider *whose* obligations we have in mind and so will define *against whom* right-holders may lodge their claims.

## 4 WOMEN'S RIGHTS

How does this matter for women, and for women's rights? A small, and once again embarrassingly commonplace, reminder may be helpful here. In speaking of women's rights most people have meant to speak of rights that men have and that women should have as well. They have not generally meant to speak of any distinctive rights which women should have and men should not. The exception – not without controversy or importance – lies in rights that are quite specifically connected to differences of sex and reproduction. Rights to maternity services would properly be women's rights and not men's. But men too may have rights not be raped, as women too may have rights to vote and rights of association.

However, it is evident that the sorts of rights to goods and services on which women and men may rely most frequently can often differ. For example, as long as women still carry more of the real work of caring for true dependants (children, those who are ill, the elderly) and as long as they have fewer resources with which to do so, they will need rights to financial support and to relevant social services more often. Equally, as long as a disproportionate amount of juvenile crime is committed by boys and young men, their need for rights of due process and for other relevant social services will be greater than that of girls and women of like age. However, such differences in (average) situation do not show that women's rights should differ from men's rights outside the areas of maternity care and the like. It is not surprising that for most of its history the women's movement has been a movement that claimed for women the *same* rights as were claimed for men – from rights to hold property, to the franchise, to rights to enter all lines of employment.

Yet from the 1980s parts of the women's movement took quite another turn. Many influential feminists stressed not the similarities of men and women, and their entitlement to the same rights, but their differences, opening the door to the thought that their ethical claims might differ. Yet surprisingly the emphasis on differences has not, on the whole, been used to develop alternative accounts of the rights of women. One reason for this has been that those who affirm the ways in which women are different from men also often stress that they differ in their moral categories or 'voice'.[7] The way was open not for a traditional feminist claim that women have been denied their due rights, or even for a revisionary claim that they should have some alternative set of rights, but for a more radical claim that any focus on justice – whether centred on obligations or on rights – uses a strident and inappropriate ethical register, and may even be seen as an aspect of the

---

[7] See in particular Carol Gilligan's *Development In a Different Voice: Psychological Theory and Women's Development* (Cambridge, Mass.: Harvard University Press, 1982; 2nd edn, 1993), 9.

oppression rather than the liberation of women. An increasing amount of radical feminist writing of the 1980s and 1990s criticized concern with justice, and hence with rights, as an abstract, adversarial, 'male' concern, and put forward conceptions of ethical life that centre on certain 'female' virtues of care and concern, of responsibility and affiliation. Some of this writing suggested that we must choose between these ethical voices or stances, that we must choose between justice (and with it obligations and rights) and care and concern, in short that justice and the virtues are the focus of antagonistic rather than of complementary visions of human life.[8]

The worry that we shall be forced to this painful choice has a number of sources. One is a lurking belief (mentioned earlier) that just as all rights need corresponding obligations, so all obligations need corresponding rights. If all obligations were the counterparts of rights, then it seems that no discussion of obligations *could* have anything to say about the virtues, about care and concern and the other matters which so many feminists, and so many virtue ethicists, have properly insisted are ethically important: for these can surely not be claimed as matters of right.

But why should one look at things in this way? While there may be many obligations to which rights correspond, why should there not be other significant obligations to which no rights correspond? The traditional distinction between *perfect* or *complete* obligations with counterpart rights and *imperfect* or *incomplete* obligations without counterpart rights of any sort reminds us that many historically important discussions of human obligations have not restricted themselves to the domain of obligations to which rights are supposed to correspond.[9] There may, for example, be obligations to show others care and concern whose recipients are not specified, and which are to be met by showing *some* others *some* appropriate form of care and concern. Such obligations could not be a matter of providing all possible care and concern to all others, which is impossible. They are inevitably selective. If, on the other hand, like so much writing on justice, we treat rights as the basic ethical category, then obligations without rights may simply

---

[8] An enormous literature on 'the ethics of care' and related virtues appeared in the wake of Gilligan's book. For reasons for thinking that justice and virtue are complementary rather than antagonistic see Onora O'Neill, *Towards Justice and Virtue: A Constructive Account of Practical Reasoning* (Cambridge: Cambridge University Press, 1996).

[9] For an account of traditional, especially early modern, views on justice and virtue that brings out these points see J. B. Schneewind, 'The Misfortunes of Virtue', *Ethics*, 101 (1990), 42–63.

be overlooked, and it may seem that all virtues must be wholly optional excellences.[10]

However, the fact that obligations with rights may not be the whole story does not mean that they are unimportant, or specifically that they are unimportant for women. To neglect obligations with corollary rights in a discussion of women's issues is no mere oversight. In a world in which women, like men, act and are acted on by the multiple complex institutions and systems of institutions, and by many distant strangers, a pretence that their significant ethical relations are entirely face-to-face, entirely a matter of virtuous relationships, of personal attachments and commitments, of care and concern, and never a matter of required action, of obligations or of rights, is both illusory and dangerous.

The danger is perhaps readily overlooked because the vision of women as using a distinct ethical 'voice' or register, which stresses care rather than justice, virtues rather than rights, is coupled with a (sometimes tacit) assumption that women still, at any rate more than men, lead their lives in a 'private' sphere whose central ethical categories are appropriately those of virtue rather than of justice. This assumption is false for two distinct reasons. First, it is straightforwardly false of many women, particularly in the more developed world, that many, let alone all, aspects of their lives are lived in anything that could be called a private sphere. Labour-force participation rates, voting patterns and dependence on publicly provided support systems all show that women's lives are no longer ensconced, either cosily or uncomfortably, in any private domain. The second reason why the assumption that women's lives are not insulated from the public sphere is false is that *no* supposedly private sphere is wholly insulated from the impact of public forces and activities. Economic, political and social forces shape and often grind all private spheres. Economic forces sustain or impoverish families and communities; political realities destroy or enable intimate and personal relationships. This is as true of undeveloped as of developed societies. The only worlds in which it may not have been true are those archaic (or at any rate obsolescent) worlds which lack any clear distinction

---

[10] In fact there is no reason to expect that all virtues will be of one kind. Some might be a matter of requirement, even if not owed either to all or to some, and hence without counterpart rights. Other virtues might be those of certain roles, relationships or traditions. Yet others might be entirely optional, hence in no way obligatory, and *a fortiori* not claimable as a matter of right.

between public and private domains – the worlds of true *Gemeinschaft*. In the worlds in which we now live women may have somewhat different lives from men, but often the difference is simply that they have more sustained real responsibility for real dependants – for children, for the seriously ill, for the elderly – although they remain economically and socially less powerful.[11] In such worlds it is mere fantasy to think that a private sphere provides a protective retreat which makes ordinary, mundane rights redundant.

## 5 REAL PATRIARCHY?

Yet the image of a sheltered space within which domestic and personal life can be insulated from the pressures of the public domain, and the virtues can flourish, has deep appeal. Perhaps its appeal has increased as the economic, social, political and cultural forces which bear on our lives are increasingly globalized. If we imagine a world in which this sheltered space is peculiarly the domain of women, in which men shelter women from the ravages of the public domain, we are drawn less to the image of *Gemeinschaft* than to the image of *Real Patriarchy*.

The proponents of women's distinctive ethical voice are not, of course, keen on patriarchy of any sort. Yet only patriarchy offers women any prospect of the very insulation from public forces whose attractions seem so persistent to some of those who over-emphasize the distinctiveness of women's moral voice and vision, and who aspire to fit all of morality into an ethic of care. Real patriarchy should at least then be taken seriously, if only because real patriarchs have, or at least had, real obligations, which could provide something worth having – if at a cost. However, all that remains of patriarchy (at least in the developed world) is remnants of patriarchal sentiment and rhetoric without much in the way of patriarchal obligations. The evidence that there isn't much real patriarchy around in the developed world can be readily assembled by any woman who demands that her male relatives shoulder the obligations of patriarchy, for example, by providing her with a suitable husband or life-long subsistence, or by forcing an erring husband back onto the straight and narrow. Since these fruits of real patriarchy are rarely on offer, the private sphere is unlikely to offer

[11] For an account of women's lives and especially of mothering which acknowledges these stark realities see Sara Ruddick, *Maternal Thinking: Towards a Politics of Peace* (Boston, Mass.: Beacon Press, 1987).

women the securities that supposedly make justice dispensable. Even
those who cling to the rhetoric of patriarchy do not now often care to
shoulder its obligations; if they try to, they are likely to find that the
powers and protected spaces by which and in which those obligations
could be discharged are no longer available. Would-be patriarchs are
almost bound to be frustrated; and probably a bit touchy. Even the
remnant patriarchs who survive in less developed corners of the world
are increasingly powerless to protect women under their sway from
larger economic, political and social forces; soon they too may find
themselves with too little power to fulfil what they take to be the obligations of patriarchy.

Yet it surely cannot be a matter for serious regret that there are now
no well-insulated private spheres, that real patriarchy is no longer an
option, and hence that there is nowhere for women to cultivate their
gardens and the virtues without concerning themselves with the obligations and rights of justice. If the remnant patriarchs are impotent, the
rights and above all the obligations of the public domain can hardly be
irrelevant to women; and if they are powerful, but unaccountably so,
they will present other dangers, and once again the rights and above all
the obligations of the public domain can hardly be irrelevant to women.
In either case, reasons for thinking that rights are irrelevant to women
or that men and women should have fundamentally different sets of
rights are lacking.

If women's rights are not redundant in our world, we need to ask what
it would be to take them seriously. I have argued that taking them seriously is pre-eminently a matter of taking the obligations which are their
counterparts seriously. Since rights may be of various sorts, so too may
obligations. The obligations that correspond to liberty rights fall on all,
and so on women as much as on men, on men as much as on women.
By contrast, some of the obligations which correspond to rights to goods
and services remain amorphous until one or another institutional
scheme is established. What matters for women is that the allocation of
those obligations to provide goods and services should itself take account
of the real resources and responsibilities, of the real capabilities and vulnerabilities, of those who are to bear the obligations. As long as some
people, and today it is often (but by no means always) women, and especially poor women in poor economies, have fewer resources and carry
higher burdens of others' dependence, as long as they are vulnerable in
ways in which others are not, a case may be made for allocations of obligations which fall more on those who have more resources or carry lower

burdens of others' dependence and consequently have greater capabilities. This, however, is not a case for differential rights for women, except in the area of maternity services and the like. It is a case for allocations of obligations to deliver goods and services that take account of the realities of different sorts of lives.[12]

[12] See Chapter 8 below.

PART II

*Political bounds of justice*

# CHAPTER 7

# Transnational economic justice[1]

## I JUSTICE ACROSS BOUNDARIES

The discussion of world-wide justice, and in particular of world-wide economic justice, is both new and messy. The messiness extends to the very terms used. The older term 'international justice' ostensibly presupposed that we begin with *nations* as units. In the modern period the units presupposed have in fact been not nations, but *states*, many of them not *nation-states*. However, the term 'interstatal justice' has gained no currency. This may be just as well, since the idea that justice could be divided into *intrastatal* and *interstatal justice* – justice within and justice between states – is also obsolete. The activities and relationships that link not only states but many other corporate bodies, including substatal political units, businesses, international and governmental agencies, non-governmental agencies, communities, professional organizations and charities, may all raise issues of justice. On the other hand, the term 'global justice' seems to beg questions by presupposing that the topic under discussion is a single regime of justice for the world. With misgivings I settle here on the relatively new terms 'transnational justice' and 'transnational economic justice', with the thought that these at least point to relations of (economic) justice that cross boundaries, that are not confined within any one set of states or institutions.

Behind this terminological messiness lie substantive difficulties. Transnational justice, and in particular transnational economic justice, is a hard topic because global economic relations and global economic distribution are also new possibilities. Moreover, principles of economic justice are themselves highly contested. One difficulty of extending any of these principles to address transnational issues is that it is unclear *to whom* they will then have to be addressed: who are the agents of change?

[1] This essay is based on an earlier one, titled 'Transnational Justice', in David Held, ed., *Political Theory Today* (Cambridge: Polity Press, 1991), 276–304.

Who can act on or flout principles of transnational justice? Which of the parties affected have what sorts of claims to have them observed?

The novelty of discussing the justice of world-wide economic relations also has technical and historical aspects. Evidently wealth and entitlements[2] have always been adequate or better for some, while poverty and hunger have been unevenly distributed and acute for many. However, traditional societies could do little to change the circumstances of distant strangers. Without modern technologies and institutions it is hard or impossible to end or reduce distant poverty, or even to send a food surplus from one region to redress deficits in others. Within the great empires of the past, grain distribution was sometimes well controlled from the centre, but the boundaries of empire were also the maximal boundaries of redistribution. Transport of grain or goods even within those boundaries was problem enough; global transport simply impossible. Global economic justice was hardly imaginable.

This being the case, traditional codes said little about economic justice to those who lived beyond the frontiers, whether of tribe, community or empire. There might be limited advice on the right treatment of 'strangers', but strangers were thought of not as distant but as outsiders (travellers, refugees) who entered a territory and were present for a limited time and in limited numbers, with limited claims to share resources. The duties of hospitality and succour and the claims of strangers cannot offer an illuminating model for the distribution of resources where investment, production and goods can be shifted and development planned across huge distances, where trade is global and globally regulated, where economic processes can surge around the world affecting vast numbers.

It is not obvious that better models for thinking about economic and distributive justice across large distances will be found within traditional Western political thought.[3] In early modern European thought and politics 'outsiders' were often denied moral standing. Their occupation of

---

[2] For the concept of entitlement as the effective command of resources see A. K. Sen, *Poverty and Famine: An Essay on Entitlement and Deprivation* (Oxford: Clarendon Press, 1981); 'Gender and Cooperative Conflicts', in I. Tinker, ed., *Persistent Inequalities* (New York: Oxford University Press, 1990); J. Drèze and A. K. Sen, eds., *Hunger and Public Action* (Oxford: Clarendon Press, 1989); Martha Nussbaum and Amartya Sen, eds., *The Quality of Life* (Oxford: Clarendon Press, 1993).

[3] European political thinking has often espoused *formal* universalism: principles were intended for all; but has then undercut many of the practical implications of universalism by *de facto* exclusion of many – at various times: women and workers, indigenous peoples and foreigners – from the scope of principles of justice.

land was not recognized as ownership; their customs and institutions were undermined and often destroyed. The European colonial expansion, which has shaped the present world economic and political order, was achieved in part by invasion, genocide, expropriation, transportation, slavery and proselytizing that Europeans would have condemned as unjust in dealings with those whose standing they acknowledged.

Today questions of transnational justice will arise whether or not we can find the theoretical resources to handle them. Modern technical and institutional possibilities make wider and more distant intervention not only possible but unavoidable. We can now hardly avoid asking how individuals, institutions and societies may change (exacerbate, alleviate) distant poverty and distress. Current answers range from the *laissez-faire* view that it is permissible, or even obligatory, to do nothing, to claims that global economic justice is required and even that it is obligatory to use any surplus to alleviate distress, wherever it may be.

These answers are not only contentious but often ill focussed. To make them more precise we would have to establish *who is (or is not) obliged to take which sorts of action for whom*. But since the agents and agencies whose action and operation produce, distribute and control resources are not only numerous but heterogeneous, no easy overview is available. The agents and agencies range from individual human beings to a great variety of corporate bodies, of which some operate only within a single jurisdiction, and others transnationally. Even corporate bodies which operate only within one jurisdiction may have complex links with and dependence on others that operate transnationally; those that operate transnationally will be affected by the laws of various states and by international agreements, and may also escape these controls in part. Equally, those who may be wronged by the present transnational economic order are scattered through many regions and jurisdictions, and have many differing forms of involvement with and dependence on others' economic activities. The very transformations that have made a degree of world-order a reality, and transnational economic justice at least a theoretical possibility, have vastly expanded the web of actions, practices and institutions that might be challenged by judgements about economic justice.

This suggests that any discussion of transnational economic justice needs to take account of the diversity of capacities and scope for action of these various agents and agencies, and of the possibility and limits of their transformation. Yet discussions of economic justice have often been conducted on the basis of very incomplete views of agency. Some writers assume that the only relevant agents are individuals; others that they also include 'sovereign' states. Most are uncertain about the agency or the responsibilities of other corporate bodies (governments, businesses, international agencies, charities). While economists and development specialists are quite ready to use the vocabulary of action when speaking of a wide variety of agencies and institutions, discussions of the ethical issues often lags for lack of any general and convincing account of the responsibilities of collectivities.[4]

Nor is it easy to agree how to describe those on the receiving end of (just) economic relations. Presumably economic justice, and in particular transnational economic justice, should take account of certain human needs. Yet much modern ethical thought makes little or no use of the category of needs.[5] In Utilitarian thinking, needs can be considered only if reflected in desires or preferences: an imperfect reflection. Some discussion of human rights takes no account at all of needs; some takes account of them in ways that place some strain on the basic structure of theories of rights. One of the more promising strategies concedes that a full account of transnational economic justice might require a complete account of human needs, but claims that less is needed for a discussion that considers basic economic rights. It is not controversial that human beings need adequate food, shelter and clothing appropriate to their climate, clean water and sanitation, and some parental and health care, without which they become ill and die prematurely. These *basic needs* may provide a basis for arguing for *basic rights*. It is controversial whether human beings need companionship, family life, education,

---

[4] Discussions of collective agency include Peter French, *Collective and Corporate Responsibility* (New York: Columbia University Press, 1984); Norman Bowie, 'The Moral Obligations of Multinational Corporations', in Stephen Luper-Foy, ed., *Problems of International Justice* (Westview, Boulder and London), 1988, 97–113; Larry May, *The Morality of Groups: Responsibilities, Group-based Harms and Corporate Right* (Notre Dame, University of Notre Dame Press, 1987); Keith Graham, 'Collective Responsibility', in T. van den Beld, ed., *Moral Responsibility and Ontology* (Dordrecht: Kluwer, forthcoming, 2000), 49–61; Margaret Gilbert, *Living Together: Rationality, Sociality and Obligation* (London: Rowman & Littlefield, 1996).

[5] The reasons for this are not obscure. The best context for an account of needs is an account of the real requirements for human beings to lead good or flourishing lives, which is difficult to provide without establishing an objective account of the good for man. See Martha Nussbaum, 'Aristotelian Social Democracy', in Bruce Douglass, Gerald Mara and Henry S. Richardson, eds., *Liberalism and the Good* (London: Routledge, 1990); Len Doyal and Ian Gough, *A Theory of Human Need* (London: Macmillan, 1991); Gillian Brock, ed., *Necessary Goods: Our Responsibilities to Meet Others' Needs* (Lanham, Md.: Rowman & Littlefield, 1998).

politics, or food for the spirit – for at least some long and not evidently stunted lives have been lived without some of these. But these issues do not have to be completely settled for a discussion of hunger and destitution to proceed; discussion of transnational economic justice can at least begin with a rudimentary account of needs. In this essay I shall survey and comment on a number of these positions, and then propose a Kantian alternative which, I argue, offers a more explicit view of agency and need. I begin with a consideration of positions that have *least* to say about transnational justice; if these positions are convincing, there will be little point in going further.

## 2 COMMUNITY AND COSMOPOLIS

The deepest disagreement about transnational justice is between those who think that there is at least *something* to be said about duties beyond borders and those who think that ethical concern cannot or should not cross boundaries.[6] Liberal and socialist thinkers have traditionally viewed justice as having unrestricted scope, and hence cosmopolitan implications. In fact both liberal and socialist practice has usually subordinated justice to the demands of nation and state; but this may have been a practical and temporary rather than a fundamental concession. By contrast, various forms of relativism, historicism and 'realist' views of international relations deny that the category of justice has implications or even makes sense beyond the boundaries of nation or community, or therefore beyond the boundaries of states that they view as properly constituted. Burke's critique of the Rights of Man, and his insistence that the revolutionaries of

---

[6] Some discussions of duties that cross borders are: Stanley Hoffman, *Duties Beyond Borders: On the Limits and Possibilities of Ethical International Politics* (Syracuse, N.Y.: Syracuse University Press, 1981); Charles R. Beitz, 'Cosmopolitan Ideals and National Sentiments', *Journal of Philosophy*, 80 (1983), 591–600; Michael Walzer, *Spheres of Justice: A Defence of Pluralism and Equality* (Oxford: Martin Robertson, 1983); Alasdair MacIntyre, *Is Patriotism a Virtue?* (Lawrence, Kan.: University of Kansas, Department of Philosophy, 1984); Onora O'Neill, *Faces of Hunger: An Essay on Poverty, Development and Justice* (London: George Allen & Unwin, 1986) and 'Ethical Reasoning and Ideological Pluralism', *Ethics*, 98 (1988), 705–22; Henry Shue, 'Mediating Duties', *Ethics*, 98 (1988), 687–704; Thomas W. Pogge, 'Cosmopolitanism and Sovereignty', in Chris Brown, ed., *Political Restructuring in Europe: Ethical Perspectives* (London: Routledge, 1994), 89–122, also in *Ethics*, 103 (1992), 48–75; Thomas Risse-Kappen, ed., *Bringing Transnational Relations Back In: Non-state Actors, Domestic Structures and International Institutions* (Cambridge: Cambridge University Press, 1995); Mervyn Frost, *Ethics in International Relations: A Constitutive Theory* (Cambridge: Cambridge University Press, 1996).

France would have done better to appeal to the traditional rights of Frenchmen, is a classic version of this thought. Contemporary communitarian critics of 'abstract' liberal justice repeat and develop many points raised by early critics of rights.[7]

The common criticism that liberal, and particularly rights-based, accounts of justice are 'too abstract' is unconvincing.[8] Abstraction, in the strict sense, is essential to all language and reasoning; predicates must be bracketed if any plurality of cases is to be brought under a single principle. The critics of 'abstract liberalism' themselves do not and cannot avoid abstraction. Even relativists and communitarians, who may think that justice differs in Athens and in Sparta, will think of the justice of Athens as formulated in principles that apply to Athenians who differ in any number of ways, from which Athenian justice abstracts. Abstraction which brackets some of the predicates true of a given reality need not damage thought or argument.

A quite different pattern of thought (also often misleadingly termed 'abstraction') introduces 'idealizing' predicates that are false of a given reality. Idealizations abound in discussions of transnational economic justice; conceptions of fully rational agents, of ideally sovereign states and of wholly impermeable boundaries, of which no actual cases are to be found, proliferate. Theories of justice which build on assumptions like these may forfeit practical relevance.

Communitarians not only question cosmopolitan conceptions of justice; they have positive things to say about justice within communities. Many of them contend that the categories, the sense and the authority of any ethical discourse are anchored within a specific community or tradition, and that attempts to apply such reasoning across the boundaries of states or societies detach it from the forms of life and thought on which it depends. On this account, any conception of transnational economic justice will be illusory, because it will assume

---

[7] On the communitarian critique of liberalism see Michael Sandel, *Liberalism and the Limits of Justice* (Cambridge: Cambridge University Press, 1982). For parallel criticism from the perspective of (a distinctive form of) virtue ethics see Alasdair MacIntyre, *After Virtue* (London: Duckworth, 1981), *Is Patriotism a Virtue?* and *Whose Justice? Which Rationality?* (London: Duckworth, 1988). See also Walzer, *Spheres of Justice*; David Miller, 'The Ethical Significance of Nationality', *Ethics*, 98 (1988), 647–62. For the historical antecedents of these criticisms of liberal theories of rights see Jeremy Waldron, '*Nonsense Upon Stilts*': *Bentham, Burke and Marx on the Rights of Man* (London: Methuen, 1987), esp. the bibliographical essay.

[8] For further comments on the implications of abstraction see Chapters 4 and 8.

falsely that those in distinct communities share categories and principles. As some communitarians see it, the largest sphere of justice is the *political community*.[9] Other communitarian critics of 'abstract liberalism' see the boundaries of justice as coterminous with those of a *cultural community*. For example, MacIntyre argues that ethical reasoning must be internal to a particular tradition, which it seeks to further, and sees an irresolvable tension between the demands of liberalism and of nationalism.[10] Rawls, in his later 'political' writing, anchors principles of justice in the agreements of citizens of a modern liberal democratic polity.[11]

If communitarians are correct, transnational economic justice is not required, perhaps not even conceivable: compatriots have legitimate priority.[12] Transnational economic justice would indeed be unthinkable if the boundaries between states, and between modes of discourse and cultures, were total and impervious. This, however, is the very respect in which the modern world is different from its predecessors, or (more accurately) from its imagined predecessors. It is not a world of closed communities with mutually impenetrable ways of thought, self-sufficient economies and ideally sovereign states. What is more, communitarians acknowledge this in practice as much as anyone else. Like the rest of us they expect to interact with foreigners, and rely on practices of translation, negotiation and trade that cross boundaries of states and cultures. If complex, reasoned communication and association breach boundaries, why should not the demands of justice do so too? Although the internationalist images of a 'world community' or 'global village' may be sentimental slogans, the view that boundaries of actual communities or states are impervious is sheer idealizing nostalgia, sometimes self-serving nostalgia. Questions of transnational economic justice cannot now be ruled out of order.

---

[9] Walzer, *Spheres of Justice*, 28–30. Walzer does not, of course, wholly neglect international (transnational) justice, for he allows that the admission of individual aliens to membership of the community and conflicts between states raise issues of justice.

[10] MacIntyre, *After Virtue* and *Is Patriotism a Virtue?*

[11] John Rawls, 'Justice as Fairness: Political not Metaphysical', *Philosophy and Public Affairs*, 14 (1985), 223–51; *Political Liberalism* (New York: Columbia University Press, 1993).

[12] See Miller, 'The Ethical Significance of Nationality', 647–62; but contrast E. Robert Goodin, 'What Is So Special about Our Fellow Countrymen?', *Ethics*, 98 (1988), 663–86 and Thomas W. Pogge, 'The Bounds of Nationalism', in Jocelyne Couture et al., eds., *Rethinking Nationalism*; *Canadian Journal of Philosophy*, supp. vol. 22 (1998), 463–504.

## 3  CONSEQUENTIALIST REASONING AND TRANSNATIONAL
ECONOMIC JUSTICE

Consequentialist reasoning has two great advantages and two massive defects for thinking about global economic justice. First, the advantages. The present global economic order has stark consequences: it leaves hundreds of millions in profound poverty, with all its associated insecurities, ill-health and powerlessness. Consequentialist thought, and specifically Utilitarian thought, is geared to judge action and structures by their consequences, and so will take cognizance of these realities. The second advantage is that by concentrating on results rather than on action, consequentialist reasoning might (it seems) be able not merely to bracket but wholly to avoid intractable questions about agency.

These advantages have been widely embraced, and there is plenty of consequentialist reasoning about global distribution. It ranges from the simple publicity of some charities that work in the Third World ('Save a child's sight for £5.00') to sophisticated economic models.

Consequentialist theorizing about justice often deploys a Utilitarian account of value, and judges between policies and actions by reference to their probable contribution to human happiness or well-being. Right acts and policies (obligatory acts and policies) are those that contribute maximally to global expected well-being.

Consequentialist, and specifically Utilitarian, accounts of transnational economic justice have been thought to support a number of wholly different, indeed incompatible, lines of action. There are those who think that it requires the rich to transfer resources to the poor until further transfer would reduce aggregate well-being.[13] Marginalist considerations suggest that any given unit of resources will be more valued by the poor than by the rich, so that transfers would have to go a long way towards an equal distribution of resources before well-being was maximized. There have been others, especially various neo-Malthusian writers, who use consequentialist reasoning to argue that, on the contrary, the rich should transfer nothing to the poor: transfers of resources encourage the poor to have

---

[13] For a well-known and continually discussed statement of this position see Peter Singer, 'Famine, Affluence and Morality', *Philosophy and Public Affairs*, 1 (1972), 229–43; see also Garrett Cullity, 'International Aid and the Scope of Kindness', *Ethics*, 105 (1994), 99–127.

children they cannot support, and so lead to 'unsustainable' population growth and, eventually, to more harm than benefit.[14] There are many others – including many development agencies, and NGOs – who argue that consequentialist reasoning justifies selective redistribution from rich to poor, and in particular development aid aimed at securing economic entitlements, but not food aid, which perpetuates cultures of dependency.

These radical disagreements arise because consequentialist reasoning is more plastic and malleable than initially appears. Consequentialism raises hopes of replacing disagreement with calculation, but dashes them by providing overly pliant instruments of calculation. Although it appears to offer an algorithm for right action, the algorithm could be used only if we had a method for generating all the 'options' to be compared, adequate causal understanding for predicting the likely results of each 'option' and an adequate theory of value (Utilitarian or other) for evaluating each result with sufficient precision to rank the 'options'. This procedure can perhaps be approximately followed for some quite limited problems. It is a non-starter for dealing with transnational justice. Here neither 'problems' nor 'options' for solving them can be uncontentiously listed, and the results of most 'options' are uncertain and of disputed value. The supposedly precise recommendations which consequentialism might in principle provide elude us; in their stead we find recommendations whose spurious precision reflects contextual (perhaps ideologically contentious) views of the available 'options', their likely results and the value of those results. Consequentialist reasoning about actual problems is irremediably impressionistic rather than scientific.[15]

This defect is internal to consequentialism. The second major defect is external. Consequentialism overlooks much that others think central to justice. In taking the production of benefit (welfare, happiness) as the criterion for right action, consequentialism not only permits but requires some lives to be used and used up in order to produce benefit in other lives. Moreover, since most consequentialists use a subjective account of the good as the measure of benefit, they treat all preferences as on a par:

---

[14] Garret Hardin, 'Lifeboat Ethics: The Case against Helping the Poor', *Psychology Today*, 8 (1974), 38–43. For further discussion of and references to neo-Malthusian writing on world hunger see O'Neill, *Faces of Hunger*, chs. 2 and 4.

[15] See O'Neill, *Faces of Hunger*, chs. 4 and 5.

meeting urgent needs may have to take second place to satisfying strong preferences. This is not trivial in the context of global economic justice, because extreme deprivation can blunt rather than sharpen preferences.[16]

Even if we knew (how?) that actual preferences reflected the urgency of need, the use of some for others' benefit raises countless questions in development ethics. How far is it permissible to take what has been produced with much effort to alleviate others' poverty? Or to demand a 'generation of sacrifice' (or many generations) for the benefit of future generations? Or to use non-renewable resources or to increase population if this will harm future generations? How much freedom may be traded for how much equality? Consequentialists have not replaced quarrel with calculation in discussions of transnational economic justice: the evidence is the diversity of their own proposals for virtually all policies that might affect economic entitlements.

### 4 ACTION-BASED REASONING: RIGHTS AND OBLIGATIONS

If consequentialist ethical reasoning cannot avoid these problems, the most appealing alternative may be to consider less ambitious forms of ethical reasoning. Action-based ethical reasoning is less ambitious in that it seeks for morally significant constraints on action rather than presuming that we should try to identify optimal results, and thereby optimal action. Most action-based approaches to justice aim to offer accounts of the rights and the obligations which constitute justice.

Much reasoning about required action begins with rights, deriving obligations as their corollaries. It favours the perspective of recipience over that of action and agency. This could have advantages. It might allow support for bracketing contentious questions about agents and agency; it might help to harness the political resonance of appeals to rights to issues of transnational economic justice. However, there are also costs to beginning with an account of rights.

One evident cost is that in starting from rights we overlook obligations without counterpart rights. Whereas a right which nobody was obliged

---

[16] If strength of preference is the measure of moral claims, those who adapt their preferences to their misfortune will find their claims weakened. See the discussion of adaptive preferences in Jon Elster, *Sour Grapes: Studies in the Subversion of Rationality* (Cambridge: Cambridge University Press, 1983), 109–40; specific illustrations and discussion of adapting to deprivation can be found in Martha Nussbaum and Jonathan Glover, eds., *Women, Culture and Development: A Study of Human Capabilities* (Oxford: Clarendon Press, 1995).

to respect would be an illusion, an obligation which nobody was entitled to claim could be rather important. However, such obligations are not generally seen as aspects of justice, and I shall set them aside. More significantly, even if rights are the starting point, their implications for action can remain deeply unclear. Rights are usually individuated by indicating *what should be accorded or provided* (rights to take up abode, to free speech, to food, to work), rather than by indicating *what action will be required of whom* if the right is to be respected. It is straightforward to work out who will have to do what for whom in order to respect certain types of rights, but not at all straightforward in the case of other types of rights.

The easy cases are *universal liberty rights* and *special rights*. *Universal liberty rights* must have corresponding obligations which are held by all others: a right to freedom of movement is impaired if there are *any* others without obligations to respect it. *Special rights* to receive goods and services from identifiable agents and agencies require those particular agents and agencies to act to respect or fulfil that right: if I have bought goods from a particular shopkeeper, it is that shopkeeper who has an obligation to provide me with the goods purchased. Other rights are not so obligingly structured, in that the right can be referred to without specifying to whom the counterpart obligations are allocated.

Some much-discussed rights that would be economically significant do not specify the allocation of their counterpart obligations. Economically important liberty rights (rights to contract, to buy and sell) and special rights between identifiable parties (a right to have a contract observed, to be paid as agreed) have clearly allocated counterpart obligations, but universal rights to goods and services do not. Who would bear the obligations that would be required if there were universal rights to food, rights to work (in the sense of rights to employment) or rights to development? Universal rights to goods and services are distinctive in that they could be satisfied in countless different ways. A 'right to food' could be satisfied by earning enough money to buy food, by having enough land to grow it or by having friends and family with obligations to provide it; in each case there would be an entitlement to food, in Sen's sense of the term. But without one or other determinate institutional structure, these supposed economic rights amount to rhetoric rather than entitlement. Beyond the most abstract level of action-centred reasoning, a gap opens between rights and obligations: rights specify what is to be received; obligations also specify who is to provide it. This gap reflects the fact that a focus on rights adopts the passive perspective of the recipient, indeed claimant, of others' action. Within the recipient perspective, the attitude of claimants is indeed *less* passive than other possible attitudes. Claimants are not humble petitioners or loyal subjects. They do not beg boons or favours. They speak as equals who are wronged. They demand others' action. This is why the early modern innovation of the perspective of rights had both heady power and political import. It could be used by the down-trodden to reject and hector existing powers and their conceptions of political and economic obligations. This rhetoric was vibrant in a world of rulers and subjects, and still resonant in the later worlds of empires and colonies, of superpowers and their clients. Nevertheless, those who claim their rights still view themselves within an overall framework of recipience. Rights are *demands on others*. Liberty rights demand that others not interfere with or obstruct the right-holder, rights to goods and services that others provide for the right-holder.

This suggests that the rhetoric of rights is not the fundamental idiom of action-centred reasoning, but a derivative (and potentially rancorous) way of thought in which others, sometimes unspecified others, are seen as the primary agents, while right-holders see themselves as secondary agents, whose action depends on restraint or provision by others. This may be the most nearly active form of ethical and political discourse for the needy and vulnerable. For the more powerful, who could do most to reduce others' need, concentration on rights and recipience may mask recognition of their own power and of the real demands of obligations.

The most questionable effect of putting rights first is that those rights for which no allocation of obligations has been institutionalized may not be taken seriously. When obligations are unallocated it is indeed right that they should be met, but nobody can have an effective right – an enforceable, claimable or waiveable right – to their being met. Such abstract rights are not effective entitlements. If the claimants of supposed 'rights' to food or development cannot find where to lodge their claims, these are empty 'manifesto' rights.[17] If a 'right to food' is promulgated without

---

[17] For the phrase 'manifesto right' see Joel Feinberg, 'The Nature and Value of Rights', in *Rights, Justice and the Bounds of Liberty: Essays in Social Philosophy* (Princeton, N.J.: Princeton University Press, 1980). More generally see Henry Shue, *Basic Rights: Subsistence, Affluence and U.S. Foreign Policy* (Princeton, N.J.: Princeton University Press, 1980); Onora O'Neill, 'Rights, Obligations and Needs', *Logos*, 6 (1985), 29–47; and Joseph Raz, 'Right-based Moralities', in Jeremy Waldron, ed., *Theories of Rights* (Oxford: Oxford University Press, 1984), 182–200.

obligations to provide food for particular right-holders being allocated to specified agents, those without food are guaranteed meagre pickings.

Differing approaches to the problems raised by treating rights as fundamental to justice have been proposed by libertarians, by advocates of compensatory justice and by the very numerous advocates of forms of 'social justice' or 'welfare' liberalism. These responses have differing implications for transnational economic justice.

### 5 LIBERTARIAN JUSTICE

Libertarian writers have a crisp response to those who object that rights to goods and services are problematic without allocated obligations. They agree, indeed insist, that all rights are either universal liberty rights, whose counterpart obligations demand only universal forbearance, or special rights, growing out of voluntary relationships and agreements between specified parties. Any other supposed universal rights – for example, rights to food, welfare or development – would impose obligations that violate some obligation-bearers' rights to liberty, and so are denied by libertarians, who see taxation for others' benefit, including taxation to provide development aid, as unjust taking of property from those taxed. The central demand of libertarian justice, whether national or transnational, is: do not redistribute.

Libertarian claims require convincing arguments in favour of a particularly strong interpretation of property rights; liberty rights are seen as protecting all outcomes of freely entered transactions. The arguments actually provided have been much criticized. Some critics simply deny that liberty should be given unconditional priority over other goods.[18] Others are less concerned about liberty having priority over other goods, but interpret freedom more broadly, and claim that rights to freedom of the person must be buttressed by rights to those forms of welfare or provision of basic needs without which human beings cannot develop, act freely or make use of liberty rights. They conclude that even if liberty is given priority, property rights must be restricted in certain ways.[19]

[18] For discussions of the priority of liberty in a libertarian and in a Rawlsian context see respectively Jeffrey Paul, ed., *Reading Nozick: Essays on Anarchy, State and Utopia* (Oxford: Blackwell, 1981) and Norman Daniels, ed., *Reading Rawls: Critical Studies on A Theory of Justice* (Oxford: Blackwell, 1975).

[19] Consider Rawls's insistence on his second principle of justice; Alan Gewirth, 'Starvation and Human Rights', in his *Human Rights: Essays on Justification and Applications* (Chicago: University of Chicago Press, 1982), 197–217; Shue, *Basic Rights*; see also the discussion in section 7 below.

Others think that the central libertarian idea of a maximal equal liberty for all is simply indeterminate.[20]

The insistence that redistribution by state powers or agencies is unjust determines libertarian views on aid, welfare and poverty. Libertarians hold that 'voluntary giving' (to use a favoured pleonasm) and charity are the only acceptable forms of help to those in need, since they alone do not violate justice. Some worry that charity too will be wrong if it establishes or fosters dependence.[21] Voluntary giving, however, is entirely inadequate for dealing with massive phenomena such as global poverty.[22] Libertarians are in any case wholly ill-placed for saying much in favour of charity. Since they deny themselves the conceptual resources which could make sense of obligations that are not the corollaries of rights, they have nothing instructive to say about such obligations, or about the virtues that might be expressed in philanthropic work and giving. Some libertarian writing gives matters a rosy gloss by suggesting that charity, since it is not a matter of obligation, is supererogatory. This is only rhetorical flourish: since they offer and can offer no account of what makes action that goes 'beyond' the limited obligations which they recognize morally admirable, libertarians would be more accurate to describe charitable giving just as one possible expression of personal preference.[23]

Yet despite their horror of economic redistribution, libertarians could hold, and a few have held, positions that have powerful and perhaps helpful implications for the poor of the Third World. Since they base their thought on respect for individuals and their rights, and judge any but minimal states unjust, libertarians should presumably view actual states, none of them minimal, as exceeding their just powers, and in particular should view state restrictions on individuals' freedom to move, to take up abode and to seek employment as violating rights. On an obvious

---

[20] O'Neill, *Faces of Hunger*, ch. 6, 'The Most Extensive Liberty', *Proceedings of the Aristotelian Society*, 53 (1979–80), 45–59 and 'Children's Rights and Children's Lives', *Ethics*, 98 (1988), 445–63.

[21] See the papers in Ellen Frankel Paul et al., eds., *Beneficence, Philanthropy and the Public Good* (Oxford: Blackwell, 1987), esp. Alan Gewirth, 'Private Philanthropy and Positive Rights', 55–78 and John O'Connor, 'Philanthropy and Selfishness', 113–27; Alan Buchanan, 'Justice and Charity', *Ethics*, 97 (1987), 558–75; Onora O'Neill, 'The Great Maxims of Justice and Charity', in *Constructions of Reason: Explorations of Kant's Practical Philosophy* (Cambridge: Cambridge University Press, 1989), 219–33.

[22] Thomas Nagel, 'Poverty and Food: Why Charity is not Enough', in Peter Brown and Henry Shue, eds., *Food Policy: The Responsibility of the United States in Life and Death Choices* (New York: Free Press, 1977), 54–62.

[23] Onora O'Neill, *Towards Justice and Virtue: A Constructive Account of Practical Reasoning* (Cambridge: Cambridge University Press, 1996), 142–4.

reading, this suggests that libertarians should champion rights to migrate and live anywhere, and to undercut any local wage level. Work and residence permits, like protectionist trade barriers, violate libertarian rights. Yet libertarians are well known for advocating free trade and opposing wage regulation, but not for advocating the dismantling of immigration laws. This may be because their stress on property rights so limits public space that it damages the freedom of movement and rights of abode of the unpropertied, even within national jurisdictions.[24]

What would the global import of radically cosmopolitan libertarianism be? Presumably such policies would greatly weaken the position of the relatively poor within rich economies, by undercutting their bargaining power. Perhaps ostensibly 'perfected' global markets might spread opportunities and thereby resources more and more evenly across the world's population. Or would removal of restrictions on movement, abode and trade achieve quite different results? In an era of automated production, the poor and unskilled may find that they have little to sell in the global market: even their labour power may lack market value. Concentrations of economic power have been able to form and survive in relatively free internal markets; transnational concentrations of economic power look likely to ride the waves of wider competition equally successfully.

## 6 COMPENSATORY JUSTICE AND TRANSNATIONAL ECONOMIC JUSTICE

Rights to compensation offer another approach to transnational economic justice. Even if the poor lack universal rights to economic support either from fellow-citizens or across state boundaries, some of them may have special rights to compensation against specified others who have injured or are injuring them.[25]

---

[24] For writing on the ethics of immigration and emigration see Walzer, *Spheres of Justice*, esp. ch. 1; Herman R. van Gunsteren, 'Admission to Citizenship', *Ethics*, 98 (1988), 731–41; Hillel Steiner, 'Libertarians and Transnational Migration', in Brian Barry and Robert E. Goodin, eds., *Free Movement: Ethical Issues in the Transnational Migration of People and Money* (London: Harvester Wheatsheaf, 1992), 87–94; Joseph Carens, 'Immigration and the Welfare State', in Amy Gutman, ed., *Democracy and the Welfare State* (Princeton, N.J.: Princeton University Press, 1988), 207–30; 'Aliens and Citizens: The Case for Open Borders', *Review of Politics*, 49 (1987), 251–73; Warren F. Schwartz, ed., *Justice in Immigration* (Cambridge: Cambridge University Press, 1995).

[25] See George Sher, 'Ancient Wrongs and Modern Rights', *Philosophy and Public Affairs*, 10, (1981), 3–17; David Lyons, 'The New Indian Claims and Original Rights to Land', in Paul, *Reading Nozick*, 355–79.

Special rights to compensation are rooted in specific historical or current facts and relationships. The present plight of the underdeveloped world was caused in part by past actions by the states, businesses and individuals of the developed world (no doubt also by more local agents and forces). Colonialism began with invasion and massive violations of liberty. Many Third World economies were developed to the advantage of the imperial powers. Profits made in the South were 'repatriated' rather than reinvested; colonial industry and trade were restricted; development in the North was partly based on exploitation of the South. However, the causal patterns of colonial violation of rights are complex and obscure: much is hidden in the heart of far-off darkness. Many former colonies were economically backward when colonized; some colonial powers did a good deal to modernize and develop their colonies; in some cases Third World economies prospered under colonial administrations. And it is always uncertain what the present would have been had the past not been colonial.

Still, where the present plight of the poor in the Third World can be traced to past injustices inflicted by *surviving* agents or agencies, it may be possible to argue that some have rights to be compensated by those agents and agencies. However, the individuals whose rights were violated in the more distant past, and those who violated them, are long dead, and the relevant institutions usually transformed or defunct. Rights to compensation could nevertheless be helpful to some if connected to an adequate account of institutional agency which showed which still-existing agents and agencies can reasonably be held responsible for which past injuries, and to whom supposed obligations are owed. Failing that, nobody will be able to tell where supposed obligations to compensate for past injustices are now located, or who (if anyone) now has rights to be compensated. However, even where the facts of past oppression, injury and exploitation can be well established, they may provide no determinate basis for showing which present individuals, groups, states or regions have special rights to compensation. We are often unsure to what extent the predicaments of the present were produced by ancient wrongs, or which of our contemporaries have been harmed by past wrongs, or which of them have benefited from past wrongs. Unsurprisingly, then, we cannot easily tell who owes whom compensation for what. States are probably the best example of obligation-bearers that last through long periods; yet even states transform their identities. Is the present Russian state, for example, responsible not only for the treaty obligations of the Soviet state it in part replaced, but for the economic injuries of forced collectivization? If so, who should pay to compensate whom? What – if anything – can special rights to compensation provide for those, however poor, who were barely touched by the activities of the colonial period? Would not their needs be wholly ignored in an account of transnational economic justice that relied mainly on appeals to special rights to compensation for the injuries of the past?

A parallel set of considerations attributes much of the plight of the Third World not to ancient but to present wrong. Sometimes clear cases of present wrong are identifiable: wars and violence, genocide, pillaging and dumping of toxic waste have perpetrators. If these perpetrators can be identified, a context for punishment or compensation is in place. However, often perpetrators cannot be identified, or if identified will be wholly unable (not to mention unwilling) to compensate. Moreover, there are many other instances of poverty and lack of basic needs which cannot be ascribed to any agent, past or present. Economic systems working in their routine ways may erode economic security or endanger prosperity for millions; yet the identification of wrongdoers may be elusive. Libertarians, in particular, do not see the harms suffered by the more vulnerable in a world of unequal competitors as unjust. On the other hand, some non-libertarian advocates of universal rights allege that *laissez-faire* is a mockery in a world where the rich and powerful control the ground rules of the transnational economic order and in particular the framework of monetary and trading arrangements.

The details of such charges are enormously intricate, but their basic pattern is simple. Others' rights are not respected if there is massive interference in the basic circumstances of their lives. The exercise of political and economic powers sometimes helps and sometimes injures the lives of distant and impoverished people in the Third World. Where injury is done, responsibility for compensation should lie with the powerful. More pointedly, a common charge is that transnational businesses, trade treaties, banking and credit institutions and the operation of the IMF and the World Bank set the ground rules of economic life for the whole world, so that the suffering of the poor and powerless is in some measure their doing. In these circumstances, it is argued, any claim that justice requires non-interference in the liberties of the powerful is rank hypocrisy.

Such arguments are often impressive in outline, but their detailed implications are once again obscure. What assumptions about rights, over and above those which libertarians would accept, are needed if the operation of economic power is to be seen as rights-violating?

Does the argument point to rejection of policies of open markets and foreign investment ('dependent development') in favour of indigenous and autonomous, perhaps slower, paths of development? Does it point to a massive scheme of compensatory payments from the developed world to the developing world? If it does, is the present range of investment and 'aid' measures adequate compensation, despite the misleading label? Or are present policies inadequate because unevenly spread, too often constrained by the interests of 'donors' and not directed on compensatory principles? Can policies which have produced developed enclaves in the Third World, while leaving vast areas of rural hinterland impoverished, count as compensation for present – or for past – injury? Are these arrangements sufficient because consented to by those whom they affect, or perhaps by their governments? Or are the powerful within the Third World more likely to owe compensation to their fellow-citizens? And what is to happen when those who ought to compensate cannot do so?

Poverty either in or beyond the Third World cannot easily be remedied by compensatory justice. To claim special rights we must show a special relationship; but the causal links between specific individuals or institutions who injured and were injured, or who now injure others and suffer injuries, are too often not clear enough to allocate rights of compensation: without allocation, rights are only the rhetoric of manifestos.

## 7  RIGHTS TO GOODS AND SERVICES AND TRANSNATIONAL ECONOMIC JUSTICE

A third, more ambitious and more popular approach to transnational economic justice argues that human rights include not only liberty rights and those special rights (including rights to compensation) that can arise once any universal rights are acknowledged, but also universal rights to certain goods and services. Several theories of justice claim that there are also rights to (some level of) economic provision or welfare, such as rights to whatever goods and services are required to meet basic needs. This type of claim is also basic to UN and other declarations of economic, social and cultural rights. Positions that allow for substantive economic rights should surely provide friendly terrain for an account of transnational economic justice. Yet this is not always the case.

One well-known account of economic justice that includes more than liberty and special rights is John Rawls's *A Theory of Justice*.[26] His theory of justice is designed for the basic structure of a society, conceived of as a more or less self-contained and self-sufficient community.[27] He argues for two principles of justice for such societies. The first echoes the libertarian view that all should have equal and maximal liberties; the second, the so-called difference principle, qualifies this with the requirement that inequalities be permitted only where they would be to the advantage of the representative worst-off person. Since the construction assumes the framework of a closed society, the 'representative worst-off person' is not thought of as representing the worst off of the whole world. When Rawls finally relaxes the assumption that justice is internal to states, he argues only for selected principles of transnational justice.[28] He repeats the thought experiment of the original position on the hypothesis that the parties are representatives of states, conceived of as relatively self-sufficient entities, but claims to establish only those principles of international justice which are analogues of his first principle of justice: non-intervention, self-determination, *pacta sunt servanda*, principles of self-defence and of just war. There is no international analogue of the difference principle, and hence no account of transnational economic justice.

Several writers have tried to rectify Rawls's omission within a basically Rawlsian framework. For example, Charles Beitz proposes an analogue of Rawls's procedure for vindicating principles for intrastatal justice, in which representatives of states meet behind a veil of ignorance, to choose principles of global resource distribution.[29] Beitz argues that they would choose a global difference principle that required sufficient

---

[26] John Rawls, *A Theory of Justice* (Cambridge, Mass.: Harvard University Press, 1971). Rawls proposes principles for just institutions, and does not give rights priority over obligations. However, I have discussed his work in this rather than the next section because, like rights-based theorists, he sometimes backgrounds questions about agency.

[27] Throughout his writings Rawls emphasizes that he begins by assuming that the context of justice is a bounded society, whose members enter by birth and leave by death. International justice is very much an appendix to his fundamentally 'domestic', perhaps statist view of the context of justice.

[28] Rawls, *A Theory of Justice*, 378ff.; see also *Political Liberalism* (New York: Columbia University Press, 1993) and *The Law of Peoples*, in his *Collected Papers*, ed. Sam Freeman, 2nd edn (Cambridge, Mass.: Harvard University Press, 1999), 529–64.

[29] Charles Beitz, *Political Theory and International Relations* (Princeton, N.J.: Princeton University Press, 1979). See also Bernard Boxill, 'Global Equality of Opportunity', *Social Philosophy and Policy*, 5 (1987), 143–68 for an application of Rawlsian equality of opportunity on a global scale.

redistribution of resources to protect those states that found themselves with nothing but resource-poor territories. A quite different revision of Rawls's position has been proposed by Thomas Pogge, who argues that a cosmopolitan rather than a statist perspective should be assumed from the start in constructing the original position, and that all principles of justice should have cosmopolitan scope.[30]

The actual implications of such extensions of Rawlsian thought are hard to discern. Rawls's account of justice constrains institutions: his second principle demands the evaluation and comparison of entire institutional structures. Some of the difficulties of evaluation and comparison which plague consequentialists recur here: deploying a maximin principle requires much of the information needed for ranking judgements. Since transnational interdependence is vastly complex, views about which institutional changes would most improve the lot of the poorest are bound to be hotly contested.

Other accounts that go beyond a libertarian view of rights argue that individuals have rights to basic well-being, which require that their material needs be met. On such accounts – for example, those of Gewirth and Shue[31] – arrangements will be unjust if they do not provide welfare and meet basic needs. Without minimal standards of subsistence, agency itself fails, and so the point of liberty of action and hence even of liberty rights is gone. The point is not, of course, to neglect institutional arrangements: the basic needs of many millions could only be secured by building an appropriate economic order. The point is to find some set of arrangements that secures rights that meet those needs.

Economic rights, so conceived, make hefty demands. If any universal rights to goods and services are to be taken seriously, some set of obligations that are adequate counterparts of these rights must be allocated. Yet it is not obvious which allocation of these obligations is to be preferred. Usually rights theorists assume that the counterparts to universal rights are universal obligations, although aspects of fulfilling and enforcing the corresponding institutional right may be allocated to specific agencies. This assumption sits well in discussions of liberty rights, where the corresponding universal obligations are negative. A right to liberty is

---

[30] Thomas W. Pogge, *Realizing Rawls* (Ithaca, N.Y.: Cornell University Press, 1989); also 'A Global Resources Dividend', in David A. Crocker and Toby Linden, eds., *Ethics of Consumption: The Good Life, Justice and Global Stewardship* (Lanham, Md.: Rowman & Littlefield, 1998), 501–36.

[31] Gewirth, 'Starvation and Human Rights'; Shue, *Basic Rights*; Gillian Brock, ed., *Necessary Goods: Our Responsibilities to Meet Others' Needs* (Lanham, Md.: Rowman & Littlefield, 1998).

not respected unless all agents and agencies refrain from violating that liberty. But economic rights to a level of goods or services are different. It is impossible for everyone to take on the same obligations here, for example, by making the same contribution to ending poverty or hunger. A universal right to be fed or to receive basic shelter or health care is unlike a universal right not to be killed or to speak freely. It is plausible to think that rights not to be killed or to speak freely are matched by and require universal obligations not to kill or not to obstruct free speech; but a universal right to food cannot simply be matched by a universal obligation to provide an aliquot morsel of food. The asymmetry of liberty and 'welfare' rights, on which libertarians rest so much of their refusal to broaden their conception of justice, is, I think, well grounded. (This offers little comfort to libertarians if they cannot establish that liberty has priority or what maximal liberty comprises.)

Broadly speaking, these and other 'social justice' theories propose accounts of economic justice that include rights to claim basic needs. Yet typically these theories identify these rights so abstractly that they fail to fix their allocation to obligation-bearers; they do not determine against whom claims may be lodged. Such theories allow us to *talk* quite fluently about, say, rights to food or rights to a minimal standard of life or rights to basic health care; but they obscure the real asymmetry between rights to such goods and services and universal liberty rights whose counterpart obligations are straightforwardly universal obligations of forbearance. When we think of rights to goods or services against the background of twentieth-century welfare states, with established institutions for securing and paying for 'welfare' rights, this lack of allocation may not be obvious. When we extend 'social justice' theories beyond states, we discover that the implications of economic rights whose counterpart obligations are not allocated are radically indeterminate.

Some advocates of universal economic rights to goods or services hope to make progress by challenging the very distinction between different sorts of universal right. Henry Shue, for example, correctly pointed out that once we start talking about the enforcement of rights, the distinction between liberty rights and substantive economic rights which require positive action from others fades. He writes: 'the very most "negative"-seeming right to liberty . . . requires positive action by society to protect it and . . . to restore it when avoidance and protection both fail'.[32] However, enforcement presupposes that the proper allocation of

---

[32] Shue, *Basic Rights*, 53.

obligations has been identified. It is, after all, obligations, and not rights, that will need enforcing. Arguments from the demands of enforceability cannot settle who holds the obligations that would correspond to supposed rights to goods and services. While it is true that the enforcement of a right not to be tortured demands positive action, just as enforcement of a right to food does, the asymmetry between the two rights remains. Suppose we think that there are both rights not to be tortured and rights to food. If, in the absence of enforcement, A tortures B, we are quite clear who has violated B's right; but if A does not provide B with food, not even with a morsel of food, we cannot tell whether A has violated B's rights. For nothing shows that it is against A that B's claim to food holds and should be enforced.[33]

## 8 UNIVERSAL OBLIGATIONS AND TRANSNATIONAL JUSTICE

'Social justice' theories of rights come close to providing a framework for thinking about transnational economic justice. What is missing from the positions just outlined is an account of the role of institution-building that can specify and allocate obligations to meet the claims of need and poverty. Libertarians take the allocation of obligations seriously, but overlook need; 'social justice' liberals acknowledge the claims of need but sometimes do not take the allocation of obligations seriously. I shall try to meet both demands by sketching how one might make obligations rather than rights the starting point for justice, and take cognizance of the fact that obligations are held by and towards finite, needy beings.

Those who make rights basic to their account of justice start with the thought that all have equal rights. An analogous approach to identifying obligations of justice would look for principles of obligation that can be held by all, that are universally adoptable. As is well known, this is the basic move of the Kantian ethical enterprise.[34] Kant identified principles of obligation as those which must be adopted if principles that cannot be universally held are rejected. To make non-universalizable principles fundamental to institutions or to lives presumes status and privilege that cannot be open to all. Injustice on this account is a matter of basing political and other public institutions on fundamental princi-

---

[33] See also Shue, *Basic Rights* and 'Mediating Duties'; O'Neill, *Faces of Hunger*, ch. 6; *Towards Justice and Virtue*, ch. 5.

[34] The Kantian texts that lie behind this are mainly the *Groundwork of the Metaphysic of Morals* and the *Critique of Practical Reason*; for some differences between Kant's approach and the contemporary 'Kantian' approaches discussed in the last section see Chapter 4 above.

ples which cannot be adopted by all, justice a matter of basing political and other public institutions on fundamental principles which all *could* adopt.

A Kantian construction of principles of obligation is in one crucial way less ambitious than many constructions of human rights. Those constructions typically seek to determine the *greatest* possible liberty, or the *best* set of liberty rights and rights to goods or services. At some stage in these constructions an optimum or maximal arrangement must be identified. Just as the poles of a wigwam cannot stand in isolation, so these constructions of rights are all-or-nothing affairs: if one component right of 'the most extensive liberty' cannot be identified, nor can the others. When principles of obligation are constructed on Kantian lines, they may be identified seriatim. The construction uses a procedure for determining whether any basic principle for lives and institutions can be universally adopted. It may prove possible to identify some such principles even if it is not possible to identify all of them.

Discovering which principles must be adopted if non-universalizable principles are rejected will not show that very specific types of action ought to be done. Act-descriptions which refer to particular times, places, persons or scarce resources cannot be universally satisfied. Yet clearly acts, including permissible and obligatory acts, must fall under such descriptions. Evidently, then, the point is not to check whether principles incorporating every superficial and detailed act-description can be universalizable: they cannot. We cannot all of us eat the same grain, or share the same roof. A Kantian approach aims only to identify fundamental principles for structuring lives and institutions, which can then be used to guide choice among the countless more specific principles that can be embedded in the laws, policies, practices and norms of social life. Although Kantian justice requires that actions, lives or institutions must not be based on principles that cannot be universally shared, it does not require uniform action.

## 9 JUSTICE, ABILITIES AND NEEDS

On the surface it might seem that a Kantian account of universal principles of obligation would mirror others' accounts of universal rights.[35]

---

[35] Apart, that is, from the possibility which Kant's position allows for of identifying 'imperfect' obligations without counterpart rights, which Kant views as principles of virtue. See n. 38 below.

In fact, both Kant's argument and his conclusions about justice are distinctive because he combines a strong view of human capacities for action and autonomy[36] with insistence that human beings are finite and mutually vulnerable, dependent on material resources and not always well disposed to one another. If humans were not vulnerable and needy, they could not damage, destroy, coerce and deceive so successfully (or perhaps at all), and the need for justice would be gone. On Kant's view, the combination of agency and vulnerability constitutes the circumstances of justice.

The picture of human life which Kant assumes is one in which agents with limited capacities and varied vulnerabilities interact; this picture is required if a universalizability criterion is to identify obligations of justice. The easiest way to see why certain principles *cannot* be universally adopted among finite and interacting beings is by a simple *reductio ad absurdum* thought experiment. If certain sorts of principles could (*per impossibile*) be universally adopted by mutually vulnerable interacting beings, then even moderate success in acting on them (at a level any rational being must expect on the assumption that the principle is universally adopted) will render some others victims, and so unable to adopt those principles, which therefore (contrary to hypothesis) cannot be universally adopted. Examples of principles which can be identified as non-universalizable by this strategy include principles of injury, violence, coercion and deception. If (*per impossibile*) any of these principles were universally adopted among interacting but vulnerable beings, even a moderate success rate in acting on them (at a level any rational beings must expect on the assumption that the principle is universally adopted) would create at least some victims[37] who (contrary to hypothesis) would be unable to adopt that principle. On a Kantian account, it is therefore a matter of obligation not to rely on fundamental principles of injury, violence, coercion, deception and the like,[38] obligations which he

---

[36] See Chapter 2 above.

[37] In the case of deception, the problem is less that particular victims are created than that destruction of trust undercuts the possibility of adopting strategies of deception.

[38] Kant himself uses somewhat parallel arguments to establish *principles of virtue*, requiring limited forms of beneficence and (self-) development. His argument may be rendered as follows: because human beings are finite and needy, they can rationally expect that there will be times when their own abilities are insufficient and they need others' help; because human beings have to learn and develop capacities for action, they cannot rationally expect all the abilities which they may need or want to use to be automatically available. Hence universal rejection of beneficence or (self-) development, although not incoherent, is self-defeating for finite beings.

groups under the heading of 'requirements to respect others' external freedom'.[39]

The ways in which injury, violence, coercion, deception and the like can be used to undermine external freedom is not only by undermining individual capacities for action blow by blow, threat by threat, lie by lie, but also through sustaining cultures of intimidation, insecurity, deference and evasiveness. What constitutes injury, or threat, or effective deception always depends on the relative power of those agents and agencies who act unjustly and the relative lack of power, and consequently enhanced vulnerability, of those who suffer injustice. Conversely, injustice can be prevented or minimized both by prohibiting, policing and penalizing those who might inflict it and by empowering, educating and supporting those who may be exposed to it.

Evidently, these very abstract principles of justice do not guide action with any precision. Nor, in Kant's view, is it possible to achieve a flawless realization of justice under human conditions. Because human beings are not always well disposed towards one another, justice requires enforcing institutions which unavoidably curtail external freedom. In Kant's view, the first task in developing a more specific account of justice is to recognize this reality, and to accept that justice requires institutions that coerce to limit coercion. The reason for accepting this is that alternative, non-state institutions – for example, anarchic or feudal structures – secure even less respect for external freedom.

Once principles of justice are identified, we are set a task, or rather a succession of tasks. Showing the need for coercive power – specifically for the state's right to coerce – is only a first step towards justice. Thereafter interlocking political and economic institutions are needed, which jointly provide an extensive and effective set of guarantees of external freedom. Unsurprisingly, Kant's own account of the institutions of justice is dated in many respects, although its insistence on the cosmopolitan scope of justice lends it contemporary resonance. Any version of Kantian justice which has contemporary relevance will need to show that the principles of justice he identifies could be embedded in

---

[39] Kant's 'Universal Principle of Right' – his fundamental principle of justice – is stated variously as 'Any action is right if it can coexist with everyone's freedom in accordance with a universal law' and 'the universal law of right, so act externally that the free use of your choice can coexist with the freedom of everyone in accordance with a universal law, is indeed a law that lays an obligation on me', *Doctrine of Right*, *The Metaphysics of Morals*, in Immanuel Kant, *Practical Philosophy*, VI:203–493, tr. and ed. Mary Gregor (Cambridge: Cambridge University Press, 1996).

the institutions, practices and policies of a global political and economic system.

Some have argued that any accurate view of Kant's account of justice, which requires security for external freedom, will recognize only the obligations that are the counterparts of liberty rights. His account of economic justice would then resemble the libertarian account. This may be one way in which Kantian principles could be developed. However, I do not believe that it gives adequate weight to Kant's insistence that the human beings who are to live by these principles are mutually vulnerable and needy. Their capacities to act freely are so easily undermined, whether by poverty, powerlessness, insecurity or dependence on others, that mere respect for liberty rights is highly unlikely to achieve an extensive and effective realization of Kantian justice. On the contrary, where agents are intensely mutually vulnerable, justice can be sought only by a dual strategy of disciplining the action of the powerful and of seeking to empower the powerless, so making them less vulnerable.

Just economic systems must therefore support the capacities of vulnerable agents. An aspect of this support must be to secure at least minimal entitlements to the necessities of life for all. However, it would be a mistake to think of Kantian economic justice simply as endorsing the addition of welfare rights to liberty rights. Welfare rights are only *one* way in which entitlements to basic necessities might be secured. Employment, ownership of land or other productive assets, extensive hunting or fishing rights, membership of a cooperative, strong familial obligations or the institution of a citizens' wage could also secure the relevant entitlements. Entitlements do not have to be secured in the same way for all, provided they are secured in some way for each. Kantian economic justice does not point simply to increasing average income or wealth, let alone to achieving economic uniformities of any sort. Like other aspects of justice, it is a matter of limiting relative power and powerlessness, so securing the external freedom within which people can seek to obtain the means to lead their lives. Many differing institutional structures can support economic justice.

These considerations have large implications for transnational economic justice, since there is no arena in which disparities of powers to act and be acted upon is greater. Poor and relatively powerless states and institutions, like poor and relatively powerless individuals, may make dismal 'bargains', trading their only resources for inadequate returns, 'agreeing' to damaging terms of trade and taking out loans that they cannot service. They may 'agree' to accept dirty manufacturing or 'offer' excessive tax concessions for foreign investors. They may be dominated by corrupt elites. They may waste resources. All of this reflects their vulnerability. For, miscalculation apart, public institutions fail comprehensively because they are too weak for their supposed tasks. A more just transnational economic order will need both efforts to limit the disparities of power and vulnerabilities by which some institutions, and hence many individuals, readily and repeatedly become victims of others' action and sustained efforts not to take advantage of remaining vulnerabilities. Seeking *just reforms* and seeking *just transactions* (amid unjust current institutions) both make huge demands. If justice is fundamentally a matter of securing external freedom for all, reforms which build a more just transnational economic order might have to regulate and police international markets, transactions and relations so that the conditions that make some local markets and transactions and domestic social relations relatively secure even for the weak obtain more widely. More generally, progress towards just institutions might strengthen regional and international organizations for security and economic coordination and improve their accountability, so as to prevent both state and non-state powers from oppressing, exploiting or dominating the relatively weak.

Large-scale institutional change is almost always a slow and hazardous process, and its results are often patchy. Moreover, even if just institutions can be built, this will not be enough. Just transactions, whether before, during or after any process of institution building, are also needed. Just transactions demand most where institutions are still unjust: taking advantage of others' institutionally buttressed vulnerability is often all too easy, indeed routine and accepted practice. Justice in transactions cannot then be only a matter of respecting institutionally required outward forms of contract, bargain and negotiation, or other legal requirements: a spurious consent or agreement can all too easily be elicited from the vulnerable. If vulnerable others are not to be coerced or exploited – not to have their external freedom unjustly restricted – no undue or irresistible pressure may be brought on them, especially when this is all too easy.

Of course, commitments not to take advantage of others' weakness are invariably frail. The strong are easily tempted: after all, they are not that strong, and most of them live amid many competitors and stronger powers. It can seem unrealistic to demand that institutions and agents who will be squeezed by others unless they pursue their own advantage must not lean on the weak. In particular, the boundaries between acceptable commerce and transactions that use unacceptable pressure are often hard to discern. So, despite the importance of just transactions, any approach to transnational economic justice must in the end put demands for institutional reform centre stage.

But is not an emphasis on reform a genteel way of conceding that little can be done? Perhaps it is sometimes just that. But it is worth reflecting how much reform has been achieved in a reasonably short time. Many of the agents and agencies that now affect one another transnationally are quite new. Few existed before the end of the Second World War. In 1945 there were no transnational corporations of the late twentieth-century sort, and few independent ex-colonies, other than those whose population was of European descent. The corporations, international governmental bodies, banks, development agencies and NGOs that operate transnationally are new types of corporate agents. Some may have exacerbated transnational economic injustice; others may have reduced it. This shows that immense institutional changes can be achieved in relatively short historical periods. Looked at from the bottom of the hill, the task of reform appears Sisyphean; looked at retrospectively its ability to proceed at a gallop is plain.

# CHAPTER 8

## *Justice, gender and international boundaries*[*]

### I JUSTICE FOR IMPOVERISHED PROVIDERS

Questions about justice to women and about international justice are often raised in discussions of development. Yet many influential theories of justice have difficulty in handling either topic. I shall first compare some theoretical difficulties that have arisen in these two domains and then sketch an account of justice that may be better suited to handling questions both of gender and of international justice.

I begin by distinguishing abstract from relativized theories of justice. Abstract accounts of justice claim simply to abstract from the particularities of persons and their circumstances. They paint justice as blind to gender and nationality. Its principles are tailored for 'abstract individuals', and hence take no account of differences between men and women and transcend international boundaries. Relativized accounts of justice not only acknowledge the variety and differences among humankind but ground principles of justice in the discourse and traditions of actual communities. Since nearly all of these relegate (varying portions of) women's lives to a 'private' sphere, within which the political virtue of justice has no place, and see state boundaries as limits of justice, appeals to actual traditions tend both to endorse institutions that exclude women from the 'public' sphere, where justice is properly an issue, and to insulate one 'public' sphere from another.

Both abstract and relativized accounts of justice look inadequate from the perspective of those whom they marginalize. Women, in particular poor women, will find that neither approach takes account of the reality of carrying both reproductive and productive tasks, while having relatively little control over the circumstances of one's life. Women's lives are not well conceived just as those of abstract individuals. A world of such individuals assumes away relations of dependence and interdependence; yet these are central to most lives actually available to women.

[*] An earlier version of this essay appeared in Martha Nussbaum and Amartya Sen, eds., *The Quality of Life* (Oxford: Clarendon Press, 1992), 303–35.

Nor are women's lives well conceived solely in terms of traditions that relegate them to a 'private' sphere. The productive contributions and the cognitive and practical independence of actual women are too extensive, evident and economically significant to be eclipsed by ideologies of total domesticity and dependence.

The awkward fit of theory to actuality is most vivid for poor women in poor economies. These women may depend on others but lack the supposed securities of dependence. They are impoverished but are often providers. They are powerless, yet others who are yet more vulnerable depend on them for protection.[1] Their vulnerability reflects heavy demands as much as slender resources. They may find that they are relegated to and subordinated within a domestic sphere, whose separate and distinctive existence is legitimated not by appeals to justice but by entrenched views of family life and honour. They may also find that this domestic sphere is embedded in an economy that is subordinate to distant and richer economies. They not only raise children in poverty; they grow crops and do other ill-paid and insecure work, their rewards fluctuating to the beat of distant economic forces. This second subordination too is legitimated in varied discourses which endorse an internationalized economic order but only 'domestic' regimes of taxation and welfare. A serious account of justice cannot gloss over the predicaments of impoverished providers in marginalized and developing economies.

## 2 ABSTRACT PRINCIPLES AND CONTEXT-SENSITIVE JUDGEMENT

The demand that justice abstract from the particularities of persons seems legitimate. Is not blindness to difference a traditional image of justice, and guarantee of impartiality? Yet principles of justice that are supposedly blind to differences of power and resources often endorse practices and policies that suit the privileged. So a demand that justice take account of context can seem equally reasonable. Justice, it is argued, needs more than abstract principles: it must guide judgements that take account of actual contexts and predicaments and of the differences among human beings. Relativized principles of justice meet this

---

[1] See Sara Ruddick, 'Maternal Thinking', in her *Maternal Thinking: Towards a Politics of Peace* (Boston, Mass.: Beacon Press, 1989), 13–27. Her account of women's predicament stresses that it reflects heavy demands as much as meagre resources. It is to be preferred, I think, because it does not take for granted that lack of resources is significant because 'public' while the press of others' demands is less so because merely 'private'.

demand: but since they are rooted in history, tradition or local context, they will endorse traditional sexism, nationalism and other forms of exclusion. Any relativism tends to prejudice the position of the weak, whose weakness is mirrored and partly constituted by their marginalization in received ways of thought and by their subordination and oppression in established orders. Yet many abstract approaches to justice do no better. Where relativist approaches are uncritical of established privilege, abstract approaches are sometimes uncritical of privileges from which they abstract.

A deeper problem is that many abstract approaches to justice are not merely abstract. They indeed propose abstract principles of universal scope, but they also (in a sense to be explained) import idealized conceptions of certain crucial matters. Much contemporary moral reasoning, and in particular 'abstract liberalism' (whether 'deontological' or Utilitarian), handles issues of gender and international justice badly not strictly because it abstracts (for example, from sex, race, nationality), but because it also almost always idealizes specific conceptions for example of human agents, of rationality, of family relations or of national sovereignty, which are often admired and are more (nearly) feasible for men rather than women and for developed rather than developing societies. Yet, abstraction by itself, without idealization, is part of the route rather than the obstacle to broad scope, and so is unobjectionable in principles of justice.

However, abstraction (in the strict sense) is not enough for an account of justice. Abstract principles alone will not be empty, but they may be too indeterminate; an adequate account of justice will need to link abstract principles to particular cases, yet avoid automatically incorporating features of those cases into the principle of justice, thereby relativizing principles to accepted beliefs, traditions or practices: cultural specificity confers no automatic normative weight. A complete non-relativist account of justice would need to combine abstract principles with context-sensitive judgement of cases.

## 3 ABSTRACT JUSTICE AND HUMAN DIFFERENCES: FEMINIST DEBATES

Many discussions of gender justice include disputes about the extent and import of differences between men and women. Starting with Wollstonecraft and John Stuart Mill, liberals have defended abstract principles of justice and argued that women are not fundamentally different from men, and so are entitled to equal rights. It has been embarrassing for these liberals that the Rights of Man were taken for so long and by so many of their predecessors as the rights of men, and that liberal practice failed for so long to end male privilege.[2] (Socialist feminists suffer analogous embarrassments.) Moreover, when achieved the liberal remedies appeared inadequate: even when women had equal political and legal rights, their political participation and economic rewards remained less than those of men, less even than those of men whose qualifications and labour-force participation women matched. Supposedly gender-neutral and neutralizing institutions, such as democratic political structures and markets, did not eliminate gender differentials.[3] Approximations to political and legal justice were seemingly not enough to close the radical gap between men's and women's paths and prospects.[4]

In response, some liberal feminists argued, particularly in the 1980s, that justice demands superficially and temporarily unequal treatment, such as forms of affirmative action and reverse discrimination in education and employment, as well as improved welfare rights to social support for the poor and those with heavy family responsibilities. Certain types of differences were to be taken account of by principles of justice. This move raised two difficulties.

The first difficulty is that liberals think that positional goods, such as certain forms of education and employment, should be allocated by competitive and meritocratic procedures. So all forms of preferential treatment are hard to reconcile with liberal principles. This difficulty has

---

[2] These have been leading themes in writing by liberal feminists – eclipsed more recently by feminist writing that stresses differences and separate treatment rather than universal principles and equal treatment. See Susan Moller Okin, *Women in Western Political Thought* (Princeton, N.J.: Princeton University Press, 1979); John Charvet, *Feminism* (London: Dent, 1982); Carole Pateman, *The Sexual Contract* (Cambridge: Polity Press, 1988); Alison M. Jaggar, *Feminist Politics and Human Nature* (Brighton: Harvester Press, 1983).

[3] Alison Scott, 'Industrialization, Gender Segregation and Stratification Theory', in Rosemary Crompton and Michael Mann, eds., *Gender and Stratification* (Cambridge: Polity Press, 1986), 154–89.

[4] The differences run the gamut of social indicators. Most dramatically in some Third World countries women and girls do worse on a constellation of very basic social indicators: they die earlier, have worse health, eat less than other family members, earn less and go to school less. See I. Tinker, ed., *Persistent Inequalities* (New York: Oxford University Press, 1990); Barbara Harriss, 'Differential Female Mortality and Health Care in South Asia', *Queen Elizabeth House, Working Paper*, 13 (Oxford, 1989), and 'Intrafamily Distribution of Hunger in South Asia', in Jean Drèze and Amartya K. Sen, eds., *The Political Economy of Hunger*, vol. I, *Entitlement and Well-being* (Oxford: Clarendon Press, 1991), 351–424; Martha Nussbaum and Jonathan Glover, eds., *Women, Culture and Development: A Study of Human Capabilities* (Oxford: Clarendon Press, 1995).

had particular resonance in the developed world. The second difficulty arises even where the goods to be distributed are not positional, and is particularly significant in the Third World. Where resources are scarce, non-positional goods such as basic health care or income support or children's allowances or unemployment insurance may be unfundable out of a slender 'domestic' tax base. So if social justice demands basic welfare provision, it will demand institutions that reach across boundaries. An account of gender justice would then have to be linked to one of transnational economic justice.[5]

This decreasingly liberal debate continued; its terms were increasingly questioned by feminists during the 1980s. Some argued that, despite liberalism's aspirations, gender bias is integral to its account of justice.[6] Their suspicions focussed on the very abstraction from difference and diversity which was an original hallmark of liberal justice. Some 'post-liberal' feminists criticized 'abstract liberalism' by highlighting respects in which its supposedly gender-neutral theories covertly assume or endorse gendered accounts of the human subject and of rationality. Many aspects of these critiques are convincing.

Some of these feminist challenges impugned not only abstract liberalism but reliance on abstraction itself. For example, Carol Gilligan's influential work claimed that an emphasis on justice excludes and marginalizes the 'other voice' of ethical thought. 'Abstract liberalism' simply and unacceptably devalues care and concern for particular others, which are the core of women's moral life and thought, seeing them as moral immaturity.[7] Justice as conceived of by liberals provides

---

[5] The problem is not *merely* one of resources. Where funds have been adequate for publicly funded welfare provision, this too has been inadequate to eliminate the differences between the economic and political prospects of men and of women. For example, many women in the former socialist countries found that they had secured greater equality in productive labour with no reduction in reproductive tasks. This is a reason for doubting that arguments establishing welfare rights – for example, a right to food – take a broad enough view of disparities between men's and women's prospects.

[6] See Pateman, *The Sexual Contract*; Susan Moller Okin, 'Justice and Gender', *Philosophy and Public Affairs*, 16 (1987), 42–72.

[7] Carol Gilligan, *In a Different Voice: Psychological Theory and Women's Development* (Cambridge, Mass.: Harvard University Press, 1982; 2nd edn, 1993); Eva Feder Kittay and Diana T. Meyers, eds., *Women and Moral Theory* (Totowa, N.J.: Rowman & Littlefield, 1987); Genevieve Lloyd, *The Man of Reason: 'Male' and 'Female' in Western Philosophy* (London: Methuen, 1984); Carol McMillan, *Women, Reason and Nature: Some Philosophical Problems with Feminism* (Oxford: Blackwell, 1982); Sara Ruddick, 'Remarks on the Sexual Politics of Reason', in Kittay and Meyers, *Women and Moral Theory*, 237–60; Nel Noddings, *Caring: A Feminine Approach to Ethics and Moral Education* (Berkeley, Calif.: University of California Press, 1984); Nancy Chodorow, *The Reproduction of Mothering: Psychoanalysis and the Sociology of Gender* (Berkeley, Calif.: University of California Press, 1978).

an incomplete, perhaps even a defective approach to moral issues. It fails to grasp the actualities of human difference; it lacks a sound view of the human good; it neglects the virtues; it is dismissive of love and care. This line of thought usually concludes that the proper ambition should not be to secure like treatment for women, but to secure differentiated treatment for all.

In locating the distinction between justice and care (and other virtues) in a disagreement over the legitimacy of relying on abstract principles, some feminist critics of 'abstract liberalism' view concern for care not merely as different from, but as opposed to, concern for justice. Some downgrade justice so emphatically that they endorse rather than challenge social and economic structures that marginalize women and confine them to a private sphere. Separatism at the level of ethical theory can march with acceptance of the powers and traditions that be. A stress on caring and relationships to the exclusion of abstract justice may endorse relegation to the nursery and the kitchen, to purdah and to poverty. In rejecting 'abstract liberalism' such feminists converge with traditions that have excluded women from economic and public life. Appeals to 'women's experience', 'women's traditions' and 'women's discourse' do not escape but rather echo ways in which women have been marginalized or oppressed. Some who celebrate the other 'voice' risk being thought to insist that differences are taken seriously only when actual differences are endorsed.[8]

The disputes that now divide liberal feminists and their many critics ostensibly pose an unwelcome dilemma about gender justice. If we adopt an abstract account of justice which is blind to differences between people, and so to the ways in which women's lives in the developed and in the undeveloped world differ from men's lives, we commit ourselves (it is said) to uniform treatment regardless of differences. But if we acknowledge the ethical importance of human differences, we are likely to endorse traditional social forms that sustain those differences, including those that subordinate and oppress women.

---

[8] Others insist that they urge respect for the 'other' voice, but do not reject the demands of justice: they see the two 'voices' as complementary rather than alternative. The positions taken by different writers, and by the same writers at different times, vary. The protests must be taken in context: those who appeal to 'women's experience' or 'women's thinking' appeal to a source that mirrors the traditional relegation of women to a 'private' sphere, and cannot readily shed those commitments. Not without reason, those who do the caring have traditionally been thought to have many cares.

## 4  ABSTRACT JUSTICE AND NATIONAL DIFFERENCES:
### COMMUNITARIAN DEBATES

A similar pattern of dilemmas recurs in certain discussions of international justice. Abstract liberalism proclaims the Rights of Man. As Burke was quick to complain, this is quite a different matter from proclaiming the traditional rights of Englishmen, or of Frenchmen, or of any particular group. Abstraction was the price to be paid for ethical discourse that could cross the boundaries of states and nations and have universal appeal; and Burke found the price unacceptable. The internationalist, cosmopolitan commitments that were implicit in the ideals of the Enlightenment and of subsequent liberal and socialist thinking have often been targets of similar conservative and communitarian criticism.

Liberal practice has, however, once again been quite different. It has not been universalist in action, but clearly subordinated to the boundaries and demands of states. This is evident in relations between rich and poor states. Like treatment for like cases is partially secured by laws and practices within many democratic states; only a few enthusiasts argue for world government, or think that rights of residence, work and welfare, as well as burdens of taxation, should be global. Such enthusiasm is often dismissed by practical people who hold that a plurality of jurisdictions provides the framework(s) within which liberal ideals can be pursued. Liberals may not be generally willing to take differences seriously; but they have taken differences between states remarkably seriously.[9]

Many of the varied critics of liberal justice want to take differences and boundaries seriously in theory as well as in practice.[10] When boundaries are taken wholly seriously, however, transnational justice is not just played down but largely wiped off the ethical map. Walzer's work is a good case in point. He holds that the largest sphere of justice is the political community and that the only issues not internal to such communities are about membership of them and conflicts between them. The issues of membership concern the admission of individual aliens: rights and

[9] See Chapter 9 below.
[10] See Michael Walzer, *Spheres of Justice: A Defence of Pluralism and Equality* (Oxford: Martin Robertson, 1983); Michael J. Sandel, *Liberalism and the Limits of Justice* (Cambridge: Cambridge University Press, 1982; 2nd edn, 1996); Alasdair MacIntyre, *After Virtue* (London: Duckworth, 1981) and *Is Patriotism a Virtue?* (Lawrence, Kan.: University of Kansas, Department of Philosophy, 1984); Bernard Williams, *Ethics and the Limits of Philosophy* (London: Fontana, 1985); and, more surprisingly, John Rawls, both in 'Justice as Fairness: Political not Metaphysical', *Philosophy and Public Affairs*, 14 (1985), 223–51 and in *Political Liberalism* (New York: Columbia University Press, 1993).

duties do not go beyond borders.[11] A commitment to community is a commitment to the historical boundaries of political communities, whatever these happen to be and whatever injustices their constitution and their preservation cost. Communitarians cannot easily take any wider view of ethical boundaries since their critique of abstraction is in part a demand for ethical discourse that takes 'our' language, 'our' culture and 'our' traditions seriously.[12]

Like current debates on gender justice, discussions of international justice apparently pose an unwelcome choice. Either we can abstract from the reality of boundaries and think about principles of justice that assume an ideal, cosmopolitan world, in which justice and human rights do not stop at the boundaries of states; or we can acknowledge the reality of boundaries and construe the principles of justice as subordinate to those of state sovereignty. Cosmopolitan ideals are evident in the discourse of much of the human rights movement; but some recent liberal theorists have shifted in the direction of their communitarian critics and even argued that liberal principles of justice are to be justified as the principles on which democratic citizens would agree. Rawls in his later writing hinged his theory of justice not on the abstract, indeed idealized, construction of an original position, but on the actual ideals of citizens of liberal democratic societies.[13] Here we see a surprising and perhaps unstable convergence between 'abstract' liberal theorists and some of their critics.

## 5 ABSTRACTION WITH AND WITHOUT IDEALIZATION

Debates about gender and international justice are not merely similar in that each is structured by a confrontation between advocates of abstract principles and of context-sensitive judgements. In each debate these demands are depicted as incompatible. However, the reason for the incompatibility may be that many advocates of abstraction and of sensitivity to context are making other, stronger claims that are indeed incompatible. What these debates term 'abstraction' is often a set of

[11] Walzer acknowledges that this means that he can 'only begin to address the problems raised by mass poverty in many parts of the globe'. *Spheres of Justice*, 30. Critics may think that his approach in fact pre-empts answers to questions of global justice.

[12] Communitarians can, however, take lesser loyalties seriously: where a state is divided into distinct national or ethical communities, those distinct traditions may in fact be the widest boundaries within which issues of justice can be debated and determined. They could argue for secession from a multinational state; but they can say nothing about what goes on beyond the boundaries of 'our' community. Walzer, *Spheres of Justice*, 319.

[13] Rawls, 'Justice as Fairness: Political not Metaphysical' and *Political Liberalism*.

specific, unargued idealizations of human agency, rationality and life and of the sovereignty and independence of states. And in each debate what is described as attention to actual situations and contexts in judging in fact often extends to building recognition of actual differences into fundamental principles – and so tends to relativism. Both conflations are avoidable.

Abstraction, taken strictly, is simply a matter of detaching certain claims from others. Abstract reasoning hinges nothing on the satisfaction or non-satisfaction of predicates from which it abstracts. All uses of language must abstract more or less: the most detailed describing cannot dent the indeterminacy of language. Indeed, it is not obvious that there is anything to object to in very abstract principles of justice. Highly abstract ways of reasoning are often admired (mathematics, physics), even well paid (accountancy, law). What is different about abstract ethical reasoning? A closer look at objections to 'abstract' ethical principles and reasoning shows that the more plausible criticisms are often objections not to *detachment from certain predicates*, but to the *assertion of predicates that are false of the objects of the domains to which a theory is then applied*. Reasoning that abstracts from some predicate makes claims that do not hinge on the objects to which the reasoning is applied satisfying that predicate; there is nothing untoward with this. Reasoning that idealizes makes claims that hinge on the objects to which it is applied satisfying certain 'ideal' predicates. Where those predicates are unsatisfied, the reasoning simply does not apply.

The principles and theories of justice to which the critics of 'abstract liberalism' object are indeed abstract. They take no account of many features of agents and societies. However, many of these principles and theories not only abstract but idealize. They assume, for example, accounts of rational choice whose claims about information, coherence, capacities to calculate and the like are not merely not satisfied by some deficient or backward agents, but are actually satisfied by no human agents (they are perhaps approximated, or at least admired, in artificially restricted shopping and gambling contexts!). They also assume idealized accounts of the mutual independence of persons and their opportunities to pursue their individual 'conceptions of the good', and of the sovereignty and independence of states, that are false of all human beings and all states. Such idealizations no doubt have theoretical advantages: above all they allow us to construct theoretical models that can readily be manipulated. However, taken strictly they do not apply to most, if not all, practical problems of human choice and public policy.

If idealized descriptions are not simply abstracted from descriptions that are true of actual agents, they are not innocuous ways of extending the scope of reasoning. Each idealization posits an 'enhanced' version of the objects of the domain to which the model is applied. Idealizations may privilege certain sorts of human agent and life and certain sorts of society by covertly presenting (enhanced versions of) their specific characteristics as true of all human action and life. In this way, covert gender chauvinism and an exaggerated conception of state sovereignty can be combined with liberal principles. Idealization masquerading as abstraction yields theories that appear superficially to apply widely, but which covertly exclude those who do not match a certain ideal, or match it less well than others. Those who are excluded are then seen as defective or inadequate. A reconsideration of some ways of thinking about gender and international justice shows that critics of liberal justice could legitimately attack spurious idealizations without impugning abstraction that eschews idealization.

## 6 GENDER AND IDEALIZED AGENTS

Liberal discussions of justice ostensibly hinge nothing on gender differences. They apply to individuals, considered in abstraction from specific identities, commitments and circumstances. Recent critics insist that liberal theories of justice are far from being as gender blind as their advocates claim. An instructive example is Rawls's *A Theory of Justice*. Rawls was particularly concerned to avoid an extravagant view of human agents. His principles of justice are those that would be chosen by agents in an 'original position' in which they know less rather than more than actual human agents. He conceives his work as carrying the social contract tradition to 'a higher level of abstraction'. In particular, agents in the original position do not know their social and economic position, their natural assets or their conceptions of the good.[14] The original position operationalizes the image of justice as blind to difference.

However, Rawls has at a certain point to introduce grounds for those in the original position to care about their successors. He suggests that we may think of them as heads or at other times as representatives of families, 'as being so to speak deputies for an everlasting moral agent or institution',[15] and that some form of family would be just. In doing so,

---

[14] Rawls, *A Theory of Justice* (Cambridge, Mass.: Harvard University Press, 1971), 11–12.
[15] Ibid., 128.

he pre-empts the question of intra-familial justice. He pre-empts the question not by crude insistence that heads of families must be men, but by taking it as read that there is some just form of family which allows the interests of some to be justly represented by others. The shift from individuals to heads of families as agents of construction is not a mere abstraction: it assumes a family structure which secures identity of interests between distinct individuals. It takes for granted that there is some just 'sexual contract',[16] that justice can presuppose a legitimate separation of 'private' from 'public' domains. This is idealization indeed: it buries the question of gender justice rather than resolving it. Rawls's text leaves it surprisingly obscure whether some (women?) are to be relegated to a 'private' sphere and represented by others (men?) in the construction of justice, whether both 'public' and 'private' realms are to be shared by all on equal terms or whether some (women?) are to carry the burdens of both spheres.[17]

A more radical feminist critique of abstract liberalism targets not merely the covert gendering of the subject which Pateman and Okin detect in some classical and contemporary liberal writers, but abstraction itself. In advocating an ethic of care and the marginalization of justice, some of these critics have come close both to traditional misogynist positions and to ethical relativism. When the 'voices' of justice and of care are presented as alternatives between which we must choose, each is put forward as a complete approach to moral issues. However, the two in fact focus on different aspects of life. Justice is concerned with public institutions, care and other virtues with character, which is vital in unmediated relationships with particular others (often also important in institutionally mediated relationships). The central difference between the 'voices' of justice and of care is not that they demand that we reason in different ways. Justice requires judgements about cases as

---

[16] Pateman, *The Sexual Contract*; Linda Nicholson, 'Feminism and Marx: Integrating Kinship with the Economic', in Seyla Benhabib and Drucilla Cornell, eds., *Feminism as Critique: Essays on the Politics of Gender in Late-Capitalist Societies* (Cambridge: Polity Press, 1987), 16–30.

[17] See Okin, 'Justice and Gender', 46–7. Okin asks whether Rawls's original position abstracts from knowledge of one's sex. Even if she is right in thinking that Rawls relies on a covertly gendered account of the subject, this idealization may have little effect on his theory of justice if the thought experiment of the original position has so relentlessly suppressed difference that the supposed plurality of voices is a fiction. In that case, we should read the work as taking an idealized rather than a merely abstract view of rational choice from the very start, and in effect appealing to a single, ideally informed and dispassionate and genderless figure as the generator of the principles of justice.

well as abstract principles; care is principled as well as responsive to differences. Justice matters hugely for impoverished providers because their predicament is one of institutionally structured poverty, which cannot be banished by idealizing an ethic of care which has its most significant role in face-to-face relationships.

## 7 IDEALIZED BOUNDARIES

A comparable slide from unavoidable abstraction to suspect idealization can be found in discussions of international justice. Discussions of global economic and political issues often take it for granted that the principal actors are states. Traditionally, the main divide in these discussions has been between *realists*, who contend that states, although agents, are exempt from moral obligations and criticism, and *idealists*, who insist that states are not merely agents but accountable agents, who must meet the demands of justice.[18]

However, in discussions of justice, the conflict between idealists and realists has been less significant than their shared assumption that states are the important actors in international affairs. These shared terms of debate endorse an exaggerated, idealized view of the agency and mutual independence of sovereign states, and neglect both the incapacity of some states and the importance of many differing non-state actors. This stance is increasingly obsolete. The common ground on which realists and idealists traditionally debated international relations is being eroded as other actors, including transnational corporations, international agencies, regional associations, NGOs and many other corporate bodies take a more and more significant role in world affairs. A world that is partitioned into discrete and mutually impervious sovereign states is not an abstraction from our world, but an idealized version of it, or perhaps an idealized version of what parts of it once were. Although idealists in international relations did not think of states as exempt from moral standards, they, like realists, idealized the sovereignty of states.

Idealized conceptions both of state sovereignty and of state boundaries limit discussions of justice, and particularly of transnational economic justice. Although advocates of human rights, who deny that states should be sovereign in determining the fates of individuals, have often depicted cosmopolitan just institutions as an ideal, they have in

---

[18] See Charles Beitz, *Political Theory and International Relations* (Princeton, N.J.: Princeton University Press, 1979), for an account of debates between realists and idealists.

practice been coy about criticizing the violation of rights beyond boundaries. Although there is nowadays massive and vehement criticism of violations of liberty rights in other states, there is great hesitation in intervening in other states' affairs even for strong 'humanitarian' reasons. There is even less certainty that justice requires breaching of state boundaries to reduce poverty that lies beyond them: aid and development proceed by agreement, and where states do not accept them, little happens. We still speak of *international* rather than of *transnational* justice, and talk of global justice is still more associated with ideals than with practicalities. As a result, even those who support rights to minimal goods and services are often concerned mainly with welfare in one (rich) country. It is still common to see development in other poorer states as optional 'aid', not obligatory justice. Those who have tried to argue for global rights to minimal goods or services have found it hard to show who bears the obligations that correspond to these rights, and this has proved an uphill task. In effect, those with cosmopolitan aspirations often converge with communitarians, relativists and others in confining justice within state boundaries. Liberals and socialists do so somewhat shamefacedly and provisionally, communitarians, relativists and various pluralists on principle and unapologetically, others tacitly and without discussion.

## 8 ABSTRACTION WITHOUT IDEALIZATION

The only way to find theories that have wide scope is to abstract from the particularities of agents; but, when abstraction is displaced by idealization, we are not led to theories with wide scope but to theories that apply only to idealized agents.

This suggests that if we are interested in international or in gender justice, we should resist the temptation to rely on idealizing models of human agency or state sovereignty. We should instead consider what sort of theory of justice we would have if we abstracted but refused to idealize any one conception of rationality or independence, and so avoided marginalizing or excluding those human beings and political and economic structures which did not live up to specific ideals of rationality or of independence from others. Abstraction without idealization may allow us to consider a wide range of human agents and institutional arrangements without hinging anything on the specific features of specific traditions, institutions or ideologies, or on the capacities to act that particular agents have developed. If we could do this, we might avoid idealized accounts of agency and sovereignty without following feminist and communitarian critics of abstract liberalism into uncritically endorsing aspects of the status quo.

Recent discussions may, I suggest, have been mistaken in treating appeals to idealized and to relativized standards of rationality and agency as the only options. There are other possibilities. We do not have to hinge liberal arguments for rights or for the limits of government power either on the hypothetical consent of those who meet some ideal standard of rationality and mutual independence or on the actual acceptance of an outlook and its categories that relativizes consent to an established order. We could instead begin simply by abstracting from existing social orders, and from existing configurations of desires and capacities to act. We could consider what principles of action must be adopted by agents who are numerous, diverse and neither ideally rational nor ideally independent of one another without importing socially specific assumptions about agents. We can bracket both idealizations and the status quo. The issues then become: how powerful and convincing an account of justice can we offer if we appeal neither to fictions of ideal rationality and independence nor to the contingencies of actual agents and institutions? What happens if we abstract without idealizing?

## 9 PLURALITY AND JUSTICE: WHO COUNTS?

Let us begin with the thought of a plurality of potentially interacting and diverse agents. This rules out two cases. First, it rules out the case in which justice is not a problem because there is no plurality, or no genuine plurality, of agents, and hence no potential for conflict between agents. (The action of agents in such a degenerate plurality[19] might be automatically or necessarily coordinated, for example, by instinct or by a pre-established harmony.) Second, it rules out hinging an account of justice on an assumed, contingent and determinate limit to the diversity of its members, which provides a common ground between them and permits contingent, socially guaranteed convergence and coordination. The two cases that are ruled out are once again those that would base principles of justice on an assumed ideal convergence between persons or an assumed actual historical or social convergence between them.

---

[19] Why degenerate? Because the assumption that conflict has been eliminated assumes away the context of politics and of justice.

What does justice require of such a plurality? At least, we can see, it demands that their most basic principles be ones that *could be adopted by all*. If they were not, at least some agents would have to be excluded from the plurality for whom the principles can hold, the boundaries of which would have to be drawn more narrowly.

Such a redrawing of boundaries is, of course, the very move often used to exclude women and foreigners, let alone foreign women, from the domain of justice. Those who exclude simply refuse to count certain others as members of a plurality of potentially interacting human agents. The cosmopolitan aspirations of an account of justice that hinges on the sharability of principles can easily be derailed by excluding some from the domain of justice without argument. So it is important to see the move for what it is. This can be done by asking who makes the move.

The move is not made by idealized, genderless theorists who live outside state and society. It is made by people who generally expect women to interact with them, to follow language and reason, to understand and take part in elaborate traditions and institutions, perhaps even to love, honour and obey. It is made by people who expect ordinary processes of translation, trade and negotiation to work with foreigners. To deny the agency of others with whom we interact in these complex ways reeks of bad faith. Bad faith can be avoided only by counting as members of the plurality for whom principles of justice are to hold anybody with whom interaction is to be undertaken or held possible. The question then becomes: are there any principles which must be adopted by all members of a plurality of potentially interacting agents? We cannot simply stipulate that such principles are irrelevant for interactions with certain others on whose (no doubt imperfect) capacities to reason and (no doubt limited) abilities to act independently we know we depend.

If women were all transported to Betelgeuse, and so beyond all interaction with the remnant men on earth, neither men nor women would have to see one another as falling within the domain of justice. Less fancifully, since the ancient inhabitants of the Andes and their contemporaries in Anglo-Saxon England could not and did not interact, neither would have acted in bad faith if they excluded the other from the domain of justice. Neither of them could practise either justice or injustice to the other. Things are different for the actual men and women who inhabit the earth now: the potential for interaction cannot be assumed away, and it would be arbitrary to exclude distant others from the domain of justice. We rely on numerous transnational economic and political processes and institutions, and so cannot consistently insist that justice (conveniently for the developed world) stops at state frontiers, any more than we can rely on women's rationality and their productive contribution and then argue that justice (conveniently for some men) stops at the edge of a supposed 'private' sphere, whose existence and demarcation are in fact presupposed in defining a 'public' sphere.

### 9  PLURALITY AND JUSTICE: WHAT PRINCIPLES?

Justice is then in the first place a matter of keeping to principles that can be adopted by all members of any plurality of potentially interacting beings. But if we eschew both idealization and relativism, and rely on mere abstraction, will we have strong enough premises to identify those principles? Does a universalizability test cut any ice? Granted that universalizability is not uniformity (as some critics of abstract liberalism suppose), is it not too weak a demand on which to ground an account of justice? In particular, will not any internally coherent principle for individual action be a universalizable principle?[20]

We have, however, to remember that we are considering the case of a plurality of potentially interacting beings, that is of beings who share a world. Any principle of action that is adopted by all members of such pluralities affects their action in systematic and foreseeable ways and so changes the world they share and others' possibilities for action (for this we do not have to assume that people always act, let alone act successfully, on principles they adopt, but that only that universal failure to act, and so with some success, would be an unreasonable assumption). This is why certain principles of action which can coherently be held by one agent cannot be coherently proposed as principles for all. Examples of non-universalizable principles can illustrate the point. A principle of deception, which undermines trust, would, if universally adopted, make trusting, and hence any aim to deceive, incoherent. Selective deception is a coherent project; universal deception is not. Since nobody who

---

[20] This is the hoary problem of the supposed formalism of Kantian ethics. For some textual suggestions on Kantian principles of action see Rüdiger Bittner, 'Maximen', in G. Funke, ed., *Akten des 4. Internationalen Kant-Kongresses* (Berlin: De Gruyter, 1974), 485–9; Otfried Höffe, 'Kants kategorischer Imperativ als Kriterium des Sittlichen', *Zeitschrift für philosophische Forschung*, 31 (1977), 354–84; Onora O'Neill, *Constructions of Reason: Explorations of Kant's Practical Philosophy* (Cambridge: Cambridge University Press, 1989), pt II. For discussion whether formally universal principles require uniformity of action see Chapter 7 above.

hopes to deceive can coherently will that a principle of deception be adopted by all, justice requires that they should not make deception basic to institutions or lives. Equally, those who make violence or coercion fundamental to their action aim to destroy or undercut others' agency and independence, and so cannot universalize their principle. Universal adoption of principles of doing violence or coercing would put some others' agency at risk, and thereby undercut the assumption that fundamental principles of violence or coercion can be proposed or recommended for all.[21] Selective violence and coercion are coherent projects; recommending or willing them as universal policies are not.

To keep matters under control, let us imagine only that justice demands (at least) that action and institutions should not be based on principles of deception, violence and coercion. (There may be many other principles of justice.) Still, we are far from showing just what justice demands, since we do not know what rejecting fundamental principles of deceiving, doing violence or coercing may demand *in specific circumstances*. These guide-lines are highly indeterminate. We seem to have paid the classic price of abstraction: impressive abstract principles that do not tell us what to do in specific contexts.

However, abstract principles are only part of any practical reasoning, including ethical reasoning. Principles never determine their own applications; even the culturally specific principles that relativists, communitarians and virtue ethicists favour do not determine their own applications. All practical reasoning requires judgement and deliberation by which principles are applied to particular cases. An account of gender and international justice is no exception. We need in particular to be able to judge what specific institutions and action are needed if poor women in poor economies are to be accorded justice.

## 10 PLURALITY AND JUSTICE: DELIBERATION WITHOUT RELATIVISM

I shall set aside two background issues summarily before considering moves from abstract principles to determinate judgements. First, we have no reason to expect that principles of justice will provide any algorithm

---

[21] It does not follow that every violent or coercive act is unjust – some violence and coercion, such as the use of legal sanctions, may even be the condition of any reliable space for uncoerced action. In such cases, the appropriate expression of an underlying principle of rejecting coercion is, surprisingly (and crucially for political argument), one that, taken out of context, might express an underlying principle of coercion.

of rational choice. Nor do we need any algorithm for principles to be important. Even principles that provide only a set of side constraints on action may make exigent demands. Second, we have no reason to think that principles of justice are relevant only to the action of individuals. A full account of the agency of institutions would be a complex matter, which I shall not discuss here; I shall assume that it can be given and that institutions and practices, like individuals, can be required to meet the demands of justice.

These moves, however, at least set some limits to the main task of giving a more determinate account of what may be required if principles of deception, violence or coercion are rejected. Still, it is not easy to see how we can judge whether specific types of family life or economic structures and activity are based on deception, violence or coercion and so unjust. Are all forms of hierarchy and subordination coercive? If not, how do we discern which are acceptable and which are not? It is not hard to see that certain categories of individual economic action and gender relations – for example, theft and fraud, wife burning or battering – deceive, do violence or coerce. But other cases of deception, violence and coercion are hard to adjudicate. In particular, it can be hard to judge whether social traditions that isolate or exclude women, or economic and familial arrangements that ensure their acute economic vulnerability, should be seen as evidence of failure to renounce fundamental principles of deception, violence and coercion.

However, it is possible to say a little about acceptable moves from abstract principles towards more specific principles, whose relevance and application to particular cases may be easier to assess. In making these moves it is not enough to lean on received criteria by which 'our' tradition or community picks out ethically significant 'cases' or 'options' for approaching them. We beg questions if we assume that categories of thought that have been hospitable to male dominance, to patriarchal social relations, to imperialism and to isolationism can be decisive in discerning or judging justice to those whose problems have been marginalized and whose agency and capacities have been formed, perhaps deformed, by unjust institutions. We cannot rely uncritically on the categories of established discourse, not even on the discourse of social scientists and of the 'helping' professions, to pick out the significant problems. These categories are themselves matters for ethical concern and criticism.[22] We have,

---

[22] Murray Edelman, 'The Political Language of the Helping Professions', in Michael J. Shapiro, ed., *Language and Politics* (New York: New York University Press, 1984).

after all, no more reason to trust relativized discussions of justice, gender or boundaries than to trust idealized approaches unequivocally. Those discussions are no more free of theory and ideology than are idealized discussions of justice. Their ways of individuating typical problem cases may be more familiar than those of theories that use more abstract categories, but familiarity may mask contentious and unjust delimitations. If the received views of a society or tradition are taken as defining the domain of problems to which abstract principles of justice are applied, unvindicated ideals will be introduced and privileged, just as they are in idealized approaches to justice.

Some confirmation of the ways in which received descriptions of social relations reflect larger and disputed ideals is suggestive. Consider, for example, how issues of gender can be passed over as if invisible. We often find an enormous amount of shifting around in the choice of basic units of social analysis. In the shifts between descriptions that focus on individuals, wage-earners and heads of families, there is enough flexibility for the blunt facts of economic and other subordination of women to be veiled. Women's low wages can seem unworrying if the women are wives for whom others provide; their dependence on husbands and fathers can seem acceptable if they are after all wage-earning individuals, and so not dangerously dependent. Reproductive labour may (with convenient ambiguity!) be thought of as priceless. Wage-earning women's low pay can be seen as fitting their low skills and vindicating their domestic subordination to wage-earning men, who as 'heads of families' are entitled to discretionary expenditure and leisure that wage-earning women must do without because they (unlike men!) have family commitments. The gloomy evidence of social structures and habits of thought that classify women's contributions as less valuable, even when more onerous or more skilled, is evident enough. We continually find ourselves 'thinking about men as individuals who direct households and about women as family members'.[23]

There are equally serious reasons to mistrust the move from abstract principles to determinate judgements in discussions of individual motivation. These too are shaped by received views, and in milieux which are strongly individualistic are easily diverted into attempts to pin blame for injustice on individuals, even on its victims. Women, after all, commonly

---

[23] Judith Hicks Stiehm, 'The Unit of Political Analysis: Our Aristotelian Hangover', in Sandra Harding and Merrill B. Hintikka, eds., *Discovering Reality: Feminist Perspectives on Epistemology, Metaphysics, Methodology and Philosophy of Science* (Dordrecht: Reidel, 1983), 31–3; Scott, 'Industrialization, Gender Segregation and Stratification Theory'.

acquiesce in their social and economic subordination. Are they then to
be blamed for servility? Or are men to be blamed for oppressing or
exploiting women?[24] Or do discussions of blame lead no further than
the higher bickering? It can seem that we have reasons to mistrust not
only relativist approaches to gender justice but even the attempt to apply
abstract, non-idealized principles of justice. But we do not inhabit an
ideal world. Idealized conceptions of justice simply do not apply to international relations, social relations or individual acts in a world in which
states, men and women always lack the capacities and the opportunities
of idealized agents. States are not really sovereign; even superpowers
have limited powers; and men and women are always more or less vulnerable, ignorant, insecure, lacking in confidence or means to challenge
or oppose the status quo. In a world of agents with finite capacities and
opportunities, poor women in poor economies differ not in kind but in
degree in their dependence on others and in others' demands on them.

## 11 JUST DELIBERATION IN A WORLD OF VULNERABLE AGENTS

If we are to apply principles of justice that are neither idealized nor
merely relative to actual societies to vulnerable lives and their predicaments, we must see how to move towards determinate judgements about
actual cases. The principles of justice for which I have argued take us in
this direction because they focus neither on the arrangements to which
ideally rational and mutually independent beings *would consent* nor on the
arrangements to which others in possibly oppressive situations *do consent*.
Rather they look for arrangements to which a plurality of interacting
agents with finite capacities *could consent*. I have suggested, provisionally,
that a non-idealizing yet abstract way of constructing an account of
justice will identify the rejection of deception, violence and coercion,
and of similar principles of victimizing, as principles of justice.

But principles are not enough. Non-idealizing abstraction avoids
some problems but not others. If we are to move from abstract principles to determinate judgements, we need to operationalize the idea of
avoiding acting on unsharable principles, without subordinating it to the

---

[24] Thomas Hill, 'Servility and Self-respect', *Monist*, 57 (1973), 87–104 and in his *Autonomy and
Self-Respect* (Cambridge: Cambridge University Press, 1991), 4–18; Raymond Pfeiffer, 'The
Responsibility of Men for the Oppression of Women', *Journal of Applied Philosophy*, 2 (1985),
217–29; B. C. Postow, 'Economic Dependence and Self-respect', *The Philosophical Forum*, 10
(1978–9), 181–201. See also the discussion of adaptive preferences in Jon Elster, *Sour Grapes:
Studies in the Subversion of Rationality* (Cambridge: Cambridge University Press, 1983), 109–40.

categories and views of the status quo. One reasonable way of doing so might be to ask to what extent the variable aspects of any arrangements that structure vulnerable lives can be refused or renegotiated by those whom they actually constrain. If those affected by a given set of arrangements *that could in principle be changed* can in fact refuse or renegotiate what affects them, their consent is no mere formality, but genuine, legitimating consent. If they cannot but 'accept' those arrangements, their 'consent' will not legitimate. The point of this way of operationalizing the notion of possible consent is that it neither ascribes ideal reasoning capacities and ideal independence from others to agents nor hinges legitimation on an actual consent that may mirror injustice. On this account, justice requires that institutions, like acts, allow those on the receiving end, even if frail and dependent, to refuse or renegotiate alterable aspects of the roles and tasks assigned to them.

Dissent becomes harder when capacities to act are less developed and more vulnerable, and when opportunities for independent action are restricted. Capacities to act are constrained both by lack of knowledge and abilities and by commitments to others. Institutional arrangements can disable agency both by limiting capacities to reason and act independently and by raising the demands to meet the needs and satisfy the desires of others. Apparent 'consent' to such arrangements does not show that they are just. Whenever 'consent' reflects ignorance, or lack of capacity or opportunity to do anything but 'consent', it does not legitimate. Thinking in this way about justice we can see that it demands more, not less, to be just to the vulnerable, who are easier to deceive and to victimize than the strong because their 'consent' is all too easily elicited.[25] Yet both idealized and relativized accounts of justice tend to conceal the fact that justice to the weak demands more than justice to the strong. Idealized accounts of justice tend to ignore vulnerability and relativized accounts to legitimate it.

## 12 JUSTICE FOR IMPOVERISHED PROVIDERS

The lives of poor women in poor economies illustrate these points well. Consider, for example, daily commercial transactions and practices. The

---

[25] I focus here on the obligations of the strong rather than the rights of the weak. This is not to deny that agitation and resistance by the weak can help remind and persuade the strong of their obligations and make it more difficult for them to repudiate or neglect them. However, to focus primarily on rights falsifies the predicament of the weak, who are in no position to ensure that others meet their obligations.

fact that they are generally accepted by those affected does not show that there is no injustice. Where there are great disparities of knowledge and vulnerability between agents, the 'agreement' of the weak may be spurious. They may have been duped by offers they did not understand or overwhelmed by 'offers' they dared not refuse. Within some developed societies these facts are well recognized and commercial practice is regulated to prevent pressure and fraud. Contracts can be voided for fraud; there are 'truth in lending' provisions; debt and bankruptcy will not lead to starvation; extortion is a crime; those with dependants can rely on a safety net of welfare rights, which leave them less dependent on others.

Within undeveloped societies economic transactions take place in far less regulated spaces. They may take place between agents with far greater disparities in power and resources. The weak can suffer both from particular others, who take advantage of their ignorance and vulnerability, and because nothing – no law, no consumer protection standards, no access to other customers – shields them from the intended or unintended consequences either of distant or of local economic agents and forces. The poor, and above all those who are impoverished providers, cannot refuse or renegotiate their role in economic structures or transactions which hurt them, even when these structures and transactions could in principle be changed. They are vulnerable not only to low wages, low standards of industrial safety, endemic debt and disadvantageous dependence on those who provide credit,[26] but also to disadvantageous patterns of entitlement within the family. Debtors who need further loans for survival cannot make much fuss about the terms creditors offer for purchasing their crops; the most dependent women – daughters-in-law and younger daughters in some societies – are acutely vulnerable both to market forces and to more powerful kin.[27]

Idealized pictures of justice have tended to overlook the import of economic power: by idealizing the capacities and the mutual independence of those involved in market transactions, they obscure the fact that the weak may be unable to dissent from arrangements proposed by the strong. They also tend to distinguish sharply between intended and unin-

---

[26] Henry Shue, 'The Interdependence of Duties', in Philip Alston and K. Tomasevski, eds., *The Right to Food* (Dordrecht: Nijhoff, 1984), 83–95; Barbara Harriss, 'Intrafamily Distribution of Hunger in South Asia', in Jean Drèze and Amartya K. Sen, eds., *The Political Economy of Hunger*, vol. 1, *Entitlement and well-being* (Oxford: Clarendon Press, 1991), 351–424.

[27] See Amartya K. Sen, *Poverty and Famines: An Essay on Entitlement and Deprivation* (Oxford: Clarendon Press, 1981), Tinker, *Persistent Inequalities*; Nussbaum and Glover, eds., *Women, Culture and Development*.

tended consequences and to view the latter as unavoidable 'forces'. Yet these forces are themselves the outcome of institutional arrangements and could be changed or modified, as they have been within many jurisdictions. The problem of shielding the weak from these forces is nothing to do with 'natural' processes and everything to do with the weakness of the voices that call for change and the difficulty of reform. This is hardly surprising. Market institutions magnify the security and so the voices of the 'haves', and projects of reform can easily seem no more than wishful thinking; even formal democracy provides only slender and partial redress for the weak, and is often lacking.

Typical family structures also illustrate the gulf between ideally independent agents (whom market structures might suit) and actual powerlessness. These structures often draw a boundary between 'public' and 'private' domains, and assign women (seen as wives and daughters) to the 'private' domain and leave them with slender control of resources but heavy commitments to meet others' needs. They may lack adequate economic entitlements, effective enfranchisement or access to sources of information or debate by which to check or challenge the proposals and plans of more powerful family members. Women in this predicament lack security and must meet the demands of others (depicted as fathers and husbands) who dominate them. Some family structures can enable, even impose, forms of deception, coercion and domination. Where women are isolated, secluded, barred from education or wage-earning, or have access to information only via the filter of more powerful family members, their judgement is weakened and their independence stunted. Sometimes this vulnerability will be shielded by matching concern and restraint; sometimes it will not. A rhetoric of familial concern and protective paternalism can easily camouflage callous lack of concern and legitimate deceptive acts and practices.[28]

If agents were all ideally independent of one another, it might not be hard to avoid undercutting others' agency. In practice things are different. Family structures always limit independence, and usually limit women's independence more; women who have no adequate entitlements of their own and insecure rights to a share in family property or income will not always be coerced, but are always vulnerable to coercion. Women whose effective independence is restricted by family responsibilities will be easier to coerce. In such circumstances ostensible consent reveals little; it certainly does not legitimate forms of domination and

---

[28] For some consideration of the benefits, costs and risks of patriarchy see Chapter 6 above.

subordination. Relations of dependence are not always or overtly coercive; but they provide structures of subordination within which it is all too easy to silence or trivialize the articulation of dissent, which can be dismissed as mere squabbling. To guarantee that action is not based on principles which others cannot share, it is necessary to ensure that proposals that affect others are ones from which they can dissent. Institutionalized dependence tends to make dissent hard or impossible. Those who cannot secure economic independence or who cannot rely on others to take a share in caring for genuine dependants (children, the elderly) cannot easily say 'no' or set their own terms. They must go along with the proposals of the more powerful.

Genuine, legitimating consent is unfortunately often undermined by some of the institutions and practices which most readily secure an appearance of consent. The more relations with others are ones of structural dependence, the more the weak have to depend on trusting that the (relatively) strong will not exercise the advantages which proximity and superior status give them. When the strong reliably show this restraint, there may in fact be no injustice within relationships which institutionalize dependence. However, institutions that rely too heavily on the self-restraint of the stronger cannot reliably avoid injustice. Whether the proposals of the strong are economic or sexual, whether they rely on the ignorance and isolation of the weak to deceive them, or on their diminished opportunities for independent action, or on the habits of deference and appeasement which become second nature for the weak, they ride on unjust social practices. The weak risk recurrent injustice unless institutions are structured to secure the option of refusal or renegotiation of variable arrangements for those whose capacities and opportunities are limited.

A woman who has no entitlements of her own lives at the discretion of other family members who have them, and so is likely to have to go along even with proposals she greatly dislikes, judges imprudent or knows to be damaging to herself or her children. If she were an ideally independent agent, or even had the ordinary independence and opportunities of those who have entitlements adequate for themselves and their dependants, she could risk dissent from or at least seek to renegotiate variable aspects of proposals that are put by those who control her means of life. Being powerless and vulnerable she cannot readily do either. Hence any consent that she offers is compromised and does not legitimate others' proposals. Just as we would find it absurd to hinge legitimating consent to medical treatment on procedures geared to the cognitive capacities and independence of a notional 'ideal rational patient', so we should find it absurd to hinge legitimating consent to others' plans on the cognitive capacities and independence of a notional ideal rational impoverished and dependent provider for others.

This is not to say that impoverished providers are irrational or wholly dependent or cannot consent. However, it is a matter of taking seriously the ways in which their effective capacities and their opportunities for action (in Sen's terms, their capabilities and entitlements) constrain their possibilities for refusal and negotiation. If they are to be treated with justice, others who interact with them must not rely on these reduced capacities and opportunities to impose their will. Those who do so rely on unjust institutional structures that enable deceit, coercion and other forms of victimization.

In applying abstract, non-idealizing principles we have to take account not indeed of the actual beliefs, ideals or categories of others, which may reflect unjust traditions, but of others' actual, effective capacities and opportunities to act – and of their incapacities and lack of opportunities. This move does not lead back to relativism: no principle is endorsed because it is actually accepted. In general terms, we can use modal notions to identify principles but indicative ones to apply them. The principles of justice can be determined for any possible plurality: for they demand only the rejection of principles that cannot be shared by all members of a plurality. Judgements of the justice of actual situations are regulated but not entailed by these principles. The most significant features of actual situations that must be taken into account in judgements of justice are the security and entitlements, or insecurity and vulnerability, that determine whether people *can* dissent from or seek to change alterable aspects of arrangements and activities which structure their lives.

# CHAPTER 9

# *Identities, boundaries and states*[1]

## I  BOUNDARIES IN POLITICAL PHILOSOPHY

Boundaries creep into political philosophy almost without our noticing. For example, within the liberal tradition of political discourse a theory of justice is often deployed to give some account of rights of universal scope – human rights – and of the corresponding limits of legitimate state powers. Yet before we know it we are talking about the justice not of a state but of *states*. As soon as we have states, we also, of course, have boundaries between states. The new arrivals are hardly noticeable until somebody raises a question about the just location of boundaries. At that point familiar discussions, such as those about self-determination and supposed rights to secession, may get going, without prior consideration of the nature or justice of boundaries. Yet it might be worth reflecting on the justice of boundaries *before* beginning these debates, and before asking which boundaries should exist.

Ostensibly boundaries are going to look problematic for all conceptions of justice – for example, liberal or socialist conceptions – which claim cosmopolitan scope. How can any form of moral cosmopolitanism be combined with a refusal of institutional cosmopolitanism? But it may seem at first sight as if boundaries are going to be unproblematic for those who in any case reject moral cosmopolitanism. Communitarians, relativists and other historicists look at politics and justice from some determinate location, from within and as legitimately

---

[1] This chapter brings together themes from three connected earlier essays: 'Justice and Boundaries', in Chris Brown, ed., *Political Restructuring in Europe: Ethical Perspectives* (London: Routledge, 1994), 69–88; 'From Statist to Global Conceptions of Justice', in Christoph von Hübig, ed., *XVII Deutscher Kongress für Philosophie, 1996: Vorträge und Kolloquien* (Berlin: Akademie Verlag, 1997), 368–79; and 'Transnational Justice: Permeable Boundaries and Multiple Identities', in Preston King, ed., *Socialism and the Common Good: New Fabian Essays* (London: Frank Cass and Co., 1996), 291–302.

limited by some set of boundaries. For example, Walzer takes it that political boundaries are the context of justice; MacIntyre takes it that cultural traditions are the context of all ethical categories and reasoning. Why should boundaries be problematic for anti-cosmopolitan positions of this sort?

It is true that for communitarians, and for others who hold anti-cosmopolitan positions, boundaries are, so to speak, only visible from the inside. That is perhaps why some of them are drawn to the metaphor of *horizon*, rather than boundary: horizons are limits that we neither reach nor cross, nor see beyond, as we do boundaries, but which we may enlarge or shrink. Where some actual boundary is taken to be the horizon of thought, what lies beyond that pale is viewed either as invisible or incomprehensible for insiders, or no concern of theirs. An attempt to think of actual boundaries as horizons that are constitutive of identities and understandings can only disorient all discourse about global concerns. Indeed, the effect of taking boundaries, or rather what they enclose, as constitutive for ethical discourse is dangerous as well as disorienting, since it takes the legitimacy not merely of the institution of boundaries but of the ways of life and thought they enclose as immune to any but internal criticism, and those of outsiders as incomprehensible.[2]

Those who see boundaries as the limits of justificatory reasoning will not take seriously – indeed may not be able to acknowledge – either the predicaments of those who are excluded or the alternatives for those who have been included. A ruthless relativism may suppress these concerns, at costs so high and implausible that I shall leave them unexplored. In fact, I suspect, the supposed myopia of communitarian and kindred positions about the ways of thought and life which lie beyond their boundaries may be a little contrived.

Setting aside the particular difficulties of taking any type of communitarian – or more broadly relativist – view of boundaries, it is notable that boundaries are also often overlooked by political philosophers who ostensibly argue for some version of *moral cosmopolitanism*, yet reject *institutional cosmopolitanism*.[3] What, for example, justifies Rawls's assumption

---

[2] Wittgensteinians and communitarians have both treated boundaries as constitutive of ethical discourse. Sophisticated examples of the two approaches include Peter Winch, *Ethics and Action* (London: Routledge & Kegan Paul, 1972), and Michael Walzer, *Spheres of Justice: A Defence of Pluralism and Equality* (Oxford: Martin Robertson, 1983).

[3] For this distinction see Thomas W. Pogge, 'Cosmopolitanism and Sovereignty' and Charles R. Beitz, 'Cosmopolitan Liberalism and the States System', both in Brown, *Political*

that justice for a society 'conceived for the time being as a closed system isolated from other societies' can serve as the paradigm for all justice?[4] How convincingly did Nozick get from the assumption that individuals have rights, which will need enforcing, to the claim not merely that some minimal state is just, but that there may justly be a plurality of such minimal states, although this will curtail the rights of those outside their 'own' state?[5] More generally, how can those who argue for principles of justice of universal scope, or for human rights, endorse structures that entail that the rights people actually have depend on where they are, or more precisely on which place recognizes them as citizen rather than as alien? Would not a consistent cosmopolitan account of justice reject as unjust the differentiated restrictions on rights that boundaries must entail?

These themes remain as topical as they are murky: perhaps fittingly, the topic of boundaries has no very clear boundaries of its own. So I start by considering a jamboree of arguments; some of them have been around for many years, while many seem to me not to answer questions they are sometimes thought to address. In the last part of the chapter I shall try to sketch an approach to justice which takes a different and a more explicit view of boundaries and territory.

## 2 JUSTICE, STATES AND TERRITORIES

It is often said that a plurality of political units, and hence of states, is needed for justice, because world government would concentrate power too much, and so endanger the very considerations, such as order, freedom, rights, democracy, that are thought to legitimate government. The division of powers on a global scale is then said to be just because

Footnote 3 (*cont.*)
> *Restructuring in Europe*, respectively 89–122 and 123–36, as well as Beitz's earlier discussion of Rawls's handling of boundaries and international justice in *Political Theory and International Relations* (Princeton, N.J.:Princeton University Press, 1979). Since the revolutions of 1989–90 there has been a truly gigantic resurgence of anti-cosmopolitan thinking, mainly in the form of discussions of nationalism and pluralism.

[4] John Rawls, *A Theory of Justice* (Cambridge, Mass.: Harvard University Press, 1971), 8, 378–82. For discussion of Rawls's earlier views on international distributive justice see Beitz, *Political Theory* and Thomas W. Pogge, *Realizing Rawls* (Ithaca, N.Y.: Cornell University Press, 1989). For Rawls's later account of international justice see his *The Law of Peoples*, reprinted in John Rawls, *Collected Papers*, ed. Sam Freeman (Cambridge, Mass.: Harvard University Press, 1999), 529–64.

[5] Robert Nozick, *Anarchy, State and Utopia* (Oxford: Blackwell, 1974).

it is needed to safeguard us from global tyranny, just as a domestic division of powers safeguards us from lesser tyrannies.

This argument takes us a certain distance, but it fails to show that the appropriate form of global division of powers is a division into territorially defined states, whose boundaries limit *all* government functions and *all* citizens' rights at a single set of spatial demarcations. After all, the division of powers that people have in mind as important when they put forward the same argument for the constitutions of particular states is not a division into distinct territories.

Moreover, it does not look as if a system of territorially defined sovereign states has proved a particularly good way of avoiding tyranny – even if it does avoid global tyranny. Sovereign states often abuse their citizens, and there are dangerously few restraints on the methods they use to settle their disputes with other sovereign states. The arguments that were brought against absolutist, undivided conceptions of 'internal' sovereignty during the Enlightenment, above all in the many criticisms of Hobbes, may be matched by contemporary criticism of exaggerated 'realist' insistence on the need for absolute 'external' sovereignty. Excess concentration of power within states is dangerous; so is excess independence of states from one another. The vast effort that goes into the construction of regional, intergovernmental and international (interstatal) structures and organizations testifies that a division into territorially defined sovereign states has long been seen as a risky and imperfect way of avoiding the tyranny of world government.

A modified argument in favour of a plurality of territorially defined states might be this. Although a territorially demarcated division of powers is not by itself a safeguard against tyranny, it is a component of any set of institutions which provides an adequate safeguard.[6] At least some powers of government have to be exercised across contiguous and spatially limited territories. We may think of police powers and public services. We may think that we don't want a world police force or a world sewerage system. Neither would be alert to local needs; both would concentrate excess powers.

However, this argument also can be turned in two other ways. In the first place, there are numerous territorially based functions of government which we have reason to want globally coordinated. We do want global regulation of air waves, air traffic, drug traffic and environmental standards. So we have reason to hope that even police forces and

---

[6] Even here there are exceptions: former Pakistan; island states.

waste-disposal policies are coordinated across state boundaries. Second, even when we think that some government functions, or at least some aspects of those functions, are best exercised within territorial demarcations, still we would need an argument to show why all units should coincide for a vast range of distinct functions – for it is only by superimposing the demarcations for many intrinsically distinguishable matters that we arrive at a world of bounded states. A diversity of territorial limitations would not otherwise add up to a system of state boundaries. The evident link between territoriality and *some* tasks of government does not then provide clear reasons for thinking that justice is best achieved by establishing or maintaining a plurality of sovereign states, which will circumscribe all the functions of government at a single set of territorial boundaries. Would it not make more sense to start with functional rather than territorial divisions of the tasks of government? And if we did so, would not the optimal territorial arrangements probably differ for different types of governmental function? It seems unlikely that any straightforwardly functional or instrumental argument would lead from an account of the ends of government or of just government (for example, order, freedom, rights, democracy) to a vindication of a system of territorially defined sovereign states. Of course, there may be other ways in which such an argument might be constructed.[7]

### 3 TERRITORIES AND IDENTITIES

At this point some of the less radical arguments deployed by the communitarians and their predecessors are tempting. For it may be said that territory isn't really the basic issue. What makes it just to limit all government powers at the boundaries of territorial states is a deeper argument, which starts from claims about nations, peoples or communities, that is from what are now called identities. It is because groups of people recognize one another as members of one community, and recognize certain others as outsiders, that they can legitimately aim to establish states, which are divided from other states, and hence from other nations and communities, by boundaries. Within those boundaries they can then do things in their own way and preserve and develop their own tradi-

---

[7] See Thomas Baldwin, 'Territoriality', in Hyman Gross and Ross Harrison, eds., *Jurisprudence: Cambridge Essays* (Cambridge: Cambridge University Press, 1992), 207–30, for a stimulating exploration of the links – and missing links – between statehood and territoriality.

tions; beyond those boundaries they make either no claim or claims of a different and more questionable sort, such as irredentist or imperialist claims.

Such arguments are typically strengthened by pointing out that a feeling of affiliation to nations or communities is not a mere matter of preference, but the basis of the very sense of self and identity of the persons so linked. Thus the romance of the nation-state, and more everyday stories of community life.

There are some difficulties in linking this romance with the banalities of boundaries and territories. The most fundamental of these is that membership of communities and nations is often, perhaps mostly, neither inclusive nor exclusive within any given territory. That is to say that a given community or nation will often share a territory with others whom it does not regard, or who do not regard themselves, as members, and that many who are regarded as members by themselves and by others will also be regarded as members of other communities or nations both by themselves and by others. Both problems are recalcitrant.

Consider first the case of those who are not regarded as (full) members, but live in the same territory as some well-defined nation or community. There may, of course, be ways of forcing on such people some outsider status – they may be physically displaced (for example, expelled, 'resettled', pushed onto reservations) or socially marginalized, (for example, ghettoized or assigned a more or less uncomfortable minority status). Alternatively there may be ways of subjecting outsiders to policies of cultural, social and religious assimilation and incorporation, which would destroy or damage not them but their differing sense of identity. However, if the basic argument in favour of the justice of boundaries and a plurality of states appeals to the importance of nationality or community for a sense of identity, it can hardly be just either to displace or to marginalize or to assimilate those whose sense of identity is other: if identities matter, minority identities matter.

Second, there are many members of most communities who sense themselves to be simultaneously members of other communities. Sometimes a dual identity is assumed to be obviously coherent and unproblematic – at least by most people. This is often the case with dual identities of which one is thought to fall 'within' the other – for example provincial and national, national and religious identities. Many people today take it that there is now no problem in being Breton and French, or Scots and British, or Irish and Protestant – although there are still people who see a problem in each of these dual identities.

Yet there are good reasons for doubting any insistence that identities must be mutually exclusive. The concepts by which people define who they are – in which they articulate their sense of identity – are all of them concepts without sharp borders, and hence cannot provide a basis for sharp demarcations such as those provided by the political boundaries between states. These concepts not merely permit borderline cases but are strictly *boundaryless*, in that their sense is given by a pair or a larger number of contrasts, rather than by the existence of a well-defined set of items of which the concept is true.[8] Although we have clear ideas of what it means to be red as opposed to yellow, or a child as opposed to an adult, or Irish as opposed to British, this is not because anybody can form the sets that contain all and only those items that are red, are children or are Irish. Our understanding of national and community identity is always framed in terms of boundaryless concepts – and so cannot in all cases provide an adequate basis for fixing sharp boundaries. These considerations also suggest why our understanding of national identity is so often given in terms of certain contrasts – we identify who counts as fellow-countrymen only in so far as we identify others as foreigners or even as enemies. When furthest from home we greet as compatriots others to whom we have tenuous links; when closest to home we may see those from the next valley as foreign.

Moreover, the compatibilities and incompatibilities between identities are not static. Once it was unremarkable to be German and Jewish: notoriously it became impossible.[9] In other cases the compossibility of senses of identity is a matter of context. To be Irish and British is unproblematic in turn-of-the-century Britain but has become problematic in Ireland. (In the United States I was even once told that it was a contradiction to be Irish and Protestant, and by implication that nobody could have the identity which I had all my life taken myself to have.) If membership of a community is essential to somebody's sense of identity, it is clearly a grave injury if they are required to give up either all or part of what they are, or if what they are is not recognized by others.

## 4 ALIGNING IDENTITY WITH TERRITORY: DEFINITIONAL MOVES

Arguments about these matters are sometimes badly tangled by trying to splice the vocabularies of identity (those of nation, community, patri-

---

[8] Mark Sainsbury, *Concepts without Boundaries*, Inaugural Lecture (Philosophy Department, King's College London, 1990).

[9] For a deep exploration of the theme see Viktor Klemperer, *Ich will Zeugnis ablegen bis zum letzten*, ed. Walter Nowojski (2 vols., Berlin: Aufbau Verlag, 1996).

otism) with political vocabularies (those of law, state, citizenship). For if we take it that to be a citizen is *ipso facto* to be a member of 'the community' or to have the same nationality, then any problem of non-members who inhabit the same territory can ostensibly be resolved by making citizenship available to them.

Notoriously members of minorities, whose sense of identity differs, are not always convinced by this failure to recognize who and what they are, even if they are generally pleased to get passports. And those who see themselves as members of multiple communities have similar qualms. They may insist that citizenship cannot be decisive for determining identity, that claims to the contrary represent a form of assimilation which may be more benign than exclusion from citizenship, but which refuses to recognize part of what they are.[10] In this way questions of identity can be and have been obscured in much public debate.

However, there are good reasons to keep the legal and political notions of state and citizenship and the social and cultural categories of community, nationality and identity quite separate. In particular, those who hope to use categories of identity – notions such as *community* or *nation* or *people* – as a basis for arguing for a plurality of states, divided by boundaries, cannot define these notions themselves in terms of inclusions within state boundaries, or acceptance as citizens of a state, on pain of undercutting the justifications which they seek.

## 5 ALIGNING IDENTITY WITH TERRITORY: NATION-BUILDING

These definitional approaches to the justification of states, boundaries and restricted citizenship do not work. But there are other, more political ways of aligning categories of identity and of political membership, which can be seen in broad terms as forms of nation-building.

An ancestor to these approaches can be found in Rousseau's *Social Contract*, where he writes that he would *wish* to be a member of a state whose antique origins are lost in 'the darkness of time',[11] and whose citizens see themselves as a single community with a common good. With

---

[10] Canadian debates on identities during the last thirty years are a good example. The concerns of Quebec separatists or of native peoples cannot be met by pointing out that their identity *as Canadians* is fully recognized. See James Tully, *Strange Multiplicity: Constitutionalism in an Age of Diversity* (Cambridge: Cambridge University Press, 1995) and Monique Deveaux, 'Conflicting Equalities? Cultural Group Rights and Sex Equality', *Political Studies*, 48, 2000, (forthcoming).

[11] Jean-Jacques Rousseau, *A Discourse on Inequality*, tr. Maurice Cranston (Harmondsworth: Penguin, 1984), dedication, 59.

this he looked more to the traditional world of Swiss peasant life than to the conflict-ridden realities of the Geneva he purportedly admired to assure himself that such communities were possible; and he knew well enough that his wish was not satisfied by any actual community. There are few if any communities so homogeneous that all their members identify with a single conception of the common good, and hence few for which any General Will can be defined. Rousseau's General Will is the will not of the actual inhabitants of any historical state, some of whom may lack full allegiance to any given conception of that community and its good, while others have multiple allegiances or identities, but the will of 'corrected' citizens who have been 'forced to be free', and who now correctly identify with the community – or, to put the matter in a sinister manner, identify with the corrected community. This is why Rousseau's Sovereign, the embodiment of the General Will, 'merely by virtue of what it is, is always what it should be'.[12]

Since such wished-for homogeneous communities are rarely to be found,[13] those who insist on their importance may have to view them as constructed through a process of nation-building which creates identities and aligns them with bounded states. Nation-building may proceed by a combination of nostalgic and utopian strategies. *Nostalgic* looking back to an archaic earlier time of supposed homogeneous community – Swiss peasants wisely settling affairs of state under an oak – allegedly legitimates a certain view of who now counts as a community member, and who as an outsider, as alien, as non-member. *Utopian* looking forward points to a future in which a process of nation-building will have reformed everybody within certain boundaries, by imposing a single form of identity, a single national allegiance in which all will the common good. Later nationalists often follow Rousseau in combining nostalgic and utopian elements: a mythic past is to be one of the tools for forging a united future, which is then (mis)conceived of as a 'return to roots'. Many later thinkers have believed that people who live within actual state boundaries, who are seldom homogeneous, and nearly always include some who do not share the majority identity and others who have multiple identities, may be brought to share an identity and so paradoxically may be forced to be free.[14] The weight placed on mythic

[12] Jean-Jacques Rousseau, *The Social Contract and Other Later Political Writings*, tr. Victor Gourevitch (Cambridge: Cambridge University Press, 1997), Book I, chapter vii.

[13] Ibid., book II, chapters viii–x.

[14] Nation-building can have positive aspects – education into a sense of belonging and identity; it can also be coercive. Most significantly, it is a constantly evolving process. Consider,

past and on desired future may vary greatly. Historicist conceptions of nationality stress origins more, while Rousseauian and Kantian discussions of civil religion and ethical commonwealth and contemporary discussions of 'constitutional patriotism' view community and identity as task rather than either as origin or as fate.[15]

Nation-building can, of course, be not only a theoretical construct but also a political programme. Its results can be seen, in at least partly benign forms, in the constitution of a previously missing sense of national identity in some actual states with citizens of multiple origins (for example the USA and Israel). However, once we begin to think of national or community identity as something to be constituted rather than as a *given* reality, appeals to (national) identity to vindicate state boundaries look a great deal less impressive. Any given appeal may be countered by pointing out other possible conceptions of (national) identity. If the elements and scope of a (national or community) sense of identity are not given but constructed, then it is always an open question whether they should not have been, or now be, differently constructed, and whether those who do not like the status quo should not be urged – or, if we follow Rousseau, forced – to change their sense of identity rather than to challenge existing boundaries. *A nationalism that appeals to processes of identity-formation in order to create a homogeneous identity or nation has no simple answer to those who urge assimilation into other identities.* Looked at dispassionately, nationalism and assimilationism, secession and imperialism, historicism and civil religion are just different programmes for identity-formation, which urge people to construct or fasten on differing accounts of shared origins or differing visions of shared destinies, which might then be used to 'justify' differing boundaries.

for example, Oliver MacDonagh, *States of Mind: A Study of Anglo-Irish Conflict 1780–1980* (London: George Allen & Unwin, 1983), whose work shows that Irish nationalism, the model for many later nationalisms, is not of great antiquity, and Vaclav Havel's essay 'The Power of the Powerless', in his *Living in Truth*, ed. Jan Vadislav (London: Faber & Faber, 1986), which captures the daily, persistent and yet coercive face of the attempted reformation of sense of identity under formerly existing socialism in former Czechoslovakia.

15 On civil religion, see both Rousseau, *The Social Contract* and Immanuel Kant, *Religion Within the Boundaries of Mere Reason*, vi:3–302, tr. George di Giovanni, in Immanuel Kant, *Religion and Rational Theology*, ed. Allen Wood and George di Giovanni (Cambridge: Cambridge University Press, 1996). On constitutional patriotism and related themes see Jürgen Habermas, 'Ist der Herzschlag der Revolution zum Stillstand gekommen?', in *Die Ideen von 1789 in der deutschen Rezeption*, ed. Forum für Philosophie Bad Homburg (Frankfurt-on-Main: Suhrkamp, 1989); and also Ulrich K. Preuß, *Revolution, Fortschritt und Verfassung: zu einem neuen Verfassungsverständnis* (Berlin: Wagenbach, 1990).

The flimsiness of appeals to national or other identity as justification for maintaining or changing territorial demarcations and boundaries is often obscured by adding definitional to political strategies for aligning state and identity, state and nation. In using hybrid concepts such as those of the 'nation-state' or the 'community of citizens', the very alignment of identity and territory that is in question is tacitly presupposed. However, if the social and cultural concepts of nation, tribe, community or peoples are to do the work of *justifying* states, and hence the territorial boundaries between political units, they must not be redefined in terms that *presuppose* these boundaries. Such definitional strategies undercut the aim of vindicating territorial boundaries or changes in boundaries by constructing national and other identities; they reveal that those political programmes are open to question.

## 6 ALIGNING IDENTITY WITH TERRITORY: DESTRUCTION AND EXPULSION

Another approach to the disparities between territorial realities and actual conceptions of (national) identity aims to align the two by requiring those with the 'wrong' sense of identity to end not their present sense of identity but their life within a territory. These strategies are unjust, by virtually any standards, and hardly likely to be combined with universalist political principles. Policies of forced relocation inflict huge injustice; policies of supposedly 'voluntary' transfer are often driven by fear. Moreover, any proposed alignment of identity to territory by relocation is not merely unjust but impossible when sense of identity itself is bound to territory, so that the two are not detachable. The same territories may be integral to the actual sense of identity of groups with differing, even antagonistic, conceptions of their own identity – witness the Palestinian–Israeli problem and many of the struggles in former Yugoslavia. To give up the homeland may amount to giving up sense of identity.

Of course, there are some strategies for aligning identity with territory that are even worse than forced relocation, because they rely on extermination. Events across the twentieth century in Turkey, in Nazi Germany and in some parts of former Yugoslavia provide all too vivid instances. In such cases those with the 'wrong' identity are not even given the option of assimilation or departure; they are condemned and destroyed for being who they are.

## 7 ARE TERRITORIAL STATES THE PRIMARY CONTEXT OF JUSTICE?

This scattering of arguments has so far looked back in an unsystematic way over various chapters of political philosophy and practice, in which appeals to national identity have been thought to have some justifying role in explaining why there must or may justly be a plurality of territorially bounded states. The arguments are not individually or jointly impressive. An adequate approach to these issues would reject both the fiction that all government functions for some group have to be confined within common territorial limits and the myth that the world does or ought to be made to consist of homogeneous nations lodged in mutually exclusive territories with well-defined boundaries.

If this is accepted, states and their boundaries cannot be readily justified by appeals to community or nation, and we may ask whether they are essential for justice, or whether they can be justified in some other way. Other justifications are not immediately obvious, so I shall turn first to the question of whether states and boundaries are the indispensable context of justice.

Most theories of justice of the modern period from Hobbes to Rawls[16] have simply assumed that a bounded state is the primary context of justice. Despite all the disagreement over the content of justice, its link with the bounded state as enforcing agency is taken to be secure. What is misleadingly called international justice, and would more accurately be called interstatal justice,[17] is then treated as a supplementary topic, which presupposes the existence of states – and not necessarily of just states, as debates about intervention and non-intervention in states which violate their inhabitants' rights make evident.

What licenses the thought that bounded states are the proper context of justice? One elementary, political thought is this: states are sovereign, they can make and enforce law, and so they can make and enforce just

---

[16] 'I shall be satisfied if it is possible to formulate a reasonable conception of justice for the basic structure of society conceived for the time being as a closed system isolated from other societies', Rawls, *A Theory of Justice*, 8. For consideration of some ways in which this premiss has constrained Rawls's account of international justice see Onora O'Neill, 'Political Liberalism and Public Reason: A Critical Notice of John Rawls, *Political Liberalism*', *Philosophical Review*, 106 (1997), 411–28.

[17] For reflections on these and related terms see Philip Allot, *Eunomia: New Order for a New World* (New York: Oxford University Press, 1990).

laws. This, it seems, is the role envisaged for states in the Universal Declaration of Human Rights. The supposed universality of the rights proclaimed in the Declaration is hedged with the claim that *for any individual* these rights may legitimately be differentiated at state boundaries. The Declaration proclaims that everyone has the right to a nationality (evidently intended not as (a sense of) national identity, but quite minimally as *membership of a state*) (Article 15),[18] and differentiates the freedom of movement that each is to enjoy in his or her own state (Article 13) from the much more restricted rights of asylum which he or she may enjoy in certain circumstances in other states (Article 14). A basic feature of a just international order – interstatal order – as outlined in the Declaration is that any given individual's rights to travel, take up abode, work, own property, and vote and their corresponding duties may justly be circumscribed by the boundaries of the state of which he or she is citizen, or more broadly a member.[19] The Universal Declaration does not endorse very much institutional cosmopolitanism.

Much philosophical and political writing on justice joins the Declaration in viewing states as guarantors of rights. On a rosy view, each person will have the full range of rights guaranteed by his or her state, states will be effective deliverers of those rights, and nobody's rights will be infringed or lessened by being a member of one rather than another state. In fact, as we well know, the present world order is a grotesque parody of this rosy story. Many states fail to guarantee various rights, including basic rights of the person, for some or many of their citizens; many others cannot guarantee various rights (in particular economic, social and cultural rights) for many of their citizens. And there are many stateless persons.

However, current states and current international institutions do not go very far towards securing rights for those whose states do not secure them, or for those who have no state. The situation of refugees and migrants is often harsh and uncertain, and such people rarely end up

---

[18] Article 15 of the Declaration has two parts: '1. Everyone has a right to a nationality; 2. No one shall be arbitrarily deprived of his nationality nor denied the right to change his nationality'. The second part reveals that the sense in which 'nationality' is intended has nothing to do with descent and ethnicity, but refers to membership (perhaps citizenship) of a state. See n. 19 below.

[19] The term 'citizen' is rather too narrow to define those who enjoy rights with respect to a given state. The term 'member' can be used to cover resident aliens (who have many but not all rights, and in particular no political rights), Gastarbeiter (who may have many rights but not that of permanent residence) and also children of citizens (who have many rights, but not yet those of full citizens). Cf. Walzer, *Spheres of Justice*, ch. 1.

with the full enjoyment of rights. Intervention in other states has taken place only for grossest violations of human rights, and then only occasionally, and then often for mixed motives, and then often unsuccessfully. The institutions for successful intervention are not available; the agenda of UN reform is much discussed, but little progress has been made with it.

In short, states are not always adequate guardians of their members' or citizens' rights. They are even worse at securing the rights of those who are not their citizens. For not only do they not protect those rights, but they sometimes violate them and seldom act against their violation by others. States are not reliably good at securing justice within their boundaries, and very ineffective at securing it beyond their boundaries. Why, then, should we accept the view that states are the best guardians of justice around, or even that they are better than other guardians? Is institutionally serious thinking about global justice helped by acceptance of fundamentally anti-cosmopolitan institutions such as states?

If our thinking begins from the familiar starting point of the territorial state, we shall have to repeat the long and difficult intellectual trek from accounts of justice in one state, to accounts of international (interstatal) justice, to an account of global justice. Not only is this not the only route by which to try to think about global justice, but it may be a quite unpromising route.

## 8 INSTITUTIONS AND TERRITORIALITY

One feature that distinguishes modern states from other institutions is that they are deeply and exclusively territorial. Each of them has, or claims, a certain territory as exclusively its own, and sees the limits of this territory as the limits of the state. It is no wonder that in thinking about states we now generally follow the Weberian definition and take ourselves to be focussing not merely on entities that claim the monopoly of legitimate use of force, but specifically on entities that claim the monopoly of legitimate use of force *within a given territory*. For us states are invariably associated with land, and the boundaries of a state can be represented by lines on the map. Yet we know that the linkage of the monopoly of (legitimate) use of force with territory that we find in the Weberian conception of the state is by no means inevitable. Many earlier conceptions of states represent them as exercising a monopoly of (legitimate) power over one or many peoples, and made no more immediate reference to exclusive control of territory.[20] Some entities which we call states and map as such are too weak to exercise an effective monopoly of force within what is mapped as 'their' territory (quasi states; dependent territories).

If we are to think about the ways by which we might work towards a global conception of justice, I believe we may do well not to presuppose that the sole context and guarantors of justice should be a set of mutually exclusive (and more or less jointly exhaustive) territorial units, each claiming monopoly of the legitimate use of force within its territory.

We might do better to consider a much wider range of institutions which exercise substantial power, including some that are not intrinsically territorial. Non-territorial institutions are, of course, locatable – at least in part. But their influence is not confined within any bounded territory. Many of them might be thought of as 'networking institutions', which link dispersed persons, officials and institutions. Among familiar examples of networking institutions we might include the international banking system; transnational corporations; communications networks including transnational communications organizations (satellite broadcasting; the Internet); and transnational NGOs such as Amnesty, Caritas, Oxfam, Médecins sans Frontières as well as research and educational networks.

The powers exercised by networking organizations may, of course, differ greatly from those exercised by territorial organizations. Territorial organizations are often good at exercising *coercive power*: they can enforce certain requirements on those within their territory. They are often less good at achieving certain other sorts of change: many other institutions, and in particular networking institutions, may be better able to exercise *productive power*.

This is not a novel point. It is often formulated from a statist point of view as a complaint that certain institutions, particularly networking institutions, seem to evade the exercise of state power. For example, transnational corporations can (and often do) locate dirty production processes wherever environmental legislation is weakest. Transnational companies and banks can and often do locate their profits where taxation is lowest. Global communications organizations can and often do locate their hardware, their editorial policies and their profits wherever may be advantageous – sometimes in orbit.

An alternative, non-statist view of these institutions and others like them is that they are not capable of being subordinated to states, and

---

[20] See n. 7 above.

that an approach which starts with the assumption that this is the right way forward is doomed to take too little thought about their just construction. Failure to cover these networking institutions in an account of justice is doomed to a highly selective focus on justice, because it considers only territorial institutions, although they are evidently no longer able to control networking institutions. If the networks escape the control of states, then an account of justice should look not only at the traditional question of the constitution of just states, but more broadly at the question of constructing just institutions.

## 9 NETWORKING INSTITUTIONS, SOVEREIGNTY AND JUSTICE

Networking institutions do not, of course, wholly escape the regulation of states. Their officials and offices, their technologies and laboratories are (mostly) located in state territories, or rather in the territories of many states. The problem is rather that they are not located at any one point, and thereby escape many sorts of regulation and control.

One strategy of trying to squeeze them into accounts of justice that begin with states is to construct international (interstatal) and intergovernmental bodies which can regulate the networking institutions, and possibly ensure that they meet certain standards of justice. The much noted difficulty of this strategy is that, given the assumption of state sovereignty, interstatal and intergovernmental institutions *have to* work by laborious procedures of negotiation, in some cases by procedures that demand unanimity, but that networking institutions are often flexible enough to adjust around attempted regulation. Although there are some effective international regulatory regimes – air traffic control, for example – others limp or are lacking: to choose an obvious and topical example, who regulates the Internet?

Yet international regulatory regimes may seem the obvious approach if we are in thrall to the Weberian conception of the state. For if legitimate monopolies on the use of power are *all* held by intrinsically territorial institutions, then surely ultimately the just regulation of any other institutions can only be achieved by the territorial institutions, even if they sometimes create and act through intergovernmental or interstatal bodies. Sovereignty, on this account, *must* be ultimately located in intrinsically territorial institutions.

Yet this thought is plausible only if sovereignty is intrinsically indivisible. Hobbes offered a classic formulation of the indivisibility of sovereignty: the Leviathan is a mortal God, and its sovereignty is unitary and unconditional. Already in the seventeenth century the thought that sovereignty must be indivisible was challenged for the case of internal sovereignty. The doctrine of the division of powers insists that internal sovereignty can and should be divided. The arguments for so doing have many of them been arguments against the concentration of power, and in particular against institutionalizing absolute power. The indivisibility of internal sovereignty has been challenged in the name of considerations of justice, such as liberty and democracy. Moreover, the challenge has proved institutionally sustainable and robust. Those states which institutionalize the division of powers in their constitutions are not intrinsically weakened or unable to function. On many accounts they function rather better, and go to war less often, than monolithic states.[21]

Has the time now come for reconsidering the form which external sovereignty should take? Could external sovereignty be divided? Would this threaten justice? Or might it help secure justice? Much realist thought on international relations has insisted that external sovereignty for each state is essential, the guarantor if not of justice then at least of security. Only states unite powers to tax, to fight, and to enforce law. Since only states have internal sovereignty, they alone can have external sovereignty.

This picture blurs as soon as we remember how few states *really* enjoy the sort of external sovereignty imagined. States are typically multiply interconnected with one another, with the interstatal and intergovernmental institutions and with networking institutions. A government that has to float a bond issue may find that the international banking system controls what it can do, every bit as much as a local or regional bank may find itself limited by government action. A state may find that the culture and orientation of its citizens is formed by their access to communications networks outside its territory and control. Of course, states can try to maintain the territorially limited sovereignty which they used to enjoy, when, for example, they could keep the networking institutions out of their territories. Quite apart from questions of the rights of citizens that might then be infringed, the development of technology is hostile to this sort of old-fashioned assertion of sovereignty; even the People's Republic of China, which maintains a remarkably high level of control within its borders, cannot avoid this reality.

---

[21] Michael Doyle, 'Kant, Liberal Legacies, and Foreign Affairs', in two parts, in *Philosophy and Public Affairs*, 12 (1983), 205–35 and 323–53, which presents interesting empirical material on the relative peacefulness of liberal democratic states.

If the networking institutions are not regulatable by states, acting either individually or in concert, it may be that we should view them directly as primary institutions for achieving just or unjust relations. An immediate objection may be that there is no obvious way of bringing networking institutions to account. This is an exaggeration, since networking institutions often need the support of some state – although perhaps not of any particular state. But there is no reason why accountability and indeed justice should not be aimed at: this is not intrinsically more absurd than the project of constructing states with just constitutions may have seemed in its infancy.

One route to greater accountability of networking institutions is through state regulation where that is possible, but others are imaginable and constructable. In particular there is no reason why networking institutions should not themselves take part in negotiation and regulation, in the working towards agreement about the permissible limits of their own power. For the most part networking institutions have well-structured procedures for reaching decisions and controlling their action: without them they would fall apart. The partial control that states can exercise over networking institutions because their offices and factories, their laboratories and officials need to be located somewhere may provide some leverage for negotiating their agreement to meet certain standards in domains which states cannot control. In moving in this direction we inevitably recognize limits of state sovereignty, but it does not follow that we have to recognize limits of justice. Cosmopolitan justice may be best served by recognizing that not all important institutions are, or need to be, territorially bounded.

# CHAPTER 10

# Distant strangers, moral standing and porous boundaries[1]

## I DISTANCE AND STRANGENESS

Obligations to distant strangers were traditionally thought of as hospitality and succour.[2] The stranger was one who arrived from afar, who entered market or camp or village, or who was encountered in the forest, the desert or on the high seas. Strangers in these cases are not distant: they are just strange or foreign. They are present, attractive or menacing, rich or needy, welcome or unwelcome, as the case may be. Their claims may be manageable or impossible, repudiatable or acceptable. The expectation is that these claims will be temporary, that strangers will soon distance themselves and claim no further hospitality.

The parable of the Good Samaritan belongs in this past world. On the lonely and dangerous road down to Jericho the man who fell among thieves and the Samaritan were face to face, and the Samaritan could use his strength, money, good sense and good will to treat a single nearby stranger as a neighbour. Despite the continuing resonance of the parable, the world in which hospitality and succour shown to lone strangers in our midst provide a model for all relations with strangers is now far away.

---

[1] An earlier version of this essay, under the title 'Distant Strangers, Moral Standing and State Boundaries', appeared in P. Koller and K. Puhl, eds., *Current Issues in Political Philosophy: Justice in Society and World Order* (Vienna: Hölder-Pichler-Tempsky, 1997), 118–32.

[2] Duties of hospitality were also discussed under headings such as 'common duties of humanity' or 'duties to travellers'. See Samuel Pufendorf, *On the Duty of Man and Citizen According to the Natural Law*, tr. Michael Silverthorn, ed. James Tully (Cambridge: Cambridge University Press, 1991), C. 8, section 4; 65; Immanuel Kant, *Toward Perpetual Peace*, VIII:344–86, esp. 357–60, in Immanuel Kant, *Practical Philosophy*, tr. and ed. Mary J. Gregor (Cambridge: Cambridge University Press, 1996). On Kant's account hospitality requires us to show strangers no hostility, and to allow them rights of resort (*Besuchsrecht*) and of asylum if endangered. Duties to succour or to rescue overlap traditional duties of hospitality; they too are owed to strangers and others, but only to those in present danger.

In our world, action and interaction at a distance are possible. Huge numbers of distant strangers may be benefited or harmed, even sustained or destroyed, by our action, and especially by our institutionally embodied action, or inaction – as we may be by theirs. Perhaps we have obligations not only to nearby but to distant strangers, or rights against them. Many people – let us call them (loosely) *cosmopolitans* – think that we have such rights and obligations, and that justice extends beyond borders.

Yet how could we have obligations to millions, indeed billions, of others, and how could they have rights against us? Conversely, could they all have obligations to each of us, and we rights against them? Individually we clearly cannot do much for so many distant strangers, or they for us. If there cannot be obligations to do the impossible, we must seemingly conclude that obligations and rights cannot hold on a global scale between distant strangers. Perhaps the only context for moral relations, even for justice, is local, and duties to strangers arise only when they are nearby, as in the parable of the Good Samaritan. These views about the scope of moral concern – let us call them (loosely) *communitarian* – are anti-cosmopolitan. Communitarians (and many nationalists) think that duties are owed only or mainly to others in the same community, which they may define in terms of descent, culture or common citizenship; those who identify communities in terms of citizenship often think of them as states, whose boundaries may properly limit justice and other moral concerns.[3]

Yet some action and some moral relations can link millions of distant strangers. Liberty rights and their corresponding negative universal obligations can be claimed by each and discharged by all; economic and social policies and their component rights and obligations can have global reach; global telecommunications can secure (or obstruct) cultural rights across almost any physical or social distance and for any number of people. If there is now no *general* reason to suppose that distance obstructs action, or that action must affect or respect only a few, there is no *general* reason to think that justice or other moral relations between vast numbers of distant strangers are impossible.

Even obligations and rights that focus specifically on meeting needs can have global scope. Individual action may not be able to meet mass

---

[3] Communitarians do not, I think, generally hold that foreigners have no or lesser moral standing: they merely draw conclusions that fit with that view. In the background they may rely on strong (but false) views that foreigners will have equal and equally effective claims against their states, so that accepting their moral standing has no practical implications.

needs: collective action is not so puny. Collective action has met some mass needs within states that have prosperous economies and have constructed welfare safety nets. Could these or other institutions meet mass needs on a global scale? If so, are there obligations to support or work towards some set of global institutions to meet the needs of distant strangers?

Although we live in a world where some action at a distance is highly institutionalized (trade, capital transfers, telecommunications), other familiar institutions obstruct action at a distance. The most formidable obstructions are state boundaries. Contemporary states pave the earth's surface with discrete territorial units, whose boundaries confine numerous activities and processes. For example, state boundaries may define where a given individual may travel, work, take up abode, go to school, own property, vote, pay taxes or receive welfare benefits. Cosmopolitans and communitarians disagree whether such borders obstruct or secure justice.

## 2 THE SCOPE OF MORAL CONCERN

The numerous disagreements between cosmopolitans and communitarians are not best seen as pitting universalism against particularism in ethics. Moral cosmopolitans, of course, take it that moral principles must have universal *form*, i.e. must hold for all rather than some cases within a certain domain; but universalism in this elementary formal sense is common ground between cosmopolitans and communitarians. What makes cosmopolitans distinctive is rather their view of the proper *scope* of moral principles, which they extend to include (at least) all humans, wherever they live.

The claims of moral cosmopolitans cannot be rebutted by showing that *as a matter of fact* state boundaries, backed by state power, obstruct certain sorts of boundary-crossing action: cosmopolitans can retort that those obstructions, and hence those boundaries, or those uses of state power, and systems of positive obligations and rights based on them, are unjust and wrong.[4] They point out that boundaries can vary in many ways, and may think that they would have to be changed in a just or better world.

The changes in boundaries that matter to cosmopolitans are not shifts

---

[4] Often they do not make this reply. For example, much liberal and socialist thinking, although cosmopolitan in the abstract, is statist when it comes to action and politics.

in their location, but changes in their character. Cosmopolitans think that boundaries should be (more) *porous* to persons and their activities. Free traders seek to make boundaries more porous to commerce; liberals seek to make them more porous to the passage of information, and the movement of persons.[5] At the limit, some cosmopolitan thinking argues for the abolition of boundaries, and hence for a world state or a world federation.

By contrast, communitarians, who also think that ethical principles should be of universal *form*, take an anti-cosmopolitan view of their proper *scope*, which they may restrict to the territory of communities, of nations or (more commonly) states. Communitarians think that boundaries can legitimately be (relatively) impervious. Protectionists hope to make them impervious to commerce; some nationalists want to make them impervious to (the wrong sorts of) immigrants by limiting rights of entry and abode; authoritarian regimes may want to make them impervious to immigrants, to emigrants and to the flow of ideas.

Claims about obligations and rights between distant strangers, and about institutional arrangements that secure or obstruct them, cannot be resolved unless these disputes about the proper scope of moral principles, and above all about the scope of principles of justice, can be resolved. Yet it is not obvious how either cosmopolitans or communitarians can settle questions of scope without begging questions. Communitarians will not be convinced by those moral cosmopolitans who drift with a rhetoric of universal human rights, assert that all human beings have rights to have liberties respected and basic needs met, and that everyone has obligations to respect those liberties and that someone or other – but who? – has obligations to meet those needs. Abstract cosmopolitanism of this popular sort dilutes rather than promotes understanding of universal human rights: if we are ever to take rights seriously, we cannot begin by taking them so lightly.[6] Equally, cosmopolitans will think that arbitrary exclusion matters despite communitarian insistence that we should respect the needs and interests of communities or nations and give priority to fellow-nationals and fellow-citizens.

---

[5] See Brian Barry and Robert E. Goodin, eds., *Free Movement: Ethical Issues in the Transnational Migration of People and of Money* (Pennsylvania: Pennsylvania State University Press, 1992) and Warren F. Schwartz, ed, *Justice in Immigration* (Cambridge: Cambridge University Press, 1995).

[6] Discussions of supposed 'rights to food' or 'rights to development' which fail to show who bears the counterpart obligations provide vivid examples of this failure. See Chapter 7 above.

### 3 THE ELUSIVE BASIS OF MORAL STANDING

The running disagreements between cosmopolitans and communitarians could, of course, be finally resolved if we could determine the true basis of moral standing and thereby establish the proper scope of justice and other moral concern by arguments acceptable to both parties.

Numerous conceptions of the basis of moral standing are appealed to in debates between cosmopolitans and communitarians. Cosmopolitans claim at least that all human beings have equal moral standing; communitarians typically view the matter relationally and hold, for example, that compatriots have full moral standing for one another, but foreigners (at best) lesser standing for one another.

Other discussions of the scope of moral concern can be found in work that searches for a *lower* rather than an *outer* boundary of moral standing. For example, many bioethicists hope to establish whether the foetus or those in persistent vegetative states or non-human animals have the same standing as humans 'in the maturity of their faculties'. Some adventurous writers hope to show that trees and landmarks, wildernesses and species, corporations, states and other artificial persons also have moral standing. These debates often seek to show which properties are essential, or at least central, for moral standing, and claim that beings with these properties (whether metaphysical or natural) should be ascribed (full) moral standing, and hence viewed as agents or subjects of experience, or (using the term in a sense more technical than appears) as *persons*. Only these beings will be seen as fit to bear obligations, or at least to hold rights, and as falling within the domain of justice.

Philosophical debates about the lower bound of moral standing have persisted unresolved. Some writers claim that the crucial property is possession of a soul or self, others that it is rationality or potentiality for rationality (variously construed), and yet others that it is sentience or the ability to suffer, or other more specific capacities for independent life. Similar disagreements are frequent in popular and political discussions. Notoriously, in popular discussions of abortion in the last third of the twentieth century those who think that the foetus (at various stages of gestation) has the properties essential for (full) moral standing, and in consequence have viewed abortion as murder, or at least as seriously wrong, have confronted others who think that the foetus lacks the relevant properties and hence (full) moral standing, and who are prepared to countenance abortion (at various stages of gestation). Or again, popular debates between certain advocates of animals and others are often disputes about whether beings which are sentient and capable of some sorts of independent life, yet not rational, or which lack speech, have the essential characteristics for (full) moral standing. Resolution of the more popular debates about the lower bound of moral standing has proved every bit as elusive as resolution of the more philosophical debates. Perhaps no certainty can be found unless the underlying metaphysical uncertainties can be settled by establishing what is sometimes referred to as a *metaphysics of the person*.

If neither philosophical nor popular debates about the *lower* bound of moral standing have made progress, it is not entirely surprising that debates about the *outer* boundary of moral standing, which underlie disputes about the claims of distant strangers and the moral acceptability of excluding boundaries, remain unresolved. Cosmopolitans maintain robustly that distance and strangeness do not make a difference to standing;[7] communitarians maintain that if distance itself does not, then at least strangeness does, and that we have obligations to compatriots that we do not have to foreigners.[8] In this stand-off, as in the disputes about the lower bound of moral standing, there is more assertion than demonstration.

Yet even if the philosophical and popular debates about moral standing cannot be settled, we need to determine *for quite practical purposes* whether justice, or other forms of moral concern, is owed to distant as to nearer strangers, to foreigners as to compatriots.

## 4 A PRACTICAL APPROACH TO MORAL STANDING

Questions about standing can be posed as context-specific *practical* questions, rather than as demands for comprehensive theoretical demarcations. For practical purposes it might be enough to answer the specific question 'To whom are we (or am I) committed to according moral

---

[7] For an explicit and still much-cited and much-discussed argument that distance makes no difference see Peter Singer, 'Famine, Affluence and Morality', *Philosophy and Public Affairs*, 1 (1972), 229–43; for more recent discussion of the theme, see Garret Cullity, 'International Aid and the Scope of Kindness', *Ethics*, 105 (1994), 99–127.

[8] David Miller, 'The Ethical Significance of Nationality', *Ethics*, 98 (1988), 647–62; Yael Tamir, *Liberal Nationalism* (Princeton, N.J.: Princeton University Press, 1993); contrasting views can be found in Robert E. Goodin, 'What Is So Special about Our Fellow Countrymen?', *Ethics*, 98 (1988), 663–86 and Thomas W. Pogge, 'The Bounds of Nationalism', in Jocelyne Couture et al., eds., *Nationalism*; *Canadian Journal of Philosophy*, supp. vol. 22 (1998), 463–504; see also Andrew Mason, 'Special Obligations to Compatriots', *Ethics*, 107 (1997), 427–47.

standing in acting or in living in this way?' In posing this question we ask *what assumptions we are already building into our action, habits, practices and institutions*. If in acting we already assume that others are agents and subjects, then we can hardly deny this in the next breath. This conclusion holds even if our conceptions of what it is to be an agent or a subject are metaphysically primitive and leave many cases undetermined.

This practical approach to fixing the scope of moral concern may seem to endorse the limited views of scope which communitarians hold. If it appeals to assumptions already made, will it not endorse established exclusions? In fact, I believe that, on the contrary, it will offer cosmopolitans and communitarians alike reasons for concluding that we are sometimes committed to regarding the scope of moral principles, and especially principles of justice, as *more or less cosmopolitan*. Although a practical approach does not aim to settle all disagreements about the proper basis of moral standing, it can resolve differences about the proper scope of moral concern in a given context.

The approach may be illustrated initially by considering a case that is close at hand, internal to a community, indeed where interaction is face-to-face. In shopping at my corner shop I assume that the shopkeeper has ordinary commercial capacities as well as the multiple, complex cognitive and social capacities which these require. My shopping reflects a web of assumptions, most of them unspoken, indeed unconscious, about the shopkeeper's abilities to act and to respond. It would be inconsistent for me to claim to doubt whether the shopkeeper is an agent or a subject. If I were to deny her the moral standing that I routinely accord others whom I view as agents or subjects, I would need to offer weighty reasons.[9]

The advantage of this practical, contextual approach to moral standing is that there is no need to demonstrate that the conception of agency and subjecthood on which I tacitly rely is correct, complete or metaphysically well grounded: my views on the metaphysics of the person may remain rudimentary. A practical approach to moral standing claims only that what we assume in acting, we cannot selectively revoke in reaching ethical judgements.

This practical, non-essentialist, account of the scope of moral

---

[9] Reasons might be weighty enough if they *genuinely* rebutted the assumption that the shopkeeper is an agent and subject (for example, by demonstrating that she is a robot), but not, for example, if they showed that she is a bad or dangerous agent (for example, a wanted criminal). The latter conclusion might warrant different action, but not exclusion from the domain of moral concern.

concern has clear implications for (inter)action at a distance, including (inter)action that links agents to others whom they cannot individuate. For example, householders who insure their properties against theft make no assumptions about individual thieves; they assume only that somebody, they know not who, might steal from them: their precautions reveal their assumptions. Or again, the managers of a hotel who have no idea which individuals will eat the meals they offer will make complex assumptions about numbers of diners, the sorts of meals they will want and the prices they will be prepared to pay. It would be incoherent for managers who make such preparations to doubt that the diners, whoever they may be, will be agents and subjects with complex preferences and capacities for action (and preferably credit cards). Or again, drivers with no idea who else is on the roads will make complex assumptions about the capacities of other road-users, whose content will be evident from their driving (and from the vigour with which certain failings in others' driving will be noted and criticized).

As these examples show, in acting we commonly assume that distant strangers *within our own societies* are both agents and subjects. Today we make very similar assumptions about distant strangers whose lives are separated from ours by various boundaries. Importers and exporters rely on complex assumptions about the capacities of distant trading partners. Broadcasters make complex assumptions about distant audiences; airlines about distant customers; both make assumptions about distant regulators. Banks borrow and lend on complex assumptions about a widely dispersed, possibly global, range of savers and borrowers and about their propensities to deposit and borrow given certain rates of interest. In each case it would be absurd for those who assume that distant strangers have such complex capacities to act to query whether they are agents or subjects; they would need weighty reasons to refuse them the moral standing they routinely ascribe to nearby familiars in whom they assume like capacities. The fact that other agents or subjects are foreign or far away would not be reason enough to exclude them from the domain of moral concern – although it could sometimes be a reason for expressing that concern differently.

It is, of course, quite common for people to deny that certain others are agents or subjects. Their actual assumptions will, however, be revealed not by avowals or denials, but in the ways in which they organize and adjust their action to take account of others' capacities to act, to suffer and to be influenced. Notoriously some Nazis *claimed* that some of their victims lacked moral standing, that they were *Untermenschen*. Yet the Nazis' actions reveal that they in fact assumed that those whom they persecuted were intelligent, foresighted, literate agents capable of complex mental and physical suffering. None of the organization of the deportations or of the camps makes sense except against these background assumptions. All the subterfuge, the bureaucratic formalities of deportation, the rhetoric of belittlement, the techniques of control make sense *only* on the assumption that the victims were indeed seen as intelligent agents and vulnerable subjects. Analogous points are standardly true of the way in which agents treat those whom they see as enemies or subjects, as revolutionaries or subversives, as criminals or as slaves.[10] Unless distinctive and weighty reasons to the contrary can be given in a particular case, agents will be committed to acknowledging the moral standing of those whom their action acknowledges as agents and subjects.

On this view, agents may show by their own action that they are committed to according moral standing to many others, near and far, compatriots or strangers, of whom they can individuate some, but can only specify others. However, a practical approach does not establish any view of the essential basis of moral standing of the sorts that some moral cosmopolitans have sought. It offers no account of the properties that demarcate persons from things, or that underpin moral standing or the proper boundaries of moral concern.

This can be seen in several ways. First, a practical approach may lead to different answers in different contexts: it is designed only to show who has standing *for certain agents*. For example, the approach says nothing at all about the moral standing of others on whom agents cannot act. It cannot show that the unknown inhabitants of distant planets whom agents cannot affect, and about whom they make no assumptions in any action, have moral standing for them. Or again, the approach will show that the beings who have moral standing for those who lived in Jerusalem in 500 BC will differ from the beings who have standing for those living in Oslo in AD 2500.

---

[10] Could there perhaps be action that inflicted great harm on beings normally taken to be agents and subjects that was not premised on any such assumptions? For example, may not those who conduct chemical warfare claim that they view their victims as mere vermin (as we view cockroaches if we poison them) and not as agents or subjects? It seems more likely that they assume victims who suffer and could act in other circumstances, but who *as it happens* lack means of redress and effective allies. That those who act barbarously typically don't assume that their victims are mere vermin is evident from the precautions they take or would take if they thought retaliation possible or publicity likely.

Contemporaries too may reasonably assign moral standing differently if they take a practical approach. For example, the inhabitants of Viking Dublin and their Peruvian contemporaries did not know of one another's existence: they lived beyond the pale (the *limes*) of one another's known world; they did not and could not premise action on assumptions about one another's capacities to act or to suffer. Neither Peruvians nor Dubliners saw members of the other group as agents or as subjects, or as falling within the scope of justice; it would be absurd to accuse members of either group of having acted either justly or unjustly, well or ill, to the distant strangers in the other group.

However, these notional gaps in a practical account of moral standing create no practical problems. Although a practical approach to establishing who or what has moral standing does not deliver the same answers that a comprehensive account of the metaphysical basis of moral standing might deliver, it can provide what is needed for action, since it aims to answer the question 'Whom must we (or I) count as an agent or subject in taking this action, in supporting this practice, in adopting this policy or in establishing these institutions?'[11]

A practical approach provides a relational account of moral standing, but does not return us to the much narrower relational views (relativist views) which some communitarians and nationalists take of the scope of moral concern. Conjoined with the commonplace facts of action-at-a-distance in our present social world, this relational view points us to a *contingently* more or less cosmopolitan account of the proper scope of moral concern in some contexts. We assume that others are agents and subjects as soon as we act, or are involved in practices, or adopt policies or establish institutions in which we rely on assumptions about others' capacities to act and to experience and suffer. Today we constantly assume that countless others who are strange and distant can produce and consume, trade and negotiate, translate and settle payments, pollute

[11] A harder case for a practical approach to moral standing than that of directed barbarity may arise where consequences are unintended. For example, why need those who hoard in times of scarcity, and thereby collectively and unintentionally raise prices so that the poorest die, see those who die as agents and subjects? (For cases see Amartya Sen, *Poverty and Famines: An Essay on Entitlement and Deprivation* (Oxford: Clarendon Press, 1981.) The failing here may be mere blindness to causal connections, which can arise even when others *are* taken to be agents or subjects. Nothing can guarantee that agents do not take false and myopic views about the effects of their action (even if we had a metaphysics of the person, even if strong assumptions about others' agency are made). However, false beliefs and myopia are at least corrigible, and there are often strong pressures to correct them.

or protect the environment.[12] Of course, most such assumptions will barely be conscious or articulated, just as the corresponding assumptions that lie behind action that affects familiars and nearby strangers are barely conscious or articulated. Yet the action of anyone today who did not rely on a vast web of assumptions about nearer and more distant strangers would be wholly disoriented. Without such premises of action, it is hardly possible to plan what to do or to proceed with any prudence. Hence *if* we owe justice (or other forms of moral concern) to all whose capacities to act, experience and suffer we take for granted in acting, we will owe it to strangers as well as to familiars, and to distant strangers as well as to those who are near at hand.

A practical approach to moral standing does not offer as much as a theoretical account could provide. It does not answer the impersonal question 'Who is entitled to justice (or other forms of moral concern)?' But this has few, if any, practical costs, since the approach answers the question 'To whom would I (or we) owe justice (or other forms of moral concern) in acting in this way?' Today only those few who genuinely live the hermit life can consistently view the scope of moral concern which they must acknowledge in acting as anything but broad, and in some contexts more or less cosmopolitan.[13]

A practical approach to moral standing has strong implications for action for anyone who does not live the hermit life. We live with and by the complex interlock of agents which global trade, communications and densely connected institutions have produced. For us distance is no guarantee of lack of interaction, and we constantly assume that many distant others are every bit as much agents and subjects as nearby and familiar others, and hence are beings whose claims to just treatment (and perhaps to other forms of moral concern) we cannot reasonably settle merely by arbitrary exclusion. We do not and cannot coherently deny the agency of those whose nuclear weapons or debt repudiation or

---

[12] The list suggests that assumptions about distant others are only found in institutionally mediated action, but analogous assumptions can also be present in daily life. When drinking coffee we assume that those who supply the delectable beans are agents with complex capacities, and in all likelihood know that they are poor and distant strangers living in tropical countries.

[13] Whether this approach is enough to establish the lower bound of moral concern is another matter. Perhaps assumptions about others' agency and subjecthood do not cease abruptly at some lower boundary, so that we base some action on recognition of proto-agency and of incipient subjecthood, and may accord some, but perhaps not full, moral standing in these cases. See Onora O'Neill, *Towards Justice and Virtue: A Constructive Account of Practical Reasoning* (Cambridge: Cambridge University Press, 1996), ch. 4.

habits of pollution and environmental degradation we fear, and against whom we take precautions. We do not and cannot consistently deny the agency of those whose peaceful coexistence, economic sobriety and environmental responsibility we hope to rely upon. Once we have moved beyond Rousseau's earliest State of Nature,[14] once we find ourselves, as Kant put it, sharing the surface of the earth with others,[15] we enter into competition for resources and control, we begin to coordinate and contest with distant others, and we begin to premise our action, plans and policies on there being agents and subjects. When we do this, I have argued, we are committed to ascribing to them the same moral standing that we ascribe to nearby and familiar others in whom we assume like capacities. Today we have moved so far beyond that earliest State of Nature that there can be few, if any, distant strangers whom we can coherently see as living beyond the pale or *limes* of justice (and perhaps of some other forms of moral concern).

## 5 VARIETIES OF MORAL CONCERN

The fact that we are in practice committed to a more or less cosmopolitan view of moral standing has more import for our views of justice than for our views of many other forms of moral concern, since many of the latter are inevitably selective. We cannot manifest virtues such as kindness and beneficence to all whose moral standing we acknowledge; we cannot have or discharge special duties such as those of parent or teacher to all whose moral standing we acknowledge. These virtues and duties are unavoidably and appropriately selectively exercised. By contrast, justice is owed to all whose standing is assumed, whether or not we can provide metaphysical backing for that assumption.

Nevertheless, on some accounts, the fact that the scope of justice is more or less cosmopolitan does not entail that the substantive obligations of justice must cross state boundaries. If the obligations of justice could be *wholly* allocated to the institutions of particular states, or to more local authorities, justice would not require any trans-border (transnational) obligations.[16] On such accounts, foreigners can have the very rights that

---

[14] Jean-Jacques Rousseau, *A Discourse on Inequality*, tr. Maurice Cranston (Harmondsworth: Penguin, 1984).    [15] Kant, *Toward Perpetual Peace*, VIII:358.

[16] This sort of statism is commonly combined with liberal and cosmopolitan views of justice. For a liberal argument that bounded states provide effective ways of securing justice for all see Alan Gewirth, 'Ethical Universalism and Particularism', *Journal of Philosophy*, 85 (1988), 300; for a critical view see Pogge, 'The Bounds of Nationalism'.

compatriots have: but not against us. Their rights will be obligations for their state and their fellow-citizens, not for ours or for us. This view of the appropriate institutional embodiment of cosmopolitan obligations is, perhaps surprisingly, enshrined in the United Nations Universal Declaration of Human Rights, which proclaims cosmopolitan rights then hands their protection over to states.[17] This view has harsh consequences in a world where states have unequal power and societies unequal resources, where some states are clients of others, or have hostile or cavalier views of citizens' rights, and where there are many stateless persons. An adequate account of justice to distant strangers in our world cannot be reached by pretending that the obligations of justice are or even can be entirely distributed to or discharged or enforced by and within states. *A fortiori*, an adequate account of justice cannot get off to a good start by taking the justice of existing boundaries for granted. Thinking about justice must begin, although it cannot end, by abstracting from existing institutions.

## 6 THE OBLIGATIONS OF JUSTICE

An initial, abstract account of justice could view its requirements either from the perspective of agents and their obligations or from that of claimants and their rights. Evidently a practical approach to the proper scope of justice fits more readily with a view that takes obligations rather than rights as basic. Moreover, there are independent reasons for taking this perspective as basic.[18] Here I shall note only some practical considerations.

Since the Second World War, advocates of human rights have often invoked rights in abstraction from institutions. This can leave it obscure who has to deliver the counterpart performances for certain sorts of rights. It will not be obscure who holds the obligations that correspond to liberty rights, since these must fall on all. But it matters as soon as we think either about the enforcement of liberty rights,[19] about economic, social or cultural rights, or about special rights, which hold in virtue of specific roles or relationships. In all these cases the obligations must fall on some rather than on all, and it is important to know on whom they fall. Food and health care and education cannot be delivered by the

---

[17] See Chapter 9 above.     [18] See Chapters 6 and 7 above.

[19] See Henry Shue, *Basic Rights: Subsistence, Affluence and U.S. Foreign Policy* (Princeton, N.J.: Princeton University Press, 1980).

simultaneous action of all others. Those who seek their rights must know whether to turn to their compatriots (and if so to which of them), to the state (and if so to which agencies or officials), or to other more global organizations (and if so to which).

By contrast, if we start by considering obligations, and find that it is unclear who the claimants on our action are, or how they are to lodge their claims, we at least begin with a practical task. In beginning with the traditional, Kantian question 'What ought I (or we) do?', rather than with the recipients' question 'What ought I (or we) get?', we face realities more forthrightly, and pose a question that we *can* address, even if only by beginning the task of constructing institutions. By contrast, those who put rights first and try to claim them in abstraction from institutions will not know where to lodge their claims. The perspective of obligations is simply more directly connected to action.

These are reasons enough to show that obligations provide the more coherent and more comprehensive starting point for thinking about ethical requirements, including the requirements of justice. Although the rhetoric of rights has a heady power, and that of obligations and duties few immediate attractions, it helps to view the perspective of obligations as fundamental if the political and ethical implications of normative claims are to be taken seriously. Since action at a distance is usually institutionally and technologically mediated action, it is hard and often impossible to determine just which individual's action harms or injures which others, and hence hard to discern who might have rights of redress against whom. Even if we have reasons to think that each individual has certain rights, this alone will not be enough to establish who must act, or from whom each right-holder might rightfully claim particular rights. However, if we can establish some principles of justice, and have at least a practical account of the scope of moral concern, then we may be able to start by identifying what is required in order to work towards just institutions.

Even the enforcement of obligations, including positive obligations, may often be best achieved by approaches that do not stress individual rights. In particular, many obligations that we might think important between distant strangers may not be best secured by the seemingly straightforward strategy of seeking to establish institutions which vest positive rights in all individuals. For example, obligations not to attack or invade others' states or communities may be better institutionalized by means of treaties and policies of disarmament and non-aggression, or by fostering democracy and interdependent economies than by the seemingly more direct strategy of seeking to invest potential victims of attack with rights against potential attackers. Equally, obligations to reduce poverty may be better served by mixes of investment, development and educational policies combined with efforts to relieve poverty when economies fail. A mix of institutions may do more to secure entitlements to the necessities of life for all than seemingly more direct attempt to set up 'rights to food' or 'rights to development'.

### 7  JUST BUT POROUS BOUNDARIES

These considerations are, I believe, relevant to thinking about how we might justly view state and other boundaries and the distant strangers who live beyond them. If today we are committed by some of our routine activities to a more or less cosmopolitan view of moral standing, then whatever our account of justice, we shall need to work towards an implementation of its requirements that takes account of that scope.

Does it then follow that state boundaries must be unjust, because they exclude some whose moral standing is acknowledged from the rights and benefits secured on the far side of borders? Does justice today require a world state or world federation? Or would a world state concentrate too much power and incompetence, and a plurality of states do better at limiting injustice?

Given the dangers of concentrating too much power in a borderless world, there would be many risks in a total abolition of boundaries. A better set of just institutions might be one that is constructed in the light of considering carefully to whom and to what (to movements of persons, of goods, of information, of money) any given boundary should be porous. Porosity is endlessly variable and adjustable; different filters can be institutionalized. As long as we have a plurality of states, and hence of boundaries (differing from municipal boundaries in that individuals cannot choose on which side to locate their lives), there will be exclusions.

The exclusions boundaries inflict are surely not *inevitably* unjust, in that all those whose standing I am committed to acknowledging might in theory have protections and prospects in their states which meet the demands of justice. On a rosy view, this is what the system of states is to achieve.[20] Yet we know that it wholly fails to do so. Demands for inter-

---

[20] In effect the picture of rights enforcement to which United Nations Declaration of 1948 aspires. See Chapter 9 above.

vention in cases of violations of basic rights, demands for secession, demands for asylum show that for many millions, current inclusions and exclusions are seen as sources of deep injury. These problems are not going to go away. However, I think that we may look at them differently if we do not pretend that we can vindicate a metaphysics of the person that fixes the scope of moral concern and points either to a radical institutional cosmopolitanism, in which there are no excluding boundaries, or to a bounded communitarianism, by which we legitimately deny or downplay the claims of outsiders. I have tried to suggest that in the contemporary world, even if we cannot establish a convincing account of the metaphysical basis of moral standing, we are committed by our own action to thinking that many outsiders count, but that we need not conclude that all boundaries are unjust.

Moral cosmopolitanism has had the reputation of being both a feeble and a dangerous form of idealism. I do not think that it can really be *both* of these. The charge that it is feeble expresses the thought that it has no practical implications; the charge that it is dangerous probably the fear that it points towards a world state and the dismantling of the institutions we take to protect our security – and our affluence. A more serious way in which to understand the approximate moral cosmopolitanism for which I have tried to argue here is as a background picture which frames and sets standards for attempts to work towards an appropriate degree of *institutional cosmopolitanism* – that is towards institutions which take seriously the obligations that approximate moral cosmopolitans have reason to acknowledge.

Over the last fifty years boundaries have been becoming more porous. It has happened gradually, selectively and in faltering ways, and has transformed both political and economic life for countless people. For example, most boundaries in Europe stand where they stood at the end of the Second World War, but are unimaginably more porous. Boundaries that were once impervious to capital flows and trade, to cultural and technical influence and above all to movements of people have become highly, if variably, porous. In Western Europe the changes happened incrementally over many years; in Eastern Europe everything stalled for decades but changed rapidly and dramatically after 1990. The changes in boundaries that count for most today are evidently not spatial but qualitative. One consideration that should guide us in making or working towards such qualitative transformations is a recognition of the reality that we constantly act in ways that commit us to seeing those on the far sides of existing boundaries, distant strangers though they be, as having moral standing for us. If we do so, then we shall also have reason to treat distant strangers justly, whether by making the boundaries which exclude them more porous in specific ways or by compensating them for any harms caused by otherwise unjustifiable exclusions. Moral cosmopolitanism, even approximate moral cosmopolitanism, does not point to a stateless world, but to forms of institutional cosmopolitanism in which further boundaries become porous in further ways.

# Bibliography

Allison, Henry E., *Kant's Theory of Freedom*, Cambridge, Cambridge University Press, 1990.

Allot, Philip, *Eunomia: New Order for a New World*, New York, Oxford University Press, 1990.

Aristotle, *The Politics*, tr. W.D. Ross, revised J. L. Ackrill, J. O. Urmson and Jonathan Barnes, ed. Stephen Everson, Cambridge, Cambridge University Press, 1988.

Baldwin, Thomas, 'Territoriality', in Hyman Gross and Ross Harrison, eds., *Jurisprudence: Cambridge Essays*, Oxford, Clarendon Press, 1992, 207–30.

Baron, Marcia W., *Kantian Ethics almost without Apology*, Ithaca, N.Y., Cornell University Press, 1995.

Barry, Brian and Goodin, Robert E., eds., *Free Movement: Ethical Issues in the Transnational Migration of People and Money*, London, Harvester Wheatsheaf, 1992.

Bayles, Michael D., *Morality and Population Policy*, Alabama, University of Alabama Press, 1980.

Beck, Lewis White, *A Commentary on Kant's Critique of Practical Reason*, Chicago, Ill., University of Chicago Press, 1960.

Beitz, Charles R., 'Cosmopolitan Ideals and National Sentiments', *Journal of Philosophy*, 80 (1983), 591–600.

'Cosmopolitan Liberalism and the States System', in Chris Brown, ed., *Political Restructuring in Europe: Ethical Perspectives*, London, Routledge, 1994, 123–36.

*Political Theory and International Relations*, Princeton, N.J., Princeton University Press, 1979.

Bentham, Jeremy, *Introduction to the Principles of Morals and of Legislation* (1789), in *A Fragment on Government with an Introduction to the Principles of Morals and Legislation*, ed. Wilfrid Harrison, Oxford, Blackwell, 1967.

Bittner, Rüdiger, 'Maximen', in G. Funke, ed., *Akten des 4. Internationalen Kant-Kongresses*, Berlin, De Gruyter, 1974, 485–9.

Blomstrom, Magnus and Hettne, Bjorn, *Development Theory in Transition: The Dependency Debate and Beyond: Third World Responses*, London, Zed Books, 1984.

Blum, Lawrence A., *Friendship, Altruism and Morality*, London, Routledge & Kegan Paul, 1980.

Bowie, Norman, 'The Moral Obligations of Multinational Corporations', in Stephen Luper-Foy, ed., *Problems of International Justice*, Boulder and London, Westview, 1988, 97–113.

Boxill, Bernard, 'Global Equality of Opportunity', *Social Philosophy and Policy*, 5 (1987), 143–68.

Brink, David O., 'Rawlsian Constructivism in Moral Theory', *Canadian Journal of Philosophy*, 17 (1987), 71–90.

Brock, Gillian, ed., *Necessary Goods: Our Responsibilities to Meet Others' Needs*, Lanham, Md., Rowman & Littlefield, 1998.

Buchanan, Alan, 'Justice and Charity', *Ethics*, 97 (1987), 558–75.

Camartin, Iso, *Von Sils-Maria aus Betrachtet: Ein Blick von dem Dach Europas*, Frankfurt, Suhrkamp, 1991.

Campbell, Thomas, 'Perfect and Imperfect Duties', *The Modern Schoolman*, 102 (1975), 185–94.

Carens, Joseph, 'Aliens and Citizens: The Case for Open Borders', *Review of Politics*, 49 (1987), 251–73.

'Immigration and the Welfare State', in Amy Gutmann, ed., *Democracy and the Welfare State*, Princeton, N.J., Princeton University Press, 1988, 207–30.

Charvet, John, *Feminism*, London, Dent, 1982.

Chodorow, Nancy, *The Reproduction of Mothering: Psychoanalysis and the Sociology of Gender*, Berkeley, Calif., University of California Press, 1978.

Coetzee, J. M., *Waiting for the Barbarians*, Harmondsworth, Penguin, 1982.

Cullity, Garrett, 'International Aid and the Scope of Kindness', *Ethics*, 105 (1994), 99–127.

Dancy, Jonathan, 'Ethical Particularism and Morally Relevant Properties', *Mind*, 92 (1983), 530–47.

Daniels, Norman, ed., *Reading Rawls: Critical Studies on A Theory of Justice*, Oxford, Blackwell, 1975.

Descartes, René, *Discourse on the Method of Rightly Conducting One's Reason and Seeking the Truth in the Sciences*, in *The Philosophical Writings of Descartes*, vol. 1, tr. John Cottingham, Robert Stoothof and Dugald Murdoch, Cambridge, Cambridge University Press, 1985.

Deveaux, Monique, 'Conflicting Equalities? Cultural Group Rights and Sex Equality', *Political Studies* 48 (2000).

Doyal, Len and Gough, Ian, *A Theory of Human Need*, London, Macmillan, 1991.

Doyle, Michael, 'Kant, Liberal Legacies, and Foreign Affairs', in two parts, in *Philosophy and Public Affairs*, 12 (1983), 205–35 and 323–53.

Drèze, Jean and Sen, Amartya, eds., *Hunger and Public Action*, Oxford, Clarendon Press, 1989.

Dworkin, Gerald, *The Theory and Practice of Autonomy*, Cambridge, Cambridge University Press, 1988.

Dworkin, Ronald, 'Liberalism', in Stuart Hampshire, ed., *Public and Private Morality*, Cambridge, Cambridge University Press, 1977, 113–43.

Edelman, Murray, 'The Political Language of the Helping Professions', in Michael J. Shapiro, ed., *Language and Politics*, New York, New York University Press, 1984.

Elshtain, Michelle Jean Bethke, *Public Man, Private Woman: Women in Social and Political Thought*, Princeton, N.J., Princeton University Press, 1981.

Elster, Jon, *The Cement of Society: A Study of Social Order*, London, Routledge, 1989. *Sour Grapes: Studies in the Subversion of Rationality*, Cambridge, Cambridge University Press, 1983.

Feinberg, Joel, *Rights, Justice and the Bounds of Liberty: Essays in Social Philosophy*, Princeton, N.J., Princeton University Press, 1980.

Förster, Eckhart, ed., *Kant's Transcendental Deductions: The Three Critiques and the Opus Postumum*, Stanford, Calif., Stanford University Press, 1989.

Frankfurt, Harry, 'Freedom of the Will and the Concept of a Person', *Journal of Philosophy*, 68 (1971), 5–20.

French, Peter, *Collective and Corporate Responsibility*, New York, Columbia University Press, 1984.

Frey, R. G. and Morris, Christopher W., eds., *Violence, Terrorism, and Justice*, Cambridge, Cambridge University Press, 1991.

Frost, Mervyn, *Ethics in International Relations: A Constitutive Theory*, Cambridge, Cambridge University Press, 1996.

Gauthier, David, *Morals by Agreement*, Oxford, Clarendon Press, 1986.

Gewirth, Alan, 'Ethical Universalism and Particularism', *Journal of Philosophy*, 85 (1988), 283–302.
    'Private Philanthropy and Positive Rights', in Ellen Frankel Paul et al., eds., *Beneficence, Philanthropy and the Public Good*, Oxford, Blackwell, 1987, 55–78.
    'Starvation and Human Rights', in his *Human Rights: Essays on Justification and Applications*, Chicago, University of Chicago Press, 1982, 197–217.

Gilbert, Margaret, *Living Together: Rationality, Sociality and Obligation*, London, Rowman & Littlefield, 1996.

Gilligan, Carol, *In a Different Voice: Psychological Theory and Women's Development*, Cambridge, Mass., Harvard University Press, 1982, 2nd edn, 1993.

Goodin, E. Robert, 'What Is So Special about Our Fellow Countrymen?', *Ethics*, 98 (1988), 663–86.

Graham, Keith, 'Collective Responsibility', in Ton van den Beld, ed., *Moral Responsibility and Ontology*, Dordrecht, Kluwer, 2000, 49–61.
    'The Moral Status of Collective Entities', forthcoming.

Habermas, Jürgen, 'Ist der Herzschlag der Revolution zum Stillstand gekommen?', in *Die Ideen von 1789 in der deutschen Rezeption*, ed. Forum für Philosophie Bad Homburg, Frankfurt-on-Main, Suhrkamp, 1989.

Hardin, Garret, 'Lifeboat Ethics: The Case against Helping the Poor', *Psychology Today*, 8 (1974), 38–43.

Harriss, Barbara, 'Differential Female Mortality and Health Care in South Asia', *Queen Elizabeth House, Working Paper*, Oxford, 1989.
    'Intrafamily Distribution of Hunger in South Asia', in Jean Drèze and

Amartya K. Sen, eds., *The Political Economy of Hunger*, vol. 1, *Entitlement and Well-being*, Oxford, Clarendon Press, 1991, 351–424.

Harsanyi, John, 'Morality and the Theory of Rational Behaviour', in A. Sen and B. Williams, eds., *Utilitarianism and Beyond*, Cambridge, Cambridge University Press, 39–62.

Havel, Vaclav, 'The Power of the Powerless', in his *Living in Truth*, ed. Jan Vadislav, London, Faber & Faber, 1986.

Henrich, Dieter, 'Kant's Notion of a Deduction and the Methodological Background of the First *Critique*', in Eckhart Förster, ed., *Kant's Transcendental Deductions: The Three Critiques and the Opus Postumum*, Stanford, Calif., Stanford University Press, 1989, 29–46.

Herman, Barbara, 'Obligation and Performance', in her *The Practice of Moral Judgement*, Cambridge, Mass., Harvard University Press, 1993, 159–83.

*The Practice of Moral Judgement*, Cambridge, Mass., Harvard University Press, 1993.

Hill, Thomas E., Jnr, 'The Importance of Autonomy', in his *Autonomy and Self-respect*, Cambridge, Cambridge University Press, 1991, 43–51.

'The Kantian Conception of Autonomy', in his *Dignity and Practical Reason in Kant's Moral Theory*, Ithaca, N.Y., Cornell University Press, 1992, 76–96.

'Servility and Self-respect', *Monist*, 57 (1973), 87–104 and in his *Autonomy and Self-Respect*, Cambridge, Cambridge University Press, 1991, 4–18.

Hirsch, Fred, *The Social Limits of Growth*, Cambridge, Mass., Harvard University Press, 1976.

Historisches Wörterbuch der Philosophie, vol. 1, Basle, Schwabe, 1971.

Hobbes, Thomas, *Leviathan*, ed. Richard Tuck, Cambridge, Cambridge University Press, 1996.

Höffe, Otfried, 'Kants kategorischer Imperativ als Kriterium des Sittlichen', *Zeitschrift für philosophische Forschung*, 31 (1977), 354–84.

Hoffman, Stanley, *Duties Beyond Borders: On the Limits and Possibilities of Ethical International Politics*, Syracuse, N.Y., Syracuse University Press, 1981.

Hollis, Martin, *The Cunning of Reason*, Cambridge, Cambridge University Press, 1987.

Hudson, James L., 'The Ethics of Immigration Restriction', *Social Theory and Practice*, 10 (1984), 201–39.

Hume, David, *A Treatise of Human Nature*, ed. L. A. Selby-Bigge, revised P. H. Nidditch, 2nd edn, Oxford, Clarendon Press, 1978.

Jackson, Tony with Eade, Deborah, *Against the Grain*, Oxford, Oxfam, 1982.

Jaggar, Alison M., *Feminist Politics and Human Nature*, Brighton, Harvester Press, 1983.

Kant, Immanuel, *An Answer to the Question: 'What is Enlightenment?'*, VIII:35–42, in Immanuel Kant, *Practical Philosophy*, tr. and ed. Mary Gregor, Cambridge, Cambridge University Press, 1996.

*Anthropology from a Pragmatic Point of View*, tr. Mary Gregor, The Hague, Nijhoff, 1974.

*Critique of Judgement*, tr. James Creed Meredith, Oxford, Clarendon Press, 1973.

*Critique of Pure Reason*, tr. and ed. Paul Guyer and Allen Wood, Cambridge, Cambridge University Press, 1998.

*Groundwork of the Metaphysics of Morals*, IV:387–460, in Immanuel Kant, *Practical Philosophy*, tr. and ed. Mary Gregor, Cambridge, Cambridge University Press, 1996.

*The Metaphysics of Morals*, VI:232–493, in Immanuel Kant, *Practical Philosophy*, tr. and ed. Mary Gregor, Cambridge, Cambridge University Press, 1996.

*Religion within the Boundaries of Mere Reason*, VI:3–202, tr. George di Giovanni, in Immanuel Kant, *Religion and Rational Theology*, ed. Allen W. Wood and George di Giovanni, Cambridge, Cambridge University Press, 1996.

*Toward Perpetual Peace*, in Immanuel Kant, VIII:344–86, *Practical Philosophy*, tr. and ed. Mary Gregor, Cambridge, Cambridge University Press, 1996.

*What does it Mean to Orient Oneself in Thinking?*, VIII:133–46, tr. Allen W. Wood, in Immanuel Kant, *Religion and Rational Theology*, ed. Allen W. Wood and George di Giovanni, Cambridge, Cambridge University Press, 1996.

Keohane, Robert O. and Nye, Joseph S., eds., *Transnational Relations and World Politics*, Cambridge, Mass., Harvard University Press, 1973.

Kittay, Eva Feder and Diana T. Meyers, eds., *Women and Moral Theory*, Totowa, N.J., Rowman & Littlefield, 1987.

Klemperer, Viktor, *Ich will Zeugnis ablegen bis zum letzten*, ed. Walter Nowojski, 2 vols., Berlin, Aufbau Verlag, 1996.

Kneller, Jane and Axinn, Sidney, eds., *Autonomy and Community: Readings in Contemporary Kantian Social Philosophy*, Albany, N.Y., State University of New York Press, 1998.

Larmore, Charles, 'Moral Judgment', *Review of Metaphysics*, 35 (1981), 275–96.

*Patterns of Moral Complexity*, Cambridge, Cambridge University Press, 1987.

Levine, Andrew, *The Politics of Autonomy: A Kantian Reading of Rousseau's 'Social Contract'*, Amherst, University of Massachusetts Press, 1976.

Lindley, Richard, *Autonomy*, Basingstoke, Macmillan, 1986.

Lloyd, Genevieve, *The Man of Reason: 'Male' and 'Female' in Western Philosophy*, London, Methuen, 1984.

Locke, John, *Two Treatises of Government*, ed. Peter Laslett, Cambridge, Cambridge University Press, 1988.

Luper-Foy, Steven, ed., *Problems of International Justice*, Boulder, Colo., Westview Press, 1988.

Lyons, David, 'The New Indian Claims and Original Rights to Land', in Jeffrey Paul, ed., *Reading Nozick: Essays on Anarchy, State and Utopia*, Totowa, N.J., Rowman & Littlefield, 1981, 355–79.

Makkreel, Rudolf, 'Differentiating, Regulative, and Reflective Approaches to History', in Hoke Robinson, ed., *Proceedings of the Eighth International Kant Congress*, vol. 1, pt 1, 123–37.

McCormick, D. N., 'Is Nationalism Philosophically Credible?', in William Twining, ed., *Issues of Self Determination*, Aberdeen, Aberdeen University Press, 1991.

'Nation and Nationalism', in his *Legal Right and Social Democracy*, Oxford, Clarendon, 1982, ch. 13.

MacDonagh, Oliver, *States of Mind: A Study of Anglo-Irish Conflict 1780–1980*, London, George Allen & Unwin, 1983.

McDowell, John, 'Deliberation and Moral Development', in Stephen Engstrom and Jennifer Whiting, eds., *Aristotle, Kant and the Stoics*, Cambridge, Cambridge University Press, 1996, 19–35.

MacIntyre, Alasdair, *After Virtue*, London, Duckworth, 1981.

*Is Patriotism a Virtue?*, Lawrence, Kan., University of Kansas, Department of Philosophy, 1984.

*Whose Justice? Which Rationality?*, London, Duckworth, 1988.

McMillan, Carol, *Women, Reason and Nature: Some Philosophical Problems with Feminism*, Oxford, Blackwell, 1982.

Marcus, Ruth Barcan, 'Moral Dilemmas and Consistency', *Journal of Philosophy*, 77 (1980), 121–36.

Mason, Andrew, 'Special Obligations to Compatriots', *Ethics*, 107 (1997), 427–47.

May, Larry, *The Morality of Groups: Responsibilities, Group-based Harms and Corporate Right*, Notre Dame, Ind., University of Notre Dame Press, 1987.

Mill, J. S. *Utilitarianism* (1861), in Mary Warnock, ed., *Utilitarianism; On Liberty; Essay on Bentham etc.*, London, Fontana, 1985.

Miller, David, 'The Ethical Significance of Nationality', *Ethics*, 98 (1988), 647–62.

*On Nationality*, Oxford, Clarendon Press, 1995.

Munzel, G. Felicitas, *Kant's Conception of Moral Character: The 'Critical' Link of Morality, Anthropology and Reflective Judgement*, Chicago, University of Chicago Press, 1999.

Murdoch, Iris, *The Sovereignty of Good*, London, Routledge & Kegan Paul, 1970.

Nagel, Thomas, 'Poverty and Food: Why Charity is not Enough', in Peter Brown and Henry Shue, eds., *Food Policy: The Responsibility of the United States in Life and Death Choices*, New York, Free Press, 1977, 54–62.

Nicholson, Linda, 'Feminism and Marx: Integrating Kinship with the Economic', in Seyla Benhabib and Drucilla Cornell, eds., *Feminism as Critique: Essays on the Politics of Gender in Late-capitalist Societies*, Cambridge, Polity Press, 1987, 16–30.

Noddings, Nel, *Caring: A Feminine Approach to Ethics and Moral Education*, Berkeley, Calif., University of California Press, 1984.

Nozick, Robert, *Anarchy, State and Utopia*, Oxford, Blackwell, 1974.

Nussbaum, Martha, 'Aristotelian Social Democracy', in Bruce Douglass, Gerald Mara and Henry S. Richardson, eds., *Liberalism and the Good*, London, Routledge, 1990, 203–52.

Nussbaum, Martha and Glover, Jonathan, eds., *Women, Culture and Development: A Study of Human Capabilities*, Oxford, Clarendon Press, 1995.

Nussbaum, Martha and Sen, Amartya, eds., *The Quality of Life*, Oxford, Clarendon Press, 1992.

O'Connor, John, 'Philanthropy and Selfishness', in Ellen Frankel Paul et al., eds., *Beneficence, Philanthropy and the Public Good*, Oxford, Blackwell, 1987, 113–27.

Okin, Susan Moller, 'Justice and Gender', *Philosophy and Public Affairs*, 16 (1987), 42–72.

*Women in Western Political Thought*, Princeton, N.J., Princeton University Press, 1979.

O'Neill, Onora, 'Abstraction, Idealization and Ideology', in J. G. D. Evans, ed., *Ethical Theories and Contemporary Problems*, Cambridge, Cambridge University Press, 1988, 55–69.

'Autonomy, Coherence and Independence', in David Milligan and William Watts Miller, eds., *Liberalism, Citizenship and Autonomy*, Aldershot, Avebury Press, 1992, 209–29.

'Children's Rights and Children's Lives', *Ethics*, 98 (1988), 445–63.

*Constructions of Reason: Explorations of Kant's Practical Philosophy*, Cambridge, Cambridge University Press, 1989.

'Distant Strangers, Moral Standing and State Boundaries', in P. Koller and K. Puhl, eds., *Current Issues in Political Philosophy: Justice in Society and World Order*, Vienna, Hölder-Pichler-Tempsky, 1997, 118–32.

'Enlightenment as Autonomy: Kant's Vindication of Reason', in Peter Hulme and Ludmilla Jordanova, eds., *Enlightenment and its Shadows*, London, Routledge & Kegan Paul, 1990, 184–99.

'Ethical Reasoning and Ideological Pluralism', *Ethics*, 98 (1988), 705–22.

*Faces of Hunger: An Essay on Poverty, Development and Justice*, London, George Allen & Unwin, 1986.

'From Statist to Global Conceptions of Justice', in Christoph von Hübig, ed., *XVII Deutscher Kongress für Philosophie, 1996: Vorträge und Kolloquien*, Berlin, Akademie Verlag, 1997, 368–79.

'The Great Maxims of Justice and Charity', in *Constructions of Reason: Explorations of Kant's Practical Philosophy*, Cambridge, Cambridge University Press, 1989, 219–33.

'Instituting Principles: Between Duty and Action', in Mark Timmons, ed., *Kant's Metaphysics of Morals: Interpretive Essays*, Oxford, Oxford University Press, forthcoming.

'Justice and Boundaries', in Chris Brown, ed., *Political Restructuring in Europe: Ethical Perspectives*, London, Routledge, 1994, 69–88.

'Justice, Gender and International Boundaries', in Martha Nussbaum and Amartya Sen, eds., *The Quality of Life*, Oxford, Clarendon Press, 1992, 303–35.

'Kant's Virtues', in Roger Crisp, *How Should One Live? Essays on the Virtues*, Oxford, Clarendon Press, 1996, 77–97.

'Kommunikative Rationalität und praktische Vernunft', *Philosophischer Rundschau*, 41 (1993), 329–32.

'Lifeboat Earth', *Philosophy and Public Affairs*, 4 (1975), 271–92.

'The Most Extensive Liberty', *Proceedings of the Aristotelian Society*, 53 (1979–80), 45–59.

'Political Liberalism and Public Reason: A Critical Notice of John Rawls, *Political Liberalism*', *Philosophical Review*, 106 (1997), 411–28.

'The Power of Example', in *Constructions of Reason: Explorations of Kant's Practical Philosophy*, Cambridge, Cambridge University Press, 1989, 165–86.

'Reason and Autonomy in *Grundlegung III* ', in *Constructions of Reason: Explorations of Kant's Practical Philosophy*, Cambridge, Cambridge University Press, 1989, 51–65.

'Reason and Politics in the Kantian Enterprise', *Constructions of Reason: Explorations of Kant's Practical Philosophy*, Cambridge, Cambridge University Press, 1989, 3–27.

'Rights, Obligations and Needs', *Logos*, 6 (1985), 29–47, and in Gillian Brock, ed., *Necessary Goods: Our Responsibilities to Meet Others' Needs*, Oxford, Rowman & Littlefield, 1998, 95–112.

*Towards Justice and Virtue: A Constructive Account of Practical Reasoning*, Cambridge, Cambridge University Press, 1996.

'Transnational Justice: Permeable Boundaries and Multiple Identities', in Preston King, ed., *Socialism and the Common Good: New Fabian Essays*, London, Frank Cass & Co., 1996, 291–302.

'Vier Modelle der praktischen Vernunft', in Hans Friedrich Fulda and Rolf-Peter Horstmann, eds., *Vernunftbegriffe in der Moderne*, Stuttgart, Klett-Cotta, 1994, 586–606.

'Vindicating Reason', in Paul Guyer, ed., *The Cambridge Companion to Kant*, Cambridge, Cambridge University Press, 1992, 280–308.

'Women's Rights: Whose Obligations?', in Alison Jeffries, ed., *Women's Voices, Women's Rights: Oxford Amnesty Lectures*, Boulder, Colo., Westview Press, 1999, 57–69.

Pateman, Carole, *The Sexual Contract*, Cambridge, Polity Press, 1988.

Paul, Ellen Frankel et al., eds., *Beneficence, Philanthropy and the Public Good*, Oxford, Blackwell, 1987.

Pfeiffer, Raymond, 'The Responsibility of Men for the Oppression of Women', *Journal of Applied Philosophy*, 2 (1985), 217–29.

Pogge, Thomas W., 'The Bounds of Nationalism', in Jocelyne Couture et al., eds., *Rethinking Nationalism*; *Canadian Journal of Philosophy*, supp. vol. 22 (1998), 463–504.

'Cosmopolitanism and Sovereignty', in Chris Brown, ed., *Political Restructuring in Europe: Ethical Perspectives*, London, Routledge, 1994, 89–122; also in *Ethics*, 103 (1992), 48–75.

'A Global Resources Dividend', in David A. Crocker and Toby Linden, eds., *Ethics of Consumption: The Good Life, Justice and Global Stewardship*, Lanham, Md., Rowman & Littlefield, 1998, 501–36.

*Realizing Rawls*, Ithaca, N.Y., Cornell University Press, 1989.

Postow, B. C. 'Economic Dependence and Self-respect', *The Philosophical Forum*, 10 (1978–9), 181–201.

Preuß, Ulrich K., *Revolution, Fortschritt und Verfassung: zu einem neuen Verfassungsverständnis*, Berlin, Wagenbach, 1990.

Pufendorf, Samuel, *On the Duty of Man and Citizen According to the Natural Law*, tr. Michael Silverthorn, ed. James Tully, Cambridge, Cambridge University Press, 1991.

Quine, W. V. O., 'Two Dogmas of Empiricism', in his *From a Logical Point of View*, New York, Harper & Row, 1963, 20–46.

Rawls, John, 'The Basic Structure as Subject', *American Philosophical Quarterly*, 14 (1977), 159–65.

'Justice as Fairness: Political not Metaphysical', *Philosophy and Public Affairs*, 14 (1985), 223–51.

'Kantian Constructivism in Moral Theory', *Journal of Philosophy*, 77 (1980), 515–72.

*The Law of Peoples*, in John Rawls, *Collected Papers*, Cambridge, Mass., Harvard University Press, 1999, 529–64.

*Political Liberalism*, New York, Columbia University Press, 1993.

*A Theory of Justice*, Cambridge, Mass., Harvard University Press, 1971.

Raz, Joseph, 'Right-based Moralities', in Jeremy Waldron, ed., *Theories of Rights*, Oxford, Oxford University Press, 1984, 182–200.

Risse-Kappen, Thomas, ed., *Bringing Transnational Relations Back In: Non-state Actors, Domestic Structures and International Institutions*, Cambridge, Cambridge University Press, 1995.

Rousseau, Jean-Jacques, *A Discourse on Inequality*, tr. Maurice Cranston, Harmondsworth, Penguin, 1984.

*The Social Contract and Other Later Political Writings*, tr. Victor Gourevitch, Cambridge, Cambridge University Press, 1997.

Ruddick, Sara, 'Maternal Thinking', in her *Maternal Thinking: Towards a Politics of Peace*, Boston, Mass., Beacon Press, 1989, 13–27.

'Remarks on the Sexual Politics of Reason', in Eva Feder Kittay and Diana T. Meyers, eds., *Women and Moral Theory*, Totowa, N.J., Rowman & Littlefield, 1987, 237–60.

Ryan, Cheyney C., 'Yours, Mine and Ours: Property Rights and Individual Liberty', in Jeffrey Paul, ed., *Reading Nozick: Essays on Anarchy, State and Utopia*, Oxford, Blackwell, 1981, 323–43.

Sainsbury, Mark, *Concepts without Boundaries*, Inaugural Lecture, Philosophy Department, King's College London, 1990.

Sandel, Michael J., *Liberalism and the Limits of Justice*, Cambridge, Cambridge University Press, 1982; 2nd edn, 1996.

Sartre, Jean-Paul, 'Existentialism is Humanism', in Robert C. Solomon, ed., *Existentialism*, New York, Modern Library, 1974.

Schneewind, J. B., *The Invention of Autonomy: A History of Modern Moral Philosophy*, Cambridge, Cambridge University Press, 1998.

'The Misfortunes of Virtue', *Ethics*, 101 (1990), 42–63.

Schwartz, Warren F., ed., *Justice in Immigration*, Cambridge, Cambridge University Press, 1995.

Scott, Alison, 'Industrialization, Gender Segregation and Stratification Theory', in Rosemary Crompton and Michael Mann, eds., *Gender and Stratification*, Cambridge, Polity Press, 1986, 154–89.

Sen, Amartya K., 'Behaviour and the Concept of Preference', *Economica*, 40 (1973), 241–59.

    *Choice, Welfare and Measurement*, Oxford, Blackwell, 1982.

    'Gender and Co-operative Conflicts', *Working Paper of the World Institute for Development Economics Research* (WIDER), Helsinki, United Nations University, 1987.

    *Poverty and Famines: An Essay on Entitlement and Deprivation*, Oxford, Clarendon Press, 1981.

    'Rational Fools: A Critique of the Behavioural Foundations of Economic Theory', *Philosophy and Public Affairs*, 6 (1977), 317–44.

Sher, George, 'Ancient Wrongs and Modern Rights', *Philosophy and Public Affairs*, 10 (1981), 3–17.

Shue, Henry, *Basic Rights: Subsistence, Affluence and U.S. Foreign Policy*, Princeton, N.J., Princeton University Press, 1980.

    'The Interdependence of Duties', in Philip Alston and K. Tomasevski, eds., *The Right to Food*, Dordrecht, Nijhoff, 1984, 83–95.

    'Mediating Duties', *Ethics*, 98 (1988), 687–704.

Sikora, R. I. and Barry, Brian, eds., *Obligations to Future Generations*, Pennsylvania, Temple University Press, 1978.

Silatianen, Janet and Stanworth, Michelle, *Women and the Public Sphere*, London, Hutchinson, 1984.

Singer, Peter, 'Famine, Affluence and Morality', *Philosophy and Public Affairs*, 1 (1972), 229–43.

Skinner, Quentin, 'Meaning and Understanding in the History of Ideas', *History and Theory*, 8 (1969), 3–53, reprinted in James Tully, ed., *Meaning and Context: Quentin Skinner and his Critics*, Cambridge, Polity Press, 1988, 231–88.

Steiner, Hillel, 'Individual Liberty', *Proceedings of the Aristotelian Society*, 75 (1974–5), 33–50.

    'Libertarians and Transnational Migration', in Brian Barry and Robert E. Goodin, eds., *Free Movement: Ethical Issues in the Transnational Migration of People and Money*, London, Harvester Wheatsheaf, 1992, 87–94.

Stiehm, Judith Hicks, 'The Unit of Political Analysis: Our Aristotelian Hangover', in Sandra Harding and Merrill B. Hintikka, eds., *Discovering Reality: Feminist Perspectives on Epistemology, Metaphysics, Methodology and Philosophy of Science*, Dordrecht, Reidel, 1983, 31–3.

Tamir, Yael, *Liberal Nationalism*, Princeton, N.J., Princeton University Press, 1993.

Taylor, Charles, 'What is Human Agency?', in his *Human Agency and Language: Philosophical Papers 1*, Cambridge, Cambridge University Press, 1985, 15–44.

'What's Wrong with Negative Liberty?', in his *Philosophy and the Human Sciences: Philosophical Papers 2*, Cambridge, Cambridge University Press, 1985, 211–29.

Tinker, I., ed., *Persistent Inequalities*, New York, Oxford University Press, 1990.

Tully, James, *Strange Multiplicity: Constitutionalism in an Age of Diversity*, Cambridge, Cambridge University Press, 1995.

Unamuno, Miguel, *The Tragic Sense of Life in Men and Nations*, tr. Anthony Kerrigan, Princeton, N.J., Princeton University Press, 1972.

van Gunsteren, Herman R., 'Admission to Citizenship', *Ethics*, 98 (1988), 731–41.

Velkley, Richard, *Freedom and the End of Reason: On the Moral Foundation of Kant's Critical Philosophy*, Chicago, University of Chicago Press, 1990.

Waldron, Jeremy, *'Nonsense Upon Stilts': Bentham, Burke and Marx on the Rights of Man*, London, Methuen, 1987.

Walzer, Michael, *Spheres of Justice: A Defence of Pluralism and Equality*, Martin Oxford, Robertson, 1983.

Wiggins, David, 'Deliberation and Practical Reason', in his *Needs, Values, Truth: Essays on the Philosophy of Value*, Aristotelian Society, 6, Oxford, Blackwell, 1987, 213–37.

Williams, Bernard, *Ethics and the Limits of Philosophy*, London, Fontana, 1985.

'Persons, Character and Morality', in his *Moral Luck*, Cambridge, Cambridge University Press, 1981, 1–19.

Winch, Peter, *Ethics and Action*, London, Routledge & Kegan Paul, 1972.

Wolff, Robert Paul, 'Robert Nozick's Derivation of the Minimal State', in Jeffrey Paul, ed., *Reading Nozick: essays on Anarchy, State and Utopia*, Totowa, N.J., Rowman & Littlefield, 1981, 77–104.

*Understanding Rawls*, Princeton, N.J., Princeton University Press, 1977.

Young, Robert, *Personal Autonomy: Beyond Negative and Positive Liberty*, London, Croom Helm, 1986.

# Index